Sir Alexander Grant

The story of the University of Edinburgh during its first three hundred years

Sir Alexander Grant

The story of the University of Edinburgh during its first three hundred years

ISBN/EAN: 9783742876478

Manufactured in Europe, USA, Canada, Australia, Japa

Cover: Foto ©ninafisch / pixelio.de

Manufactured and distributed by brebook publishing software (www.brebook.com)

Sir Alexander Grant

The story of the University of Edinburgh during its first three hundred years

THE STORY

OF THE

UNIVERSITY OF EDINBURGH

DURING

ITS FIRST THREE HUNDRED YEARS

BY

Sir ALEXANDER GRANT, Bart..

LL.D. (EDINBURGH, GLASGOW, CAMBRIDGE), D.C.L. (OXFORD),
PRINCIPAL AND VICE-CHANCELLOR IN THE UNIVERSITY OF EDINBURGH,
FORMERLY FELLOW AND NOW HONORARY FELLOW OF
ORIEL COLLEGE, OXFORD

WITH ILLUSTRATIONS

IN TWO VOLS.—VOL. I.

TO

MY ACADEMIC CHIEF AND VALUED FRIEND,

THE RIGHT HON. JOHN INGLIS OF GLENCORSE,

D.C.L., LL.D., ETC.

(A NAME WIDELY HONOURED IN GREAT BRITAIN),

LORD JUSTICE GENERAL OF SCOTLAND,

CHANCELLOR OF THE UNIVERSITY OF EDINBURGH,

I DEDICATE,

WITH ALL RESPECT AND AFFECTION,

THIS BOOK,

IN WHICH ARE MENTIONED

SOME OF HIS GREAT SERVICES TO THE

UNIVERSITIES OF SCOTLAND.

PREFACE.

This book was undertaken in honour of the Tercentenary of the University of Edinburgh, in order that any one who cared might be able to know by what steps the University has arrived at its present position.

There were already in existence three separate chronicles of the University of Edinburgh, produced by three of its officials. In none of these, however, has the history of the University been really written. Valuable as they are, they are only *mémoires pour servir*.

I. The excellent Thomas Craufurd, Regent of Philosophy and Professor of Mathematics, dying in 1662, left behind him a manuscript, a copy of which, in the handwriting of William Henderson, the librarian (dated 1673), is preserved in the University Library. This MS. was sometimes referred to in the last century, but it was never printed till 1808, when it was published under the title of *History of the University of Edinburgh from 1580 to 1646, by Thomas Craufurd*, etc. "Annals" would have been a more appropriate designation than "History," for no continuous account is given, but under each year occurrences connected with the origin and progress of the College of Edinburgh are detailed. It is said indeed that Craufurd himself gave the title of "Memoirs" to what he had written. In quite an early part of the book (under date 1617) there is an allusion to the Restoration, which shows that Craufurd must have been engaged in putting the work into order shortly before his own death. But probably the whole thing was commenced shortly after 1626, when Craufurd first came to be a Regent. He must then have collected, while they were fresh, particulars about the first forty-three years of the College, and have habituated himself afterwards to jotting down from year to year events which struck him. We are under great obligation to him for so doing, for he has preserved for us numerous facts which, but for him, would have been lost. And everything in his book is told in the freshest, quaintest, most graphic style. But he did not pretend to be a historian, and his honest anxiety to represent the "Town's College" as a full-blown University occasionally vitiates to some extent the accuracy of what he records.

II. Towards the close of the eighteenth century Andrew Dalzel (Professor of Greek, 1772-1805) set himself to write a *History of the University*. But he began too late, for his health soon afterwards failed. His mode of proceeding was to extract from the City Records, in chronological order, entries referring to the College, and with these to combine particulars out of the graduation lists and other documents in the University Library. He thus compiled a somewhat dry statement of appointments made and classes laureated, down to the year 1723, occasionally adding references to contemporary Scottish history, with which he was well acquainted. He had, in fact, only collected materials for his *History*, and he probably would have changed the form of what he had written, if life and strength had remained to him. His unfinished MS. had the advantage of being edited and published by David Laing in 1862. But even thus it serves only as a work of reference, being a set of annals without continuity, and on constitutional points requiring correction, for Dalzel, like Craufurd, treated the College of Edinburgh as a University.

III. Alexander Bower, Assistant Librarian in the University of Edinburgh, published in 1817 *The History of the University* (in two volumes), *chiefly compiled from original papers and records never before published;* and in 1830 he brought out a third volume, continuing his *History* from 1756, which it had before reached, down to 1829. Bower was strong in one point, that of biographical research, and weak in all other points. In his account of the origin and early history of the College he makes ludicrous mistakes, and it is pretty evident that he writes under fear of his masters, the Town Council. When he arrives at times when ticklish questions would have to be discussed, he finds it safer to say nothing about them; so in his third volume, which nominally brings down the history of the University to 1829, he omits all mention of the litigations and other events which had occurred, and in fact gives us nothing but a string of biographies of the Professors. This, in its way, was a useful thing to do, and Bower was industrious in ferreting out particulars, which would otherwise have been irrecoverable, about bygone personages. But neither biographies nor annals will constitute the history of a University.

The primary difficulty in writing a history of the kind is to find out a method under which the facts may be arranged in continuous narrative. The method which, after consideration, I have adopted in these pages is to treat the College, growing into the University, of Edinburgh, as an organism, in respect of its constitution, its staff, and its educational equipment; and to trace the development of that organism from age to age, without mention of persons, except so far as their actions contributed to the progress of the story. To supplement and relieve this somewhat abstract treatment of the history of the University, I have added appendixes containing many details. In one long appendix, which gives imperfect sketches of all defunct Professors who ever taught in the University, I have, to some extent, by placing together the successive Professors in each Chair, exhibited the progress of teaching in each separate department in the University.

The three so-called "Histories" which have been described are all equally deficient in any account of the constitutional forms of the University of Edinburgh. They speak of the College of James VI. as if it had been quite the same as a Mediæval University. And they treat its arrangements as perfectly natural and requiring no explanation. But to me the existing forms and arrangements were a perfect riddle, which I could only solve by going into antecedent history. Hence arose the necessity for my two preliminary chapters on the rise and decadence of the Papal Universities of Scotland, and on the measures adopted by the Reformers in dealing with those institutions. The events and ideas recorded in those chapters will be seen to have formed a set of conditions out of which the peculiarities in the foundation of the College of Edinburgh took their origin.

In addition to what the existing *Histories* contained, I found the following sources of information relative to the University of Edinburgh available: (1) The City Records, in which Craufurd, Dalzel, and Bower had left large gleanings behind them; (2) the Minutes of the Senatus Academicus from 1733 to the present day, of which neither Dalzel nor Bower had made use; (3) unprinted documents in the University Library, such as the Draft Charter of James II., George Drummond's Diary, etc.; (4) the Records of "the College Commissioners" for carrying out the new University buildings, 1816-1834, which are preserved in one of the offices of the Town Council; (5) the evidence before the Royal Commission to inquire into the Universities of Scotland, 1826-1830; (6) the printed Records of several actions before the Court of Session and the House of Lords between the Town Council and the Senatus Academicus; (7) old tracts and rare books of the seventeenth and eighteenth centuries; (8) published biographies of many of the Principals and Professors, from Rollock downwards; (9) scattered notices in contemporary memoirs and autobiographies, and in the *Scots Magazine*, and various other periodicals and newspapers.

Out of this copious mass of materials I dare say I have inadvertently let escape me points of interest and perhaps even of importance. I have also made many conscious omissions, because in fact my object was not to provide a work of reference containing all that can be known about the University of Edinburgh, but to produce, if possible, a readable book of moderate size, and, above all things, to tell a continuous story. Thus the reader will not find here reprints of Charters, nor the early College Regulations in full, nor a record of all the Bursaries founded from time to time, nor an account of the various Commissions which sat upon the College in the seventeenth century without really altering it, nor an examination of the Theses of the Regents or of the draft schemes of Philosophy drawn up by the different Universities of Scotland in 1690 but never adopted. Some one perhaps will say that with all these things, and others too, left out, I have not written the History of the University of Edinburgh. I am willing to admit it, but I beg that it may be remembered that my book has been composed, under some pressure of time, for a special occasion, as a birthday offering to the University on the Tercentenary of its foundation. And I hope that I have succeeded in telling, at least in outline, *The Story of the University during its first three hundred years.*

I have now a great many acknowledgments to make. This book, such as it is, owes immense obligations to my learned friend, Mr. John Small,

Librarian to the University, without whose warm sympathy, and the assistance rendered by his great bibliographical knowledge and familiarity with University traditions, it could never have been written. I have also received much kind aid from my colleagues and friends in the Senatus Academicus, among whom I especially beg to thank Professors Campbell Fraser, Turner, Malcolm Taylor, Lorimer, Muirhead, Macpherson, Chrystal, Tait, Masson, Flint, Charteris, Grainger Stewart, Dickson, T. Fraser, Ewart, Simpson, Chiene, Sir Herbert Oakeley, and *Emeritus* Professor Mackay. I have also to thank the late Lord Provost, Sir Thomas J. Boyd, and the present Lord Provost, the Right Hon. George Harrison, for the cordial permission which, with the concurrence of the Town Council, they accorded me to search the City Records; also Mr. William Skinner, the City Clerk; Mr. Alexander Harris, Depute City Clerk; and Mr. Robert Adam, City Chamberlain, for assisting my enquiries; also the Lord Justice General of Scotland, for the use of some rare books and tracts from his Lordship's Library; also the Keeper of the Records of Scotland for an opinion on the evidence which I set before him[1] relative to

[1] Having circulated as a "Case for Opinion" among various competent authorities the evidence on this curious question, I was favoured by the Keeper of the Records with the following letter:—" I received your 'Case for Opinion' relative to the question whether, besides the

the apparent loss of the original Charter of the College of Edinburgh; also Mr. Thomas Dickson, Curator of the Historical Department in the Register House; Dr. Joseph Anderson, Secretary to the Society of Antiquaries; and Mr. James Gordon, the learned Librarian to the Royal Society of Edinburgh, for their advice and assistance on several points; also Sir Alexander Christison, Bart., and his brothers Dr. David and Mr. John Christison, for kindly placing at my disposal an interesting autobiographical manuscript, written by their illustrious father, Sir Robert Christison, during the latter years of his life. I would also wish to thank the Rev. J. Anderson, an expert in old handwriting, for his assistance in exploring documents of the sixteenth and seventeenth centuries; and Mr. George

---

Charter of James VI., dated 14th April 1582, another Charter or Charters may have been granted in connection with the foundation of the College of Edinburgh. I have very carefully considered the case, in connection with Mr. Dickson, Curator of my Historical Department, upon whose judgment in such matters it is well known that great reliance may be placed. I entirely concur in the opinion which, I understand, he indicated to you verbally, that there is a strong probability that, contemporaneously with or very soon after, the Charter of 14th April 1582, another Charter was granted containing the 'irritant clause' to which reference is made in the entry in the City Records, No. 3 in your 'Case.'   STAIR AGNEW."

The learned Professor of Church History, Dr. Malcolm Taylor, took the same view, and pointed out to me how well the supposition of a lost Charter agreed with certain expressions used by Craufurd. But the reader will judge for himself on the evidence, which is fully stated in Chapter III.

Pearson, engraver, for the great pains he has taken in reproducing likenesses of some of the most celebrated persons connected with the University. I only regret that considerations of cost prevented the number of such portraits from being multiplied.

A. G.

UNIVERSITY OF EDINBURGH,
 19th November 1883.

CONTENTS OF VOL. I.

CHAPTER I.

(PRELIMINARY.)

THE UNIVERSITIES OF SCOTLAND BEFORE THE REFORMATION.

	PAGE
Reason for Preliminary Chapters	1
Foundation of the University of St. Andrews	1–8
Pædagogium of St. Andrews	9–10
College of St. Salvator	10–12
College of St. Leonard	12–14
College of St. Mary	15–17
New College	17
University of St. Andrews previous to the Reformation	18
Foundation of the University of Glasgow	19–22
The Arts Faculty at Glasgow	23
Collapse of the University of Glasgow	24–26
Foundation of the University of Aberdeen	26–31
The Charter of James IV.	31–33
Bulls of Alexander VI.	33–35
Foundation of King's College	35–39
Hector Boece and his Colleagues	39–44
Visit of James V. to the University of Aberdeen	44
Collapse of the University of Aberdeen	45–46
John Mair's Account of the Scottish Universities	47–48

What the Roman Catholic Church did for the Universities	PAGE 48–49
Abbot Myln's Letter	49–50
The "Purging" of the Scottish Universities . .	50–53

CHAPTER II.

(PRELIMINARY.)

THE VARIOUS ATTEMPTS OF THE REFORMERS TO REORGANISE UNIVERSITY EDUCATION IN SCOTLAND.

I. Commission of 1560 for making the Book of Discipline	54–58
New Scheme for Universities in the Book of Discipline	58–68
II. George Buchanan's Scheme . . .	68–69
III. Queen Mary's Gift to the University of Glasgow	69–70
IV. Queen Mary's Charters of 1567 granting Church Property to the Municipalities of Edinburgh and Glasgow	70–73
V. "New Foundation" of the College of Glasgow by the Town Council . . .	73–78
VI. Andrew Melville as Principal of the College of Glasgow	78–84
VII. The *Erectio Regia* by James VI. at Glasgow .	84–90
VIII. *Fundatio Nova* of King's College, Aberdeen .	90–91
IX. New Scheme for the University of St. Andrews (1579)	91–94
Repeal of the "New Foundations" . .	94–96

CHAPTER III.

THE ORIGINS AND OUTSET OF THE UNIVERSITY OF EDINBURGH.

Bower's Incorrect Account of the Origin of the University	97–99

CONTENTS.

	PAGE
Efforts of the Town Council of Edinburgh to obtain a Seat of Learning	99–101
Their Treaty for the Kirk-of-Field	101–103
Opposition from the Three Older Universities	104
Efforts of James Lawson to get a College in Edinburgh	105–106
Royal Sanction for a College obtained (1580)	107
Reasons for supposing that the original Charter of the College of Edinburgh has been lost	107–121
James VI.'s Charter of 1582	121–125
A College, not a University, founded in Edinburgh	125–126
The Academy of Geneva probably taken as a Model	126–127
The Town Council make Hamilton House the nucleus of their College Buildings	128–129
Rollock appointed Regent	129–134
His emoluments	134–136
The Opening of the College (14th October 1583)	137
Nairn's Appointment as Second Master	137
College Regulations	138–143
The College Classes	143–145
The Regenting System	146–148
The College Curriculum	148–151
Examinations for Degrees	151–155
Rollock made Principal	155
Also Professor of Theology	156–158
The Earl of Arran, as Lord Provost, visits the College	159

APPENDIX A. ROBERT REID, BISHOP OF ORKNEY.

External facts of Reid's life	159–160
John Knox's Account of Reid	161–162
Reid's actions as recorded by Ferrerius	163–164
Panegyric of Reid by a monk of Kinloss	165–166
Reid's bequest for a College in Edinburgh	166–167
His wishes frustrated by his executors	167–168
The Town Council receive a small portion of his bequest	168–169

CONTENTS.

APPENDIX B.   KIRK-OF-FIELD.

	PAGE
Old Edinburgh and the Flodden Wall	169
Rise and Fall of the Collegiate Church of Kirk-of-Field	170
Remains of the Kirk-of-Field after the Reformation	171

APPENDIX C.   DISPUTATION AT STIRLING.

Craufurd's Account of the Disputation of the College Regents at Stirling before James VI.	171–174
Relations of James VI. to the College of Edinburgh	174–176

APPENDIX D.   ACADEMY OF GENEVA.

Foundation of the Academy of Geneva and its Peculiar Forms	176–178

APPENDIX E.   MONTAGUE COLLEGE AND THE SCOTS COLLEGE.

History of Montague College down to the Reformation	178–179
History of the Scots College	180

CHAPTER IV.

HISTORY OF THE UNIVERSITY OF EDINBURGH UNDER ITS FIRST FORM AS A DEGREE-GIVING COLLEGE, 1583-1708.

Difference between a "College" and a "University"	181–182
Only a "College" at Edinburgh down to 1708	183–184
Foundation of a Professorship of Laws (1590)	184–189
This changed into a Tutorship of Humanity	189–195
Gift to the College from the Kirk-Session of Edinburgh	195–196
Institution of Rectorship and Professorship of Divinity	197–202
Private Subscriptions for the Chair of Divinity	202–203
The two Senior Regents made "Professors"	203–204
The Act of Confirmation of 1621	204–205
History of the Rectorship of the College	205–212
Professorship of Hebrew created	212–215
James Gregory made Professor of Mathematics	215–217

CONTENTS. xxi

	PAGE
Beginnings of the Medical School	217–218
Institution of the Physic Garden	218–219
Professor of Botany appointed	220
The Royal College of Physicians established	221–223
Three Professors of Medicine appointed	223–229
Carstares obtains a Grant for the Scotch Universities	229–231
Professor of Ecclesiastical History appointed	231
Chair of Public Law created	231–233
Bishop of Edinburgh claims to be Chancellor	233–234
James II. designs to turn the College into a University	234–237
Internal Administration of the College	237–239
Imprudent Conduct of the Regents	239–240
Visitation of the College by Town Council	240–247

APPENDIX F. MARISCHALL COLLEGE.

Origin and Constitution of Marischall College	247–250

APPENDIX G. HISTORY OF THE UNIVERSITY MACE.

The old College Mace stolen	250
University Mace presented by Town Council	251
Armorial Bearings granted to the University	252

APPENDIX H. DRAFT CHARTER OF JAMES II. 253–257

CHAPTER V.

THE DEVELOPMENT OF THE FOUR FACULTIES IN THE UNIVERSITY OF EDINBURGH, 1708–1858.

The Regents turned into Professors	258–263
The new Curriculum in Arts	263–264
Decline of Graduation in Arts	265
Professors' Programmes in 1741	266–274
Dr. A. Carlyle's Criticism of the Professors	275
Chair of Rhetoric founded	276

CONTENTS.

	PAGE
Efforts of Senatus to revive Graduation in Arts	277–282
Chair of Civil Law instituted	282–284
Chairs of Civil History and Scots Law founded	285–288
Teaching by the Faculty of Laws in 1741	289
Senatus opposes institution of Chair of Conveyancing	290–291
Also of Chair of Medical Jurisprudence	291
These two Chairs founded	291–292
Chairs of Anatomy and Chemistry instituted	292–297
Alexander Monro *primus*, Professor of Anatomy	298–302
Anatomical Theatre provided in the University	302–304
Valuable Services of Lord Provost Drummond	304–305
Foundation of the Royal Infirmary	305–306
Porterfield appointed Professor of Medicine	306–308
The use of the College Garden granted to four Physicians	308–310
The Medical Faculty in the University founded	310–315
Chair of Midwifery founded	315–316
Clinical Teaching established	317
Alston, Professor of Botany and Materia Medica	318
Separate Chair of Materia Medica	319
Regius Professorship of Natural History founded	319–320
Chair of Surgery proposed, but resisted	321–322
Regius Chair of Clinical Surgery founded (1802)	322–323
Regius Chair of Military Surgery founded (1806)	324–325
Chair of Comparative Anatomy and Veterinary Surgery resisted	325
Chairs of Surgery and of Pathology established	326–327
Full complement of the Medical Faculty	328
Growth of Medical Graduations	329
Regulations for Medical Degrees	330–333
Teaching of the Faculty of Divinity	334–337
Regius Chair of Biblical Criticism founded (1847)	337–338
Regius Chair of Practical Astronomy founded (1785)	338–341
Professor of Practical Astronomy to be Astronomer-Royal	341–344

CONTENTS. xxiii

	PAGE
Chair of Agriculture founded (1790)	344–348
General Reid's Bequest	348–352
Chair of the Theory of Music founded (1839)	352–354
Chair of Technology founded (1855)	354–356
George Wilson, Professor of Technology	357–360
Suppression of the Chair	361

APPENDIX I. ALEXANDER CUNNINGHAM.

Circumstances of Cunningham's appointment as Professor of Civil Law in Scotland, and his subsequent history 361–362

APPENDIX J. GEORGE DRUMMOND.

George Drummond's Early Life and two first Marriages	363–364
His Diary	364–369
His third and fourth Marriages	369–370
His Character, Services, and Funeral	371–373

APPENDIX K. THE NATURAL HISTORY MUSEUM OF THE UNIVERSITY OF EDINBURGH.

Collections of Dr. Andrew Balfour and Sir Robert Sibbald	374–375
Professor Walker's Collection	375
Professor Jameson's Collection	376–377
Transference of this Collection to the Government	377–378

APPENDIX L. THE EDINBURGH OBSERVATORY.

M'Laurin's efforts to obtain an Observatory	378
Short's Observatory (1776)	379
Professor Playfair's Observatory (1812-1834)	380
Present state of the Observatory	381

APPENDIX M. GENERAL REID.

Family History, Biography, and Characteristics of General Reid 382–384

LIST OF ILLUSTRATIONS.

VOL. I.

1. EAST FAÇADE OF THE UNIVERSITY OF EDINBURGH . . . . . *Frontispiece*
2. ROBERT ROLLOCK (Photolithograph) *To face page* 132
3. OLD BUILDINGS OF THE COLLEGE OF EDINBURGH . . . . ,, 171
4. ALEXANDER HENDERSON (Photolithograph) ,, 207
5. WILLIAM CARSTARES (Photolithograph) . ,, 244
6. ROBERT LEIGHTON (Photolithograph) . ,, 259
7. COLIN M'LAURIN (Photolithograph) . ,, 271
8. ALEXANDER MONRO, *Primus* . . ,, 299
9. BIRD'S-EYE VIEW OF THE COLLEGE OF EDINBURGH, 1646 (Photolithograph) . ,, 309
10. JAMES SYME . . . . ,, 328
11. GENERAL REID . . . . ,, 348
12. GEORGE DRUMMOND . . . ,, 373

The Engravings by George Pearson.

CHAPTER I.

(PRELIMINARY.)

THE UNIVERSITIES OF SCOTLAND BEFORE THE REFORMATION.

———"A dying glory smiles
O'er the far times."

THE three older Universities of Scotland were among the assets of the Roman Catholic Church which, at its disestablishment passed under the control of the Reformers. In order fully to understand the historical circumstances, and especially the academical ideas, which ushered in the foundation of the University of Edinburgh not long after the Reformation, it will be expedient to trace in outline the character and fortunes of the earlier University foundations; and then to examine, with some minuteness, the way in which the Reformers dealt with them on coming into possession. These two subjects, accordingly, will occupy the following preliminary chapters.

Bishop Henry Wardlaw, the founder of the University of St. Andrews, had been in early life a student at Oxford. "But northern men were never popular there, and it happened that the Papal schism just then made new cause of quarrel. In 1382 Richard II. of England addressed a writ to the Chancellor and Proctors of the University of Oxford, forbidding them to molest the Scotch Students, notwithstanding their 'damnable adherence' to Robert the Antipope (Clement VII.)."[1]

On the death of this Clement in 1394 the great schism was continued, Peter de Luna, a Spaniard, having been chosen by the French cardinals, under the title of Benedict XIII., while the Italian cardinals had already given their allegiance to Boniface IX. Scotland again took the side of Antipope, in the person of Benedict XIII., who got very little support from the rest of the Church, even France having soon dropped him. He was indeed a prisoner in his own palace at Avignon when visited there by Henry Wardlaw in 1404, and Scotland and Spain were then his only adherents. To Spain he presently retired, and from Paniscola in Arragon he had the honour of issuing Bulls which constituted the charter of Scotland's first University. It is curious to think that the University of St. Andrews should have had its foundation ratified, on the motion of a King[2] who was a captive away from his own dominions, by a Pope who, in the eyes of the greater part of

---

[1] Cosmo Innes, *Scotland in the Middle Ages*, p. 274.

[2] James I., who, after being for a brief period under Bishop Wardlaw's tutelage at St. Andrews, was captured by the English on his way to France for safer keeping and education. The Bulls of Benedict XIII. above referred to, cite "a petition lately submitted to us from our dear son James, the illustrious King of Scotland," etc.

Christendom, was no Pope at all. But by these peculiar circumstances the foundation was in no whit rendered less stable and permanent.

When Wardlaw found himself a Bishop, and the trusted Legate of that claimant to the Papacy whom Scotland at all events acknowledged, he may have looked back to the days, more than twenty years before, when he had seen his countrymen "molested" at Oxford. But, independently of this, there was case enough for the necessity of a University at home, for it was not merely the question of welcome or otherwise at Oxford or other foreign schools,— but how to get to any such places, amid wars and troubles, and dangers by land and sea? To the Scottish clergy, the class in the country who most required it, University instruction was as yet an affair of expatriation, risk, manifold hardship, and expense. Within seven years after his appointment as Bishop, Wardlaw had resolved on the foundation of a University at St. Andrews, and had actually founded one. And yet it is not now clear how far the idea of this foundation sprang originally from Wardlaw's own mind, and how far it was suggested by others. Indeed there seems to have been a certain amount of preparatory spontaneous growth; and the elements of a University were, to a certain extent, ready beforehand within St. Andrews itself. In the list of the first professors we find the names of John Litster, canon of St. Andrews; John Schives, official; and John Shevez, archdeacon of the same; beside William Stephen, who was probably an ecclesiastic there, and afterwards became Bishop of Dunblane. These and others not named doubtless formed the nucleus of a professorial staff, though persons of eminence were encouraged to come from a distance to supplement and add lustre to the materials which St. Andrews itself afforded. Such were Lawrence of Lindores, abbot of Scone, who lectured on the Sentences of Peter Lombard; and Richard Cornwall, doctor of decrees and archdeacon of Lothian. In all, it is said[1] that there were "thirteen doctors of theology and eight doctors of decrees, besides others. Nor was there wanting a corresponding auditory; for all who thirsted for literature resorted to the University from every quarter." Accordingly, Wardlaw addresses his deed of constitution, dated 27th February 1411 [12], "to the Reverend the doctors, masters, bachelors, and body of scholars (*scolaribus universis*) residing in our city of St. Andrews, present and to come;" and proceeds: "It is fitting for me to accede to your requests" in favour of "your University, which I have actually (*de facto*) instituted and founded, though without prejudice to the authority of the Holy See, and by these presents do institute and found, and which has been laudably inaugurated by you."

Thus the University had somehow come into existence before the execution of this deed in February 1411 [12], and the one thing which Wardlaw had now to do, for the body of teachers and scholars which had been collected, was, according to the

[1] Hector Boethius, *Scotorum Historiæ*, lib. xvi.

ideas of the times, to give them privileges. As Bulæus[1] said: "A University without privileges is like a body without a soul." The remainder of Wardlaw's deed of constitution consists, therefore, of a concession of privileges to the members of the University. They are to be freed from all exaction of customs. In all civil causes they are to be subject to the jurisdiction of their own Rector. Their lodgings in the town are to be held by them at a rent to be fixed by sworn arbitrators, half of them appointed by the University and half by the city. Beneficed clergy studying or teaching in the University are allowed to be absent from their benefices and at the same time to retain their stipends. The bedells, servitors, writers, stationers, and parchment-makers, with the wives, children, and maidservants of these, and of all members of the University, are to enjoy the privileges conceded. They are all to have free liberty of making wills. And they are exempted from all tributes, gifts, exactions, vexations, capitations, watches, guards, assessments, burdens, and services, either of person or property.[2] Any difference arising between the Rector of the University and the town bailies as to the punish-

[1] "Denique non plus stare possunt Studia Generalia sine Privilegiis, quam corpus sine anima.—*Hist. Un. Par.*, l. p. 98.

[2] *Angariis et Perangariis.—Angaria—*derived from the Greek word ἀγγαρεύειν (cf. *St. Matthew's Gospel*, v. 41), and originally from the old Persian custom of compelling private individuals to carry the post—was, in the Middle Ages, the term for a direct service levied on the person. *Perangaria* (which Ducange considers to have been a miswriting for *Parangaria*) was an indirect service levied on a man's property, as, for instance, compelling him to give the use of his horse or cart, etc.

ment of delinquents, etc., is to be referred to the Bishop and his successors, as perpetual Chancellors of the University.

In this charter of constitution we see exemplified what was understood in the fifteenth century by the terms "founding a University"—it was something more than merely establishing a school with various branches of teaching; it was, in truth, setting up a little State within the State. To this Act the consent of the Scottish Parliament had been obtained,[1] the young King in captivity had given it his good wishes, and the local ecclesiastical authorities—the Prior, Archdeacon, and Chapter of St. Andrews—had concurred. But something more was requisite in order to give the new institution the full *status* of a University, and to enable it to take rank among the Universities of Christendom—and that was the sanction of the Pope, to whom, as holding the keys of St. Peter, and wielding authority over the entire spiritual concerns of Europe, it logically belonged to allow or disallow the creation of semi-independent literary republics. Wardlaw must have had plenty of influence for an affair of this kind with the Pope, whom he represented. Yet all seems to have been done deliberately and in order. The petition before referred to was drawn up, and Benedict XIII. professes, though this was probably a mere matter of form, to have made some inquiry into the case, and to have satisfied himself that St. Andrews was a

[1] "De consilio, consensu, et communi tractatu trium statuum personarum, Regni Scotiæ."—*Bull of Benedict XIII.*

peculiarly suitable place for the seat of a University, "owing to its peaceful neighbourhood, the fertility of the surrounding country, and the number of good houses which it contained." He therefore gave his consent, and expressed a hope that "a city blessed by Providence with so many advantages and so much natural beauty might become fertile in knowledge, and in the production of men famous for their wisdom and virtue." About a year and a half after the date of Wardlaw's foundation, Benedict XIII. signed six Bulls at Paniscola in Spain, ratifying, in the most formal manner, all the privileges which Wardlaw had conceded, and denouncing the wrath of God, St. Peter, and St. Paul, upon all who should infringe the charter of the University of St. Andrews. Four months later, on the 3d of February 1413 [14], Henry Ogilvie arrived in St. Andrews bearing the precious documents, and was "welcomed by the ringing of bells from the steeples, and the tumultuous joy of all classes of the inhabitants." The next day, being Sunday, was given up to the celebration of the great event—the Bulls were read in the presence of the Bishop and the assembled clergy; they walked in procession to the cathedral, where the *Te Deum* was sung and high mass celebrated; and the remainder of the day and evening was devoted by the whole people to mirth and festivity, processions, bonfires, song, dance, and the wine-cup. So great a matter for rejoicing and pride it was to have obtained a real University, duly constituted by the Pope, and legally standing on the same level with the great Universities abroad, to which so many Scotsmen had resorted.

One point in the Papal Bulls constituting the University of St. Andrews is noticeable, and that is the strict system of examinations for degrees which they prescribe. Every candidate for the Master's or Doctor's degree (there is no mention of Bachelors) is to be presented to the Bishop, or his Vicegerent, or some one nominated by him, " who, in the presence of all the Doctors and Masters teaching in the Faculty of the candidate, shall proceed without charge, purely and freely, without trick or hindrance, to examine him in his knowledge, eloquence, mode of reading,[1] and whatever else may be required, and then with the counsel of the aforesaid Doctors and Masters (given on oath and secretly), shall, if he be found fit, admit him to his degree, and give him a license to teach; but if he be not found fit, shall, without feud or favour, by no means admit him." Such was the high conception entertained in the fifteenth century of a University degree; it was not a mere distinction to be obtained by a youth, but it was a license to teach, not to be lightly conceded, but only awarded after full scrutiny, conducted in the most solemn way by the highest authorities.

Altogether the attitude of those days towards learning was reverential, and also enthusiastic, and full of faith. Wardlaw had launched his University by giving it privileges and nothing more. He provided at first neither stipends for the teachers

[1] *i.e.* his mode of lecturing or teaching.

nor buildings or apartments of any kind in which teaching could be carried on. He appears to have assumed that when once a privileged community for learning had been established, men would not fail to join it; that beneficed clergy would gladly avail themselves of the permission to teach in it in lieu of performing their clerical duties; and that the University of St. Andrews might manage to get on, as the University of Paris at its outset had done, without the provision of any regularly-appointed lecture rooms. But "during the first twenty years after the foundation of the University of St. Andrews great inconvenience was suffered, not merely from the want of such rooms, but from the multiplying of schools in the different religious houses, all of them claiming to be considered as constituent parts of the University."[1] The first local habitation and centre was given in 1430 by Wardlaw himself, who granted to the Faculty of Arts and their Dean "a certain tenement situated on the south side of South Street" (where St. Mary's College now is), that the regents and masters might therein hold their grammatical schools, or to serve as halls and chambers of the students. This then became the *pædagogium*, the headquarters of the Arts Faculty, while the studies in the Faculties of Theology and Law continued to be held in other buildings, and the congregations of the University in the Augustinian Priory.

Under this free and primitive system the num-

---

[1] Principal Lee's *Lectures on the Church of Scotland*, vol. i. p. 16, note.

ber of the Students, according to Boethius, *excrevit in immensum.* Three separate Colleges rose up in St. Andrews, and yet the want of collegiate endowments became ultimately apparent, so that in 1512 the Pædagogium was described as "lying almost extinct for deficiency of funds and learned men." In Scotland, owing to the rudeness of the nobility, there was a lack of that private munificence and piety which in other Universities produced so many foundations. And all that was done of any importance for the University of St. Andrews, was done by successive prelates of the See, under whose auspices and authority three Colleges in course of time arose: that founded under the name of our Saviour (Sancti Salvatoris) by Bishop Kennedy in 1456; that substituted for the Hospital of St. Leonard by Prior Hepburn and Archbishop Stewart in 1512; and the College of the Assumption of the blessed Virgin Mary on the site of the Pædagogium, devised by Archbishop Stewart, actually begun by Archbishop James Beaton in 1537, continued by Cardinal David Beaton till his murder in 1546, and completed and remodelled by Archbishop Hamilton in 1558. The endowments of all the several colleges were provided by annexing to them the teinds of various parishes which had belonged to the Bishopric or Priory. But some personal expense on the part of the respective prelates was incurred in the erection of the buildings.

It is the object here, not to attempt a history of the University of St. Andrews, but only to indicate certain points in which the manner of its foundation and its early circumstances either contrast with those of the University of Edinburgh or serve to explain them. The three endowed Colleges within the University of St. Andrews, on the one hand, suggest historical contrast, as they were thoroughly mediæval in character; and yet, on the other hand, they serve as explanatory antecedents, having been undoubtedly imitated to a certain extent by the post-Reformation University-makers. The statutes of each of the three Colleges show that they were intended, not to be merely homes for scholars and places for University study, but to have a religious and semi-monastic character. St. Salvator's was defined by its founder, Bishop Kennedy, as "a college for theology and the arts, for divine worship and scholastic exercises." Maintenance in it was provided for thirteen persons ("being the number of the apostles"), namely a Master in Theology, with the title of Provost, a Licentiate in Theology, and a Bachelor in Theology; four Masters of Arts; and six poor clerks (*i.e.* young men belonging to the inferior orders of the Roman Church and aspiring to become deacons and priests). The Provost and his two theological assistants were to lecture in divinity, the Masters of Arts in logic, physics, metaphysics, and other branches of philosophy. A common table was provided, and regular religious services prescribed. To be first Provost, Bishop Kennedy called home John Athelmer, who had been educated in the Pædagogium, and was then a

Professor in the University of Paris. It was said of St. Salvator's, in reference to its buildings and paraphernalia, that "there was nothing outside or inside the College which did not evince the piety, taste, and munificence of the founder."[1] Yet, from an educational point of view, it was a tiny community, with seven teachers, and only six resident scholars. But probably other University Students, not on the foundation, were admitted to the lectures, and there can be no doubt that St. Salvator's greatly contributed to the stability and fame of the University of St. Andrews, during the latter half of the fifteenth and the first part of the sixteenth century, many distinguished men having been members of the College.

It is noticeable that a Bull of Pius II. in 1468 gave the Provost and Canons of St. Salvator's the power of granting degrees in Theology and Arts, but that two years afterwards the College renounced the right which had thus (to the prejudice of the University) been conferred upon them.

The old Hospital of St. Leonard had been founded by a former Prior of St. Andrews to accommodate the numerous pilgrims who flocked from all parts to witness the miracles wrought by the bones of Andrew the Apostle, but "these miracles having ceased," as Archbishop Stewart thinks, "on Christianity becoming thoroughly rooted in the country," pilgrims also ceased to come; and the hospital had been turned into an asylum for aged and infirm

[1] Martine, quoted in Lyon's *History of St. Andrews*, vol. i. p. 222.

women, "who, however, exhibited but little fruit either of godliness or virtue." So in 1512 the young Archbishop fully concurred with John Hepburn, Prior of St. Andrews (who was ready to find the endowments), that the hospital, with the church of St. Leonard attached to it, should, "for the sake of preserving the storm-tost bark of St. Peter," be converted into a College for maintaining one principal and four chaplains, "two of whom, being regents, shall say daily masses for the souls of both the old and the new founders; with twenty poor scholars, who shall be all well instructed in the Gregorian *cantus* and *discantus*, and six of whom shall be students in theology."

Thus a religious house was established, in which the pious founders secured an interest by enjoining daily masses for their own souls. Prior Hepburn proceeded to draw the statutes, in which a strict "order of living" was prescribed, looking like a milder copy of the rule of life at Montague College, under Standon.[1] The "poor scholars" at St. Leonard's had their occasional "flesh days," and seem, on the whole, to have fared pretty well, but they did, in turns, the cleaning of the house, the waiting at table, and other domestic duties. No female must enter the College, except the laundress, who must be more than fifty years of age. A cook and his boy appear to have been the only servants. And these were the only persons in the house who were excused from speaking always in Latin. Each

[1] See below, Appendix E to Chapter III.

candidate for admission must be between fifteen and twenty-one years of age, must be poor, virtuous, versed in the first and second parts of grammar, a good writer, and a good singer. In these accomplishments there was to be an examination. And if there were several candidates, the examination became competitive. Youths not on the foundation, being the children of the nobility, or others, might be admitted, provided they conformed strictly to the discipline, plain living, and clerical dress of the place. There were to be lectures on grammar, poetry, and oratory; and the Students, before proceeding to the degree of "Master," were to be perfected in logic, physics, philosophy, metaphysics, and ethics, and in one of the books of Solomon. The College soon acquired great repute, and was attended by many sons of the nobility and the gentry. The Students had an especial repute for their skill in church music.

After St. Salvator's College had been founded in 1456 Regents of the University of St. Andrews went on lecturing to University Students within the walls of the Pædagogium, which had, however, no endowments wherewith to secure the permanent services of competent teachers. In 1512 it was spoken of as lying "almost extinct," under a dearth of means and of learned men. Alexander Stewart, at the age of eighteen, had, in 1510, been settled in the Archbishopric, and, at the same time, made Lord Chancellor of Scotland, as well as Abbot of Dunfermline and Prior of Coldingham, *in com-*

mendam. Stewart was the natural son of James IV. by Margaret, daughter of Archibald Boyd of Bonshaw — and the only excuse which might be pleaded in palliation of the flagrant nepotism of which he was the object is, that he was really a youth of much accomplishment and literary taste, and of good disposition. He had been the pupil of Patrick Panter, James IV.'s Latin secretary, and the first Scotsman who could write good classical Latin. Afterwards, when thirteen years old, he was placed under the tuition of Erasmus, with whom he remained for five years, residing in various foreign towns and studying (ultimately) Greek, rhetoric, theology, and music. Erasmus, in one of his letters, draws a charming picture of Stewart, his quickness and untiring perseverance, and the sweetness and nobility of his character. The excellent classical education which he had received must have predisposed the boy-archbishop to take an interest in all schemes for improving the University of St. Andrews, of which he now became Chancellor, and he was warmly, either seconded or instigated, by John Hepburn, then Prior of the Monastery. After they had jointly founded and endowed the College of St. Leonard, Archbishop Stewart turned his attention to the Pædagogium, which he resolved to endow and erect into a College, for the glory of God, the defence of the faith, the increase of learning, and the celebration of *obits* for the souls of the King and the Archbishop, and their predecessors and successors. " With this view he repaired the chapel of St. John the Evangelist, which served as a place of worship to the Pædagogium;" and he executed a deed annexing to it the living of the Church of St. Michael de Tarvet, near Cupar. Any further steps in the way of erecting and equipping a college were fatally arrested next year, when Alexander Stewart was slain by his father's side on the field of Flodden.[1]

A quarter of a century passed away, and in 1537 James Beaton, then Archbishop, obtained a Bull from Pope Paul III. empowering him to erect a "college of scholars and presbyters, with a chapel in the same, under the name of the Assumption of the blessed Virgin Mary," and to endow it with the revenues of certain churches. This Bull not only sanctioned, in general terms, the foundation of a College for doctors, masters, and bursars, etc., the teaching within it of all University subjects, but also expressly granted to the regents and superiors of the College the power of conferring degrees—a privilege which, as in the case of St. Salvator's, was soon renounced and merged in the University. Buildings for St. Mary's College, on the site of the Pædagogium, were commenced by James Beaton, at his own expense, but within two years he died, and a sum of money, which he bequeathed for finishing the work, is said to have been diverted to other uses. Archbishop Beaton's buildings, however, were carried

---

[1] Even the annexation of the church of Tarvet seems to have been set aside, for this same gift was made anew to St. Mary's College by Archbishop Hamilton in 1558.

on by his nephew and successor the Cardinal, who appointed certain learned men as superiors, masters, regents, and scholars of the College, together with some presbyters and singers for the celebration of divine service therein. In 1552 Hamilton, the next Archbishop, obtained a Bull from Pope Julius III. sanctioning anew the foundation of the College, and authorising him to alter at pleasure the arrangements of his predecessors.

The principal changes introduced by Archbishop Hamilton into the foundation of the Beatons appear to have been, *first*, to discontinue the teaching of civil law and medicine in St. Mary's College, which thus became limited to a school of arts, theology, and canon law,—in short, a seminary for the training of ecclesiastics; *secondly*, to increase the number of persons on the foundation from fourteen to thirty-three, of whom four were to be professors and eight to be Students of theology and canon law; five were to be Professors and sixteen Students of philosophy, that is to say, logic, ethics, physics, and mathematics, with rhetoric and grammar. Hamilton's "foundation and erection of New College" (as St. Mary's was now called) had not only pious, but also polemical objects in view. It was a move of defence against the advance of Lutheranism, which had by this time found its way into St. Andrews, and had, as was said, especially leavened that community which should have been occupied in "preserving the storm-tost bark of St. Peter" within the walls of the College of St. Leonard. In 1558 Hamilton

executed a fresh deed of endowment in favour of
New College, in order "to oppose the heresies and
schisms of the pestiferous heretics and heresiarchs,
who, alas! have sprung up and flourished in these
times, in this as well as in many other parts of the
world." But in that same year the University books
recorded that "on account of the religious disturb-
ances very few students have come to the University;" the whole matriculation list, indeed, contains but three names. And next year (1559) the
graduation ceremonial was omitted, "because in the
universal confusion attendant on the Reformation,
it was impossible to be held."[1] Speedily thereafter
the Reformation in Scotland was accomplished, and
a new order of things was commenced in the Universities, of which more will have to be said. The
University of St. Andrews had now lasted a hundred and fifty years, and had done a great deal
towards the education of the country, a very large
proportion of the eminent men of Scotland having
been its *alumni*. After the first flush at its opening the numbers attendant at it soon fell off, and
especially after the foundation of a second University
at Glasgow. It is thought that less than two hundred
students attended it during the first half of the sixteenth century, and still fewer previously.[2] In fact,
but for the foundation of the Colleges, which pro-

---

[1] "Comitiis habitis 15 Maii anno 59 de promovendis discipulis
statuit academia omnes laureandos hujus anni pro laureatis haberi,
quod universa reipublicæ perturbatione et religionis reformatione
veteres ritus servare impediretur."

[2] M'Crie, *Life of A. Melville*, vol. i. p. 250.

vided adequate stipends for professors, and maintenance for altogether sixty poor scholars, it seems as if the University might have dwindled away altogether.

The University of Glasgow was founded nearly forty years later than that of St. Andrews, a Bull for the purpose having been obtained in 1450 from Pope Nicholas V. by Turnbull, Bishop of Glasgow. This Bull is in the same form, often in the same words, as that given by Benedict XIII. to Bishop Wardlaw. The King of Scotland, "our dearest son in Christ" (James II.), is quoted as greatly desiring the establishment of a "General Study" in his city of Glasgow. Then follows a specification of points in which the locality was suitable: namely, that the air was healthy (*aeris viget temperies*), and victuals, etc., abundant. Wherefore the Pope, moved by these considerations, founds a General Study in Glasgow, for all times, in theology, canon and civil law, and any other lawful faculty; bestows on the Bishops of Glasgow the office and jurisdiction of chancellor, with the right, after due examination, of conferring degrees and making licentiates; and grants to all persons so graduated or licensed full liberty of lecturing and teaching, without further examination, throughout the world.

It has often been said that the University of Glasgow was created after the model of that of Bologna. But the Bull of Nicholas did not prescribe any regulations by which the form and character of the University, as a teaching body, would be determined beforehand; it merely conceded to the masters and Students of Glasgow the same privileges and immunities as those enjoyed by the masters and Students of Bologna, and enacted that the Bishops of Glasgow, as Chancellors, should have the same authority over doctors, masters, and scholars, as that exercised by the *Rectores scholarum* of the University of Bologna. In short, it merely constituted a literary corporation with the usual privileges and the usual ecclesiastical head. The reference to Bologna merely defined the extent of the privileges conceded to the body corporate, and the amount of authority to be possessed by the chancellor. The distinguishing characteristic of the University of Bologna had always been that it was a school of jurisprudence. Indeed, all the Italian Universities (except Salerno, which was medical) had too exclusively devoted themselves to civil and canon law, so that Dante complained that in his time men studied "nothing but the decretals," and Roger Bacon declared that the jurisprudence of the Italians had "distracted philosophy and disturbed Church and State alike."[1] Had it been intended that the new University of Glasgow should copy Bologna, there would have been special encouragements, either in its charter or in its institutions, for the study of law, but this does not appear to have been the case. It has been observed that "the customs and technical phraseology of the new University early showed an imitation of the institutions of

[1] Quoted by Döllinger, *Die Universitaten sonst and jetzt* (Munich, 1871), p. 4.

Louvain, then and for all the following century the model university of Northern Europe;"[1] of which very recently (in 1432) a Scotsman, named John Lichton, had been Rector. This was especially the case with regard to the position of the Arts Faculty, which at Louvain had assumed a position of remarkable prominence, with four *pædagogia* for its accommodation. In the University of Glasgow, from its earliest commencement to the present day, the Faculty of Arts has always been distinguished relatively to other Faculties in the same University, and to the same Faculty in the other Universities of Scotland.

Bishop Turnbull's University was started, like Bishop Wardlaw's, with "privileges" for its portion, in lieu of endowments. Within two years fully a hundred members had joined it, chiefly, it is said, ecclesiastics, regular or secular, "for the sake of the honour attached to a learned corporation, or of the immunities to which it entitled them."[2] There appears to have been at first no stated or regular teaching in the higher Faculties. In canon and civil law and theology "the zeal of individuals prompted them to read occasional lectures, the continuance of which depended on the caprice of the hearers, whose attendance on them was optional."[3] In the year 1460 Elphinston, who had graduated in arts at Glasgow in 1456,[4] and had performed clerical

[1] Cosmo Innes, *Sketches of Early Scotch History*, p. 221.
[2] M'Crie, *Life of A. Melville*, i. p. 66.   [3] M'Crie, *ib.*, p. 67.
[4] Keith, *Catalogue of Scottish Bishops*, p. 116. The dates, however, of Elphinston's early life are somewhat uncertain. See Cosmo Innes, *Sketches*, pp. 262, 263.

duties in the meantime, crossed over to France to attend the law schools of the Continent, thus evincing that adequate instruction in this department was not to be found at home.

In the nascent University "the Faculty of Arts alone received a definite shape and constitution. The members of this Faculty annually elected a Dean (in imitation of Louvain, where the Faculty of Arts had recently changed the title of its head from *Procurator* to *Decanus*); they had stated meetings; promulgated laws for their government; and, more than all, acquired property by the munificence of benefactors, which the University as a body did not do for some time. There might be some danger of the Faculty of Arts absorbing the University. Bachelors' degrees were conferred in Arts, Licentiates and Masters of Arts were made, and these degrees were recorded, not in the University registers, but in the register of the Faculty of Arts."[1] At a very early period in the history of the University this Faculty rented a building, in which there were lecture rooms for their masters, and chambers for the lodging of Students, who had a common table. This was the "auld pedagogy" in Rotten Row. In 1460 the first Lord Hamilton bestowed on the Faculty of Arts a piece of ground, on which they gradually erected a new pedagogy, which in its turn became the site of the late College[2]

[1] Cosmo Innes, *Sketches*, p. 222.
[2] Built with funds obtained from subscriptions; begun in 1631, and completed in 1656.

of Glasgow, until in 1869 the University was removed to its present splendid domicile.

Of the academic life of the Arts Faculty of Glasgow in the fifteenth century a bright picture has been extracted from one of their statutes, prescribing the celebration of their annual gaudy day, to be held on the Sunday, or feast next after the translation of St. Nicholas (9th May), "when all the Masters, Licentiates, Bachelors, and Students, after hearing matins in the chapel of St. Thomas the Martyr, rode in solemn procession, bearing flowers and branches of trees, through the public street from the upper part of the town to the cross, and so back to the College of the Faculty; and there, amid the joy of the feast, the Masters took counsel for the welfare of the Faculty, and gave their diligence to remove all discords and quarrels, that all rejoicing in heart might honour the prince of peace and joy. After the banquet the whole crowd of Masters and Students were directed to repair to a more fitting place of amusement, and there enact some interlude or other show to rejoice the people."[1]

Such a glimpse have we of the collegiate organisation of the Faculty of Arts at Glasgow previous to the Reformation, at a time when the other Faculties and the University itself could show nothing of the kind. The Faculties of Law and Theology had to borrow the chapter-house of the Preaching Friars for the delivery of their lectures, which, as has been said before, were only intermittent; and the congre-

---

[1] Cosmo Innes, *Sketches*, p. 245.

gations of the University were held under authority of the Bishop, as Chancellor, in the chapter-house of his Cathedral. Yet all the constitutional forms of a great mediæval University were there, and continued to be in use till the last. The four "nations" continued to elect severally their four procurators, and these to elect the Rector; convocations of the University were held; bachelors, licentiates, and masters were laureated; regents performed their teaching functions; and persons matriculated in the University were duly admitted to all the privileges conferred by the Papal Bull, till the Reformation troubles brought all this to a standstill; and then the Reformers stepping in remodelled everything, and by their *erectio nova* started the University afresh under a greatly modified form.

But long before the Reformation signs of waning from inanition had been observable in the University of Glasgow. The lack of endowments, the absence of assistance from either public or private liberality, dragged down the enthusiasm of those who might have aspired to cultivate higher learning in the West of Scotland. John Mair, writing his history before the year 1522, speaks of the University of Glasgow as "parum dotata aut scholasticis abundans." Turnbull's successors in the Bishopric of Glasgow and in the Chancellorship of the University during the century which elapsed between the death of Turnbull and the Reformation—namely, Bishops Muirhead, Laing, and Carmichael; Archbishops Blacader, James Beaton the first, Gavin

Dunbar, and James Beaton the second—did but little for the University, though all were men of statecraft and influence, most of them probably having been educated at foreign Universities— Dunbar having been noted for his literary and scholastic attainments, and the first Beaton, when translated to St. Andrews, having been the zealous founder of St. Mary's College. Among them they did a good deal for the Cathedral and Episcopal palace of Glasgow, but not much to encourage or help on the University. Thus it is not to be wondered at that Scotsmen of ability saw a better market for their talents in the foreign schools, and went "regenting" in France and the Low Countries. Owing to the troubles in Scotland, and the want of stipends in the Scotch Universities, both students who could afford to go and teachers of mark still sought the Continent. Thus the University of Glasgow has not a brilliant show of names on her lists before the Reformation. Among those she educated the most notable were—Bishop Elphinston; William Manderston, afterwards Rector of the University of Paris, and then of St. Andrews; Cardinal Beaton; John Knox; and John Spottiswood, the Superintendent of Lothian. The only names, even slightly distinguished, among her professors were John Mair, David Melville, and John Ade or Adamson.[1] In 1563, when Mary Queen of Scots was advised to do something for the University, the letter written in her name describes the whole institution as a failure:

[1] M'Crie, *Life of A. Melville*, vol. i. p. 69.

"rather the decay of ane Universitie nor ony wyse to be reknit ane establisst foundatioun." And ten years later the magistrates of the city speak of the *Pædagogium* as ruinous, and its studies and discipline extinct.[1] From these ashes of its first development the University of Glasgow was destined, like the phœnix, to arise.

The fifteenth century saw the issue of another Papal Bull, signed by Alexander H. in February 1494, and founding a third University for Scotland, namely, that of Aberdeen, at the instance of James IV., who had been moved thereto by William Elphinston, Bishop of Aberdeen. Elphinston had had great and varied experience in University matters. He had been one of the earliest graduates of the University of Glasgow, and had proceeded to Paris, where, after three years' study of the canon law, he was made *primarius lector*, or Professor of the subject, an office which he held for three years. He then migrated to the University of Orleans, where for three years more he studied and lectured on the most abstruse parts of civil law.[2] Returning to Scotland with the appointment of Official-General of the Diocese of Glasgow, he became successively Dean of the Faculty of Arts, Dean of the Faculty of Law, and Rector of the University of Glasgow. He thus was intimately acquainted with two of the great foreign schools, and was personally cognisant

---

[1] Cosmo Innes, *Sketches*, p. 223.

[2] In his Statutes for King's College, Elphinston lays down that the *Canonista* in the College shall teach after the manner of Paris, and the *Legista* after the manner of Orleans.

of all the difficulties with which his own *Alma Mater* at Glasgow, hardly a generation old, had struggled and was still struggling. His character, as drawn by Hector Boece, was beautiful, and his actions prove his zeal for the promotion of all things that were lovely and of good report. He was soon in a position to give effect to his aspirations, for in 1484 he was made Bishop of Aberdeen, and thereafter Lord Chancellor of Scotland; and when, in 1488, the young King James IV. ascended the throne, Elphinston appears to have had considerable access to his person, and to have been in several matters his mentor and guide.[1] It is therefore no great stretch of legitimate conjecture to suppose that Elphinston's influence may have procured those two enlightened measures for which the reign of James IV. is famous—namely, first, the Act of 1496, which required all barons and freeholders to have their eldest sons instructed in " arts and jure;" and secondly, the introduction of printing into Scotland by means of the royal patent granted in 1507 to Walter Chepman and Andrew Myllar for setting up a press in Edinburgh. Elphinston's proclivity for legal studies would render it natural for him to promote an enactment making such studies obligatory upon the future landowners of the country; though to all appearance the celebrated Act of 1496 remained a perfect dead letter.[2] As to Elphin-

---

[1] Hector Boece, *Murthlacensium et Aberdonensium Episcoporum Vitæ* (Bannatyne Club Edition, 1825), p. 57.

[2] John Mair, writing his *History of Great Britain*, six and twenty years after the Act in question, says of the nobles of Scotland that

ston's connection with the introduction of printing, it has been observed[1] that the royal patent to Chepman and Myllar refers especially to the printing of "legendis of Scottis sanctis as is now gaderit and ekit be ane reverend fader in God, William, Bishop of Aberdene." And the Aberdeen Breviary, with its "legends of Scottis sanctis," was actually printed by Chepman in 1509-10.

To promote the foundation of a University in his own Cathedral city was doubtless a labour of love with Elphinston, and yet there are evidences in the early documents that great difficulties were to be encountered in starting it. Elphinston's representations on the subject were perhaps sanguine, for to attempt in the fifteenth century to civilise the Highlands of Scotland by a University in Aberdeen seems almost as visionary a proposal as that of Bishop Berkeley to christianise the Red Indians by means of a College in the Bermudas. Yet the preamble of the Bull of Alexander VI. cites a petition from James IV., setting forth that "there are certain places in the northern parts of his kingdom, separated by arms of the sea and high mountains from the rest, where dwell rude men, ignorant of letters, almost untamed, who, owing to their distance from Universities, cannot apply to study, nay, are

---

they had two great faults : *first*, that they were so frightfully quarrelsome with each other ; and *second*, that they took no care for the education of their children. Secundo liberos suos principes viri in literis et moribus non educant, in reipublicæ non parvam perniciem.—*Hist. Mag. Brit.* (Edinburgh edition, 1740), p. 33.

[1] Cosmo Innes, *Sketches*, p. 273, note.

so ignorant that persons cannot be found among them fit for ministering the sacraments of the church, let alone preaching to the people ; and that in a famous city, Old Aberdeen, sufficiently near those parts, a *Studium Generale* would flourish ; the precious pearl of knowledge might thus be acquired, and the rude and ignorant people might gain the means of instruction ; that there the air is healthy (*aëris viget temperies*), and there is abundance of victual and houses ; wherefore the King, who, like his predecessors, has always been an obedient son of the church, wishes that there should be in Old Aberdeen a *Universitas studii generalis*, as in the General Studies of Paris and Bologna and other privileged Universities. — We therefore ordain and appoint that there shall be in Old Aberdeen a *Universitas Studii Generalis.*"

The terms in which this Bull is couched are precise, and seem to show the perfected form for documents of the kind which had gradually come to be adopted in the offices of the Papal See. Among other points the import of the word *Universitas* comes clearly out, and we here learn how erroneous is the modern and very common idea that under the name " University" is implied *Universitas studiorum*, or an institution embracing instruction in the entire round of the sciences. This idea indeed is implied in the term *studium generale*, to which are generally added the words " in the Faculties of Theology, Canon and Civil Law, Medicine, Liberal Arts, and any other lawful Faculty." But there might be a

Studium Generale without a *Universitas*, that is, a corporate body,[1] constituted by charter, capable of holding property and enjoying certain privileges. And it was a corporation of this kind which Alexander VI. constituted at Aberdeen by the words *Statuimus et ordinamus quod in dicta civitate de cætero sit, et perpetuis futuris temporibus vigeat, Studium Generale, et Universitas existat studii generalis.*

One special novelty, however, occurs in the Bull —a clause which possibly was suggested by Elphinston himself, from his observation of the want in the Universities of St. Andrews and Aberdeen—of a regulating power, duly constituted and of sufficient weight. By this clause authority is given to the Chancellor, Rector, and resident Doctors of Aberdeen, conjoining with themselves a sufficient number of Licentiates and Scholars, and at least two of the Privy Councillors of Scotland for the time being (*ac duobus ad minus de Regis Scotiæ pro tempore existentis conciliariis*), to frame ordinances and statutes for the well-being and conduct of the University. There is something certainly remarkable in this plan of bringing in from without two high personages of the State to assist in guiding the University.

---

[1] There were many *universitates* besides the corporations which we now call "Universities." In a later Bull of Alexander VI. (July 1500) we find a mention of *universitates castrorum, oppidorum, villarum, et aliorum locorum.* It is to be noticed, however, that Hector Boece, *Murth. et Ab. Episc.*, pp. 60 and 62, uses the expressions "*schola universalis*" and "*universalis academia*" to denote Universities. He writes loosely, and uses also the phrases "*studiorum bonorum gymnasium generale*" and "*schola generalis.*" He employs the word *universalis* instead of *generalis* merely for variety of style. He does not use the word *universitas* in the sense of *studium generale.*

It was to some extent an infringement on the complete independence and self-government which Universities had hitherto enjoyed. Perhaps it was suggested by certain instances of unwisdom or turbulence exhibited by those bodies. And if it was Elphinston who proposed the plan, he may have desired to have his own hands, as Chancellor, strengthened by the assistance of two experienced and authoritative statesmen, when he should have to sit in council with cloister-bred and perhaps intractable Doctors, Licentiates, and Scholars.

The Bull of Constitution, which had been signed by the Pope in February 1494, was not published by Bishop Elphinston till February 1496-7; and after all this delay the publication was not addressed to the Doctors, Masters, and Scholars of Aberdeen, nor is there any mention of their having "laudably inaugurated" the University, as Wardlaw said of the learned men at St. Andrews in his Deed of Constitution.[1] The publication is addressed to all sons of holy mother church, warning them not to infringe the Bull. It appears, then, that it was found more difficult at Aberdeen than it had been at St. Andrews to get together the materials for starting a University. From the very outset, however, Elphinston took measures for getting the University to some extent endowed, as may be seen from a charter of James IV., dated three months later than the publication (May 1497), which says: "Whereas we have considered that the aforesaid

[1] See above, page 4.

University of Old Aberdeen will be by no means endowed with fruits and revenues for the maintenance of regents, lecturers, and students,—therefore our holy lord (Bishop Elphinston) has granted the Churches of Arbuthnot, Glenmyk, and Abergarney to belong to the University, with their revenues. We also, in honour of God, the Virgin, and the Saints, grant and mortify an annual revenue of £12 : 6s. from certain specified lands in our county of Banff for support of a graduate in the Faculty of Medicine, regularly lecturing in the said Faculty, and we only ask in return the prayers of him and his successors. We grant to the regents, students, lecturers, and chaplains, and all incorporated into the University, the same rights and privileges as those granted by the most Christian Kings of the French to the University of Paris, by James I. to the University of St. Andrews, and by James II. to the University of Glasgow. We constitute and appoint our Viscount of Aberdeen, or the Bishop's Bailie, to be Conservator of the privileges of the University, with the same powers as those possessed by the Conservators of the University of Paris. And furthermore, we have thought it right, in honour of the Trinity, St. Andrew, St. Kentigern, and St. Germanus, and for the good of our soul and that of our dearest wife to be,[1] and of the souls of our father, mother, and brothers, etc., that

---

[1] This was merely a general phrase. James IV. appears to have avoided matrimony as long as he could. It was not till 1503 that he was married to Margaret, daughter of Henry VII.

a collegiate church (*i.e.* a college) to be erected and founded by you, reverend father, within the University, on the revenues of Arbuthnot, Glenmyk, and Abergarney." Thus much, or rather thus little, did Elphinston succeed in getting from the young King —a full concession of privileges for the Corporation, a grant of £12 : 6s. per annum from the royal lands for endowment of a medical lecturer, and permission to the Bishop himself to found a College out of revenues already belonging to the See of Aberdeen. None of the nobility of Scotland came forward with any contribution. Those times were different from the present, when we often see, in this country and in America, private liberality furnishing hundreds of thousands of pounds for the creation or improvement of a University.

The next document on record is in itself a curiosity, and it serves to show that the newly-created University of Aberdeen met with ill-usage rather than sympathy or assistance from the neighbouring territorial magnates. It is a Bull of Alexander VI., dated July 1500, and is addressed to the Bishop of Aberdeen and the Abbots of Cambuskenneth and Scone. It is couched in something like the following terms :—"As presiding over the church militant, we are rendered anxious with care about the Universities. We have learned by inquiry from our beloved sons, the Doctors, Masters, Graduates, Scholars, Students, and Supposts of the General Study of Old Aberdeen, that certain Archbishops, Bishops, and other Prelates, clerks, and parsons (*ecclesiasticæ per-*

sonæ), both religious and secular, also Dukes, Marquises, Earls, Barons, Nobles, Knights, and laymen, communities of cities, corporations of burghs, towns, cities,[1] and other places, as well as private individuals, have occupied, and caused to be occupied, towns, cities, and other places, lands, houses, possessions, rights, and jurisdictions, teinds, revenues, incomes, returns, and provisions of the said Study, etc. etc., and presume to impede the liberties, exemptions, and privileges granted to the University. The doctors, masters, etc., have petitioned on the subject; wherefore we entrust to the aforesaid Prelates to proceed against the occupiers, holders-back, presumers, or molesters and injurers, of whatever rank they be, and, if necessary, to invoke the aid of the secular arm." Such are the grandly vague and magniloquent terms employed by some legal scribe at Rome; as though the University of Aberdeen were possessed of large properties which had been infringed by persons from the rank of Archbishop and Duke downwards, whereas, in all probability, the petition of the masters and scholars of the poor little University was founded on some very petty grievance.

[1] Castrorum, oppidorum, villarum.—It is not easy to assign any exact distinction between these terms; they are used with the tautology of legal documents. According to Du Cange (Henschel's edition, Paris, 1842) *sub* vv. *Castrum* was used in the Middle Ages to denote any town which was not a *Civitas*—*i.e.* a capital town or seat of a bishopric. *Oppidum* appears to have been used in much the same sense. *Villa* (whence the French *ville*) had come to mean a collection of country-houses, then a country town, and finally a city. In the oath administered to members of the University of Paris, they swore—*Servare pacem villæ nostræ*, *i.e.* of the city of Paris.

Another Papal document, bearing the same date as the foregoing (July 1500), furnishes indication of Elphinston's policy for encouraging the study of civil law in Scotland, and of his desire to give a stimulus to the still flagging or impeded start of the University of Aberdeen. He had obtained a petition to the Pope from James IV., to the effect that "though a General Study had been founded in Old Aberdeen, yet that in the said kingdom of Scotland few —nay, very few—persons are got together (*conjugati sunt*) who carry their studies beyond the first rudiments (*ultra primas litteras*), and study imperial and civil law; while parish priests and rectors are prohibited by the canons from studying the subject." Accordingly, Alexander VI. issues an Indulgence granting permission to all ecclesiastics of whatever rank, and to the religious orders, "even including the Cistercians, but not the Mendicants," to lecture on or study law and take degrees in the University of Aberdeen; and to the end that their studies may not be interrupted, there is granted to them and all other members of the University exemption from being summoned before any court of justice except that of the Chancellor of the University for the time being. This Indulgence was published by Bishop Elphinston in October 1501.

We have seen before, from the charter of James IV., that as early as 1497 Elphinston had projected the foundation of a College within the University, had arranged the means for its endowment from certain parish revenues, and had obtained the royal consent thereto. He doubtless judged, both from his experience of other Universities and his observation of the feeble progress made at first in Aberdeen, that a bare grant of corporate privileges was no longer sufficient to draw together, as in the early days of Paris, Oxford, and even St. Andrews, an enthusiastic body of teachers and Students; and, in short, that the only way to establish a permanent school for the higher learning was to provide regular stipends and fixed positions of dignity for qualified professors, and even to add bursaries for poor scholars so as to train up teachers for the next generation. It is to be observed, however, that Elphinston, in carrying out this view, did not found University professorships and bursaries for scholars merely attending the University; he founded a "Collegiate Church," an institution in which the religious life of its members was the paramount object, but in which, at the same time, there was abundant provision made for the cultivation of letters.

Under date September 1505 we have Bishop Elphinston's charter of foundation for the College, subsequently known to all as King's College, but to which he originally gave the title of the Holy Virgin in Nativity, and by this title it was still designated as late as 1526 in a rescript of Pope Clement VII. No mention of the King's name in connection with the title of the College appears in the charter. Some points of minor interest occur in the terms used and regulations prescribed. We observe that the head of the College was to be a Master in Theology, who was to be called *Principalis Collegii*, an academical term apparently then for the first time introduced into Scotland. The rest of the teaching staff were to consist of a Doctor of Canon Law, a Doctor of Civil Law, a Doctor of Medicine, and two Masters of Arts, of whom the senior was to be Sub-Principal, and the junior was to act as *Grammaticus*, and teach the boys and young men their rudiments. The stipends provided were — for the Principal forty merks per annum, for the Doctors of Law thirty merks each, for the Doctor of Medicine twenty merks (from the endowment above mentioned of James IV.) and for the Sub-Principal twenty merks. The Grammaticus was to hold a prebend in the Church of St. Mary in the Snow (*ad nives*), a parish church belonging to the University. The Principal and Sub-Principal were to have free commons, provided they lectured daily in logic, philosophy, and metaphysics. All except the Professor of Medicine were to say masses for the founders.

Besides the Professors, there were to be on the foundation five Students of theology, with a bursary of £10 each; and thirteen scholars, or poor clerks, "ingenious and clever in speculative knowledge, whose parents were unable to help them to scholastic exercises;" these last were to have twelve merks each per annum. One of the Students in theology, of gentle turn of mind (*mansuetioris et melioris inclinationis*), was to be chosen to lecture to the scholars on poetry and rhetoric. He was to have free commons, while the other foundationers were to pay twelve merks per annum each for their keep. That is to say, that the theological Students got their board and £2 each per annum; the arts scholars got only their board free.

In one respect Elphinston may be considered by some to have set a bad example in his statutes, by introducing, for the first time in Scotland, preferences for names and localities in the elections to bursaries. He lays down that the two first of the thirteen scholars in arts shall be chosen from among persons bearing the name of Elphinston, and that three other bursaries (it is curious that he does not say four) shall be reserved for the parishes of Arbuthnot, Glenmyk, Abergarney, and Slains, from which the revenues of the College were to be derived. This last enactment was perhaps equitable, or at all events politic. A Procurator was to be appointed from the collegiate body to collect and apportion the revenues, and he was directed to set aside fifty merks a year for repair of buildings and vestments. Altogether, the various items of expense specified in the statutes for the educational department of the College do not amount to more than about £300 Scots, which in those days was equal to about £100 sterling. For the building of the College and the Church attached to it the Bishop provided funds out of his own resources. The statutes contain detailed instructions about the church services to be maintained. It is more to our purpose to note that the Regents in Arts were to lecture after the manner of those in Paris, and that the Professor of Canon Law was to take Paris, and the Professor of Civil Law, Orleans, as his model. The scholars in arts were appointed to have a course sufficient to enable them to obtain the degree of Master of Arts, namely, as is stated, three years and a half. The Students in theology were to have a course sufficient for obtaining the Licentiate in Theology, namely, seven years.

Perhaps this Charter of Foundation in 1505 may be taken as marking the completion, so as to be fit for use, of the Church and some of the other collegiate buildings of what was afterwards King's College. For as early as the year 1500 Elphinston had brought over from Paris, Hector Boece, who was the first to hold the office of Principal in the College, so it seems likely that the College had made some sort of a start, without having got into fully working order, before the charter and statutes were drawn up. After the death of Elphinston, borne down, as it was said, with sorrow for the disaster of Flodden, Boece set to work to write the life of his patron, and he brought it out with brief notices of the previous Bishops of Aberdeen, in 1522. In this book we might have expected to learn all about the early history of the University of Aberdeen; but Boece, while writing with brightness and elegance, and while drawing an exquisite picture of the character of Elphinston, is provokingly inexact on points where we should have liked to know the simple facts. He does not tell us whether immediately on his arrival he became Principal of the College; he only says[1] that he was "chosen to lay the foundations of the University of Aberdeen, and to be the first Professor of Arts therein," and that he was "enticed to come by gifts and promises."[2] If he was to lay the foundations of the University, it could hardly have been started before his arrival; and yet he speaks of his being welcomed by David Guthrie, Professor of Civil and Canon Law, who lectured to large audiences (frequentibus auditoribus); James Ogilvie, Professor of Theology; and other learned canons. It is not clear whether those mentioned were already Professors when he arrived, or after-

---

[1] *Episc. Vit.*, p. 60. Is Aberdonénsis scholæ generalis auctor ac institutor, qui ejus fundamenta facerem, primusque in ea liberales profiterer artes, me (licet minus aptum ad tantum munus exequendum) delegit, muneribus et pollicitationibus ad se allexit.

[2] As a specimen of the "Dichtung-und-Wahrheit" style in which Boece writes, we may notice that he expresses regret at having had to leave the school of Paris with its learned teachers while he was yet a youth who had hardly mastered the rudiments (adolescens vix primis literarum rudimentis imbutus), whereas in 1500 Boece was thirty-five years of age. With regard to the salary of forty merks which he received as Principal, Dr. Johnson made the well-known remark that "it is difficult even for the imagination so to raise the value of money, or so to diminish the demands of life as to suppose four and forty shillings a year an honourable stipend." This supposes the coins in the Scots currency to be equal to one-twelfth of the same coins sterling, a point of debasement not reached till 1601. In 1500 the degradation of Scots currency was comparatively trifling. To enable us to judge how far forty merks (£26 : 13 : 4) would go in Aberdeen in those days, we may observe that twelve merks was estimated as the cost of the board of each scholar in Elphinston's College during eleven months of the year. Boece had his own board and lodgings free; he also held the rectory of Fyvie; and in 1527, on publication of his History, he received a pension of £50 a year from James V. "These sources of income considered," says Cosmo Innes, "there is no reason to doubt that in emolument, as well as in social position, Hector Boece was greatly above any Principal of a Scotch College at the present day."—*Sketches*, p. 271, note.

wards became so. On the whole, it seems probable that Elphinston's College was at the outset practically coextensive with the University of Aberdeen, and that those who had places on the staff of the College were, in short, the Professors of the University.

From the time of its first start under Hector Boece, at the beginning of the sixteenth century, down to 1540, and perhaps a little later, King's College, or, in other words, the University of Aberdeen, had a career of great activity and success. Boece had brought with him from Paris, to assist him in his task, William Hay, who had been his friend and companion from boyhood, and who now became his Sub-Principal.[1] Boece records with pride the success of their joint labours; and how already (1522) many scholars had been turned out distinguished in theology and canon and civil law, and "very many in philosophy." He adds a list of about a dozen names, of whom several had become teachers in the University, some had got good benefices in the Church, one (though bred as a civil lawyer) had joined the order of the Preaching Friars, and one had become Provincial Grand Master of that order in Scotland. Besides William Hay, the only other one of his coadjutors whom

[1] On the death of Boece in 1536 William Hay succeeded him in the office of Principal. There is in the Library of King's College a MS. of some lectures delivered by Hay, while Sub-Principal, "On the Sacrament of Marriage and its Impediments," being a collection of the remarks of various authors on the fourth book of the *Sentences* of Peter Lombard.

Boece mentions is John Vaus, the *grammaticus* or teacher of Latin scholarship. To this name some little interest attaches, owing to the value placed by Bibliophilists on copies of his grammatical works, now become extremely rare. In 1522 both Boece and Vaus went to press with their writings, Boece with his *Lives of the Bishops*, Vaus with his commentary on the *Doctrinale*, or rhythmical elements of Latin grammar, of Alexandrinus. It is observable that neither of them are printed in Scotland. The paralysis of the higher energies of the nation which ensued from Flodden had put a stop to the operations of Chepman and Myllar, and it is said that there is no trace of printing in this country between 1513 and 1542. Our Aberdonian authors went to the firm of the Ascensii, in Paris, who were printing John Mair's *History of Great Britain* about the same time. Vaus appears to have personally gone to Paris, and perhaps he took the work of Boece with him as well as his own. His book appeared, with an introduction by Iodocus Badius Ascensius, addressed *Studiosis Abredonensis Academiæ Philosophis*, commending "the labour of Vaus, and his courage in venturing through the dangers of pirates and a stormy sea to the press of Ascensius to get his rudiments multiplied."[1] The French printer compliments the new Scotch University, and claims an interest in it on the ground that its "founders and leaders have been almost all bred in the University of Paris."

[1] Cosmo Innes, *Sketches*, p. 271, note.

In 1530 new statutes for King's College were given by Bishop Gavin Dunbar (uncle to the Archbishop of Glasgow of the same name), but the modifications in Elphinston's scheme are not worth dwelling upon. In 1534 an epistle was written at Kynloss by Joannes Ferrerius, the Italian scholar brought into this country by Bishop Reid of Orkney; this epistle was dedicatory to William Stewart, who became Bishop of Aberdeen in 1532, of a tract in defence of the poetry of Cicero, which was afterwards printed at Paris in 1540, and is now in King's College Library. Ferrerius praises the University of Aberdeen as standing highest in repute of the Scottish Universities of that time,[1] and says that it contains men who might take rank in the first University of the world. "What," he asks, "can be be more learned and elegant in the round of educational subjects, and especially in history,[2] than Hector Boece? What more finished and delightful in the mysteries of theology than William Hay? What more apt in the relief of sickness and in knowledge of geography than Robert Gray, the Professor of Medicine? In canon law you will hardly find any one to surpass Arthur Boece;[3] and to pass over other accomplished and learned men, what more exact in grammar than John Vaus?" In all this there was doubtless something courtly

---

[1] Celeberrimam apud Scotos hoc potissimum tempore (absit verbo invidia) Academiam.

[2] Cum in cyclicis disciplinis tum historiis.

[3] Brother to the Principal, and educated in King's College, in which he was appointed *Canonista*.

and complimentary. Yet still it testifies, to a certain extent, to the respectable character of the teachers of the first generation of the University of Aberdeen. Evidently they constituted an industrious hive, and did great credit to the leadership of Hector Boece.

In 1541 the University of Aberdeen appeared in its glory, when James V. and his queen, accompanied by a large train of the nobility, made a progress to the North, and for fifteen days were entertained by Bishop Stewart at Aberdeen, "apparently," says Cosmo Innes,[1] "in the College buildings." Bishop Leslie, who was one of the company, records in the Scotch, in which his history was originally written, that they were received " with diverse triumphs and plays maid be the town, and be the universitie and sculis theirof, and remainit thair the space of fiftein dayes weill entertenit be the bishop; quhair ther was exercise and disputationes in all kind of sciences in the college and sculis, with diverse oratiouns maid in Greke,[2] Latine, and uther languages, quhilk was mickell commendit be the King and Quene and all thair company."

[1] *Sketches*, p. 274.
[2] The Greek orations must have been the work of some scholar, happening to be in Aberdeen, who had picked up Greek abroad. There is no trace of Greek having been taught in any Scottish University prior to the Reformation. Andrew Melville learned it (1557-9) at the Grammar School of Montrose from Pierre de Marsilliers, a learned Frenchman who had been brought thither as master a few years previously by Erskine of Dun. But when Melville went to the University of St. Andrews, in his fourteenth year, 1559, he found himself the only person in the University who was able to read the Greek text of Aristotle.

The next glimpse of the University of Aberdeen which we obtain dates eight years after the royal visit, and shows that the first blush of success had then passed away, and that a blight had already fallen upon the institution. In a document, dated 1549, Alexander Galloway, Prebendary of Kinkell, Rector of the University for the fourth time, records the results of his rectorial visitation, made in terms of Elphinston's foundation of King's College.[1] The picture which he draws is a deplorable one. He says that there were "no lay teachers" in the University, so that James IV.'s *Doctor Medicus* must have ceased his functions; there were few in the College beside the bursars, and apparently none who were not preparing for the church or for practice in the church courts. "The teachers were negligent, perhaps from the smallness of their audience." "The College had sunk into a convent and conventual school; and the design of the University, and the great hopes of its founder and first teachers, seemed about to be frustrated."[2] The depression which had showed itself as early as 1549 was naturally only deepened by the storm of the Reformation. In August 1562 the University had sunk to zero, as may be seen from the terms used by Randolph, the English ambassador in Scotland, in writing to Cecil from Aberdeen :—" The Quene, in her progresse, is

---

[1] In Elphinston's Statutes it is ordained that the Rector of the University shall annually visit the College, unless he be himself a member of the College, in which case the visitation is to be made by the Dean of the Faculty of Arts and the Official of Aberdeen.

[2] Cosmo Innes, *Sketches*, p. 276.

now come as far as Olde Aberdine, the Bishop's seat, and where also the Universitie is, or, at the least, *one colledge with fifteen or sixteen scollers.*"[1]

The leading facts in the history of the three older Universities of Scotland down to the time of the Reformation have, in the preceding pages, been brought together. From the general survey thus afforded, we see that each of those Universities was founded in due form by Papal authority after the grand old mediæval model. They were each constituted as a free corporation of learned men, with self-government, dignities, titles, and separate internal courts of civil and criminal jurisdiction, immunities from taxation and from civic burdens, and many special privileges both for ecclesiastics and for laymen. But we see at the same time that their growth was always stunted by the extremely unfavourable circumstances which surrounded them. The smallness and poverty of the nation, of which one-half was still in a state of savagery; the continual turbulence of the times; and the general rudeness and selfishness of the nobility and landowners, were conditions which prevented the expansion of the Scottish Universities—which prevented them, indeed, from ever taking kindly root in the national soil previous to the Reformation. It was not merely that the strifes and struggles of the Reformation extinguished the Universities, though this was the case, as we have seen, with each one of them; but what we find is that, even antecedently to the middle

[1] Quoted by Chalmers, *Life of Ruddiman*, p. 7, note.

of the sixteenth century, neither of the Universities had attained to any vigorous life of its own. On this point we may accept the estimate of a contemporary Scotsman, who, having spent most of his life in the schools of Paris, regards his country from an external and somewhat critical point of view. John Mair (1522) in his naïve and simple manner, using the barbarous Latin of the Sorbonne, sums up the characteristics of three Scotch Universities.[1] All he says of St. Andrews is that "no one has done anything considerable for it, except Bishop Kennedy, who founded a small but rich and beautiful college there." Of Aberdeen he mentions the "noble college of Bishop Elphinston." Of the University of Glasgow he says that it is "poorly endowed, and with a scanty attendance of scholars." He concludes by saying: "I cannot praise this number of the Universities,[2] for, as iron is sharpened

[1] *Hist. Mag. Brit.*, I. vi.—" Est Sanctus Andreas ibi Universitas, in quam nullus adhuc aliquod magnificum egit, dempto Jacobo Kennedo, qui Collegium unum parvum sed pulchrum et opulentum fundavit. Est Abredonia altera in septentrione Universitas, in qua, Episcopus, Elphinston nomine, egregium Collegium fundavit, qui etiam Universitatis institutor extitit. Est insuper civitas Glasguensis archiepiscopalis sedes et Universitas parum dotala aut scholasticis abundans. Præbendas tamen multas et pinguissimas Ecclesia habet, sed in absentia in Scotia, sicut in præsentia, ferme tantum recipiunt, quod sine moderamine et prudentia factum est. Hunc Universitatum numerum non approbabo; Sicut enim ferrum ferro acuitur, sic multi scholastici mutuo se acuunt, sed pro naturis loci non sunt reprobandæ."

[2] The style here is very obscure. It is not clear whether Mair meant to complain that there were not more than three Universities in Scotland, or that the existing Universities were not better attended —probably the latter; he seems in the phrase "*hunc numerum*" to be referring to what he had before said about Glasgow being "*parum scholasticis abundans.*"

by iron, so numerous scholars sharpen one another; and yet, considering the local circumstances, they cannot be blamed." The two points in the Scotch Universities which appear to have struck Mair, in comparison of course with Paris, were, that they were so scantily attended by Students, and that so few endowments and collegiate foundations had been provided for them. In reference, apparently, to the latter point, he remarks: "And yet the Church in Scotland has many very rich prebends." He goes on to say that these are recklessly allowed to be enjoyed by absentees. But what, judging from the context, he seems to have had in his mind was, that some of these prebends might well have been used for the endowment of University professorships.

This remark would have been doubtless true. Perhaps rather too much[1] has been made of the services rendered to education and learning by the Catholic Church in Scotland. During a century and a half some five or six prelates were bright exceptions to the general apathy, and assisted their country in entering upon the course which all civil-

[1] As, for instance, by Mr. Lecky in his *History of England in the Eighteenth Century*, vol. ii., p. 43. "It must be acknowledged that a very large part of the credit of the movement in favour of education belongs to the Church which preceded the Reformation; nor is any fact in Scotch history more remarkable than the noble enthusiasm for learning which animated that Church during the fifteenth century." Mr. Lecky specifies, as proofs of this enthusiasm, the foundation of the three Universities, the establishment of burgh schools, and the Act of 1496 for the education of the sons of landowners. Probably one University and the Act in question were due to Bishop Elphinston. Burgh schools were very sparsely provided; and to this day secondary education has remained a weak point in Scotland.

ised Europe had long previously followed. But they were not supported by their brethren and successors, and their action, therefore, was isolated and inadequate. All honour be to the few enlightened Bishops who strove to promote learning in this country! But the wealthy Catholic Church of Scotland in general scarcely deserves praise in the matter. How far from universal on the part of the Scotch ecclesiastics was any sympathy for the native Universities may be seen from an extant letter addressed by Alexander Myln, Abbot of Cambuskenneth,[1] to the Abbé and Canons of St. Victor, an Augustinian house near Paris. In this letter,[2] which bears date 15th January 1522-3, Myln deplores the decline of learning in his fraternity. "Although," he says, "in former times men of learning abounded in our monastery, yet at present they are almost completely extinct; nor will their place be speedily supplied, unless we send a certain number of our most promising Novices to the Universities, where there is a greater frequency of literary exercises. But we do not hold it expedient for them to engage in secular studies, and are therefore solicitous that they should be educated in your college, in order that they may acquire a complete knowledge of the Sacred Scriptures, and may afterwards be instru-

---

[1] A splendid Augustinian abbey, founded by David I., on the banks of the Forth, a little below Stirling, of which one fine tower alone remains. Myln was the first president of the College of Justice (1532), and was employed by James V. on several embassies and in high State appointments.

[2] *Epistolæ Regum Scotorum*, i. 335, 336.

mental in the propagation of learning and piety." The terms of this document throw a strange light upon the relations, or rather want of relations, subsisting between the regular clergy of Scotland and the Universities in the sixteenth century. We see that the Abbey of Cambuskenneth had fallen into intellectual sloth; perhaps into that state of things so graphically depicted by Scott in his *Monastery*. For the means of reforming and educating his fraternity Myln turns, not to the Scotch Universities, but to Paris. And yet Pope Alexander VI., in his Bull of 1500 (see above, p. 33), had constituted the Abbot of Cambuskenneth one of the protectors of the University of Aberdeen; and in his Indulgence of the same date had encouraged the members of all the religious orders (except the Mendicants) to go and study at that University. Evidently the Augustinians of Cambuskenneth had not acted upon this encouragement. Myln's letter shows an attitude of standing aloof from the Scotch Universities which is not creditable to a prelate otherwise so able and enlightened. He need not have been afraid of Lutheranism in Aberdeen, for at the crisis of the Reformation the professors and other authorities there showed themselves rather as conservators of the old than adherents of the new principles of religion. In 1569, by Commission of the General Assembly, Sir John Erskine of Dun, Superintendent of Angus, made a visitation of the University, and having summoned before him the Principal, Sub-Principal, and the three Regents of King's

College, required them to subscribe the following declaration:—

"We, whose names are underwritten, do ratify and approve, from our very hearts, the Confession of Faith, together with all other acts concerning our religion, given forth in the Parliaments holden at Edinburgh, the 24th day of August 1560, and the 15th day of December 1567, and joyn ourselves as members of the true Kirk of Christ, whose visible face is described in the said acts; and shall, in time coming, be participant of the sacraments now most faithfully and publickly ministrat in the said Kirk, and submit us to the jurisdiction and discipline thereof."

Showing no signs of compliance with the requisition of the Superintendent, Principal Anderson, Sub-Principal Galloway, and Regents Anderson, Ousten, and Norrie, were called before the Regent Murray and Lords of Privy Council, before whom "most obstinately contemning his Grace's most godly admonitions, they refused to subscribe the said articles." They were then sentenced to deprivation of office, ordered to remove from "the Coledge of Old Aberdeen," and inhibited from teaching publicly or privately in any part of Scotland. "Thus that University was purged from their old Popish teachers, who had too long corrupted the youth and their parents in the North, and disseminated disaffection to the government."[1]

With St. Andrews the case was different; the University there had from a very early period been a hot-bed for the Reformation principles. We have already seen (above, p. 17) the character which St.

[1] Wodrow's *Life of John Erskine of Dun* (Maitland Club edition), pp. 22-25, from which the above account is taken.

Leonard's College acquired in this respect. Indeed, to have "drunk of St. Leonard's Well" became a proverbial phrase for those suspected of Lutheranism.[1] Archbishop Hamilton's reorganisation and endowment of St. Mary's College (see above, p. 17) was a forlorn hope against the new opinions when the battle was already lost. The endowment was speedily seized by the Reformers, and applied to support the very principles which it had been intended to controvert. Even the greater part of Hamilton's Professors and Students "changed with the times, and joined the Reformers." So also, as was only to be expected, did the Professors of St. Leonard's. The Provost and most of the Regents of St. Salvator's, on the other hand, adhered to the ancient faith, and were deprived of their appointments. But the "purging" of the University of St. Andrews was easily effected, and was not nearly so sweeping an affair, speaking relatively, as was that of the little University of Aberdeen.

This "purging" of the Scottish Universities, in order to secure their conformity in principle with the Knoxian Kirk, was the negative side of the work which the Reformers set themselves to perform for those institutions. The positive side, which for the purpose of these volumes is more interesting, consisted in the reorganising of University education, which they now took in hand.

The old Universities of Scotland had partly failed and partly been extinguished. With all their

[1] Lyon's *Hist. of St. Andrews*, ii. 206.

shortcomings, there was a romantic grace about them which was alien from all the ideas of the Reformers, and which could never more reappear. We shall now see how the old mediæval corporations lost all their salient features, and how the old terms got misapplied, and the University was confounded with a College. At the same time we shall see that the Reformation triumphant had good schemes of its own for the higher education of the country; only, unfortunately, it was not allowed to carry these out.

CHAPTER II.

(PRELIMINARY.)

THE VARIOUS ATTEMPTS OF THE REFORMERS TO REORGANISE UNIVERSITY EDUCATION IN SCOTLAND.

"The old order changeth, giving place to new."

1. THE Parliament of Scotland which abolished the Papal jurisdiction and ratified the Protestant doctrine, as contained in the Confession of Faith, was dissolved in January 1559-60. And by an order of the Privy Council, dated on the following 29th April, "commission and charge was given to Mr. John Winram, Sub-Prior of St. Andrews; Master John Spottiswood; John Willock; Mr. John Douglas, Rector of St. Andrews; Master John Row; and John Knox, to draw in a volume the Policy and Discipline of the Kirk as well as they had done the Doctrine."[1] The work was undertaken with the greatest alacrity, and the famous *Buke of Discipline* was presented, on the 20th of May 1560, to the nobility, "who," as John Knox says, "did peruse it many days. Some approved it, and willed the

[1] John Knox, *History of the Reformation* (Laing's ed.), vol. ii. p. 128.

same to have been set forth by a law. Others, perceiving their carnal liberty and worldly commodity to be impaired thereby, grudged, insomuch that the name of the *Book of Discipline* became odious unto them. Everything that repugned to their corrupt affections was termed, in their mockage, 'devout imaginations.'" At last, in January 1560-61, an approval of the *Book of Discipline* was signed in the Tolbooth of Edinburgh by twenty-six Lords of Congregation, headed by the Duke of Chatelherault, the Earl of Arran, the Earl of Argyll, and the Lord James Stuart (afterwards Regent Murray). But there were too many powerful persons throughout the country of the same mind with Lord Erskine, who, according to Knox, reflected that "if the poor, the schools, and the ministry of the Kirk had their own, his kitchen would lack two parts and more of that which he unjustly now possesses."

But, in justice to the nobility of these days, it must be added that in all probability it was not a feeling of avarice alone which set them against the *Book of Discipline*. The whole tone of its contents was high-handed and unconciliatory in the extreme. It may be questioned whether the Commissioners were wise, if they wished for the realisation of their educational schemes, to introduce into them the following compulsory clause: "The rich and potent may not be permitted to suffer their children to spend their youth in vain idleness, as heretofore they have done. But they must be exhorted and, by the censure of the Church, compelled to dedicate their sons, by good exercise, to the profit of the Church and the Commonwealth. If they be found apt to letters and learning, then may they not (we mean neither the sons of the rich, nor yet the sons of the poor) be permitted to reject learning, but must be charged to continue their study, so that the Commonwealth may have some comfort of them. And for this purpose must discreet, learned, and grave men be appointed to visit all schools for the trial of their exercise, profit, and continuance; to wit, the ministers and elders, with the best learned in every town, shall every quarter take examination how the youth hath profited." On the whole, it is hardly to be wondered at that the nobility of Scotland declined to put themselves under a yoke which would have resembled that of the Jesuits in Paraguay, and that the *Book of Discipline* was relegated to the limbo of "devout imaginations," and became a dead letter. Yet the project of national education which it contained—with a Grammar School in every Parish, and a College for "Logic, Rhetoric, and the Tongues," in every notable town—confers immortal honour on its authors. And their ideas with regard to the ordering of Universities, though never carried out, deserve notice in this place.

If we ask what were the qualifications for academical legislation of the Commissioners appointed to draw up the *Book of Discipline*, we find that none of them was especially distinguished as a scholar; and it is to be noted that the two greatest Scotch scholars of the age, George Buchanan and Andrew Melville, were, in 1560, still absent from their country.

The Commissioners, however, were all eminent men, several of whom had seen a great deal of the world. St. Andrews was well represented among them by John Winram, Sub-Prior of the Augustinians, and now Superintendent of Fife, and by John Douglas, Provost of St. Mary's College, who for twenty-three consecutive years (1551-73) was elected Rector of the University of St. Andrews. John Spottiswood graduated at the University of Glasgow, and was now Superintendent of Lothian; he had lived for five years in England, and had accompanied Lord James Stuart to the nuptials of Mary Stuart with the Dauphin in 1558. John Willock had abandoned the monastic habit of the Franciscans, and gone to live in England, where he was chaplain to the Duke of Suffolk; on the accession of Queen Mary to the throne of England he had escaped to the Continent, and practised as a physician at Embden in Friesland; on his return to Scotland at the Reformation, being an Ayrshire man, he was made Superintendent of the West. John Row, after graduating in arts and studying canon law at St. Andrews, had resided for seven years at Rome, as agent for the clergy of Scotland to the Vatican. He obtained the degree of Doctor of Laws from the University of Padua; and in 1558 arrived in Scotland as the Pope's Nuncio, to investigate the causes and devise means for arresting the progress of the heretical innovations which were spreading over the country. But, as his son remarks, he proved "a corbie messenger" to his master, for, being shocked by the exposure of a pretended miracle at Loretto, near Musselburgh, he embraced the Protestant faith, and was made minister of Perth.

Last and greatest of all these "Johns" was John Knox, of whom nothing need here be said, except that he had lived for three years at Geneva, in close intimacy with Calvin (1556-9), at the very time when Calvin's plans for the establishment of the College of Geneva were being carried out. Such were some of the antecedents of the Commissioners.

The *Book of Discipline*, in laying down regulation for the Universities, speaks of them as if they had to be created anew; thus ignoring any title to existence based on Papal Bulls or royal charters of the past, and virtually cutting short the historical continuity of national institutions. In an article headed "The Erection of Universities," the Commissioners say: "The Grammar Schools and of the Tongues being erected as we have said, next we think it necessary there be three Universities in this whole realm, established in the towns accustomed. The first in St. Andrews, the second in Glasgow, and the third in Aberdeen." It will be observed, however, that they restricted themselves to the idea of creating anew—that is to say, carrying on with certain changes—the three existing Universities. The Commissioners made no proposal for the establishment of a University in Edinburgh. According to the ideas of the Reformers in 1560, the Metropolis of Scotland was merely to reckon among the "notable towns," in each of which was to be erected "a College in which the Arts, at least Logic and Rhetoric, together with the Tongues, should be read by sufficient masters." The *Book of Discipline*, providing for the endowment, ordering, and policy of the Church, the sacraments, preaching, marriage, burial, regulation of life, the punishment of offenders, and the education of the whole people, was conceived, completed, and brought out in the astonishingly short time of twenty-two days. It necessarily, therefore, dealt with all matters in outline and not in detail. The form which the Commissioners proposed that the three Universities should take was sketched out in hurried but masterly touches. Guided by experience of the past, and a knowledge of foreign schools, the Commissioners evidently threw aside the mediæval notion that liberty of teaching, privileges to the incorporated teachers and students, and offices with high-sounding titles, would be sufficient to ensure the prosperity of a University. They saw that it was necessary to have a nucleus of adequately paid Professors of fixed subjects. And they proposed to make these Professors, or, as they called them, "Readers," not University but College officers. The teaching requisite for the curriculum of a Faculty was to be organised within a separate College. Thus the proposed Colleges were brought into the foreground; they were to constitute all that was essential in each University. The institutions and offices which had belonged to the University, properly so-called, faded into the background; they were not entirely to be abolished, but they were to be used chiefly for the purpose of regulating the Colleges and maintaining their efficiency.

The Presbyterian Superintendent was naturally to take the place of the Bishop in St. Andrews, Glasgow, or Aberdeen, respectively, as Chancellor of the University. But the title "Chancellor" is not used in the *Book of Discipline*, which merely assigns certain academical duties to the Superintendent—namely (1) to form a Chapter with the Rector and the Principals of other Colleges, for the election of a Principal of any College whose headship might be vacant; and (2) to induct the Rector, after election, to his office, and to exhort him as to his duties. The Rector of the University was to be annually elected, not, however, by Procurators nominated by the whole body of the students as in a mediæval University, but in the following way: the Principals of Colleges, with all the Regents, were to be convened in a chapter, and to nominate by most votes a leet of three. And out of these three the Rector was to be elected by the votes of Principals, Regents, and Supposts[1] who had graduated, "or at least studied their time in Ethics, Economics, and Politics." This regulation for the election of Rectors,

[1] We see the Commissioners here employing the old University terms, "Regents," and "Supposts." In the Mediæval Universities *Regere* merely meant to teach publicly, and this function was at first compulsory on all "perfect graduates," *i.e.* Masters and Doctors above the grade of the Bachelors (*bas chevaliers*) who were imperfect graduates. When the number of voluntary Regents, *i.e.* Graduates willing to teach, was sufficient, the necessary regency was remitted to

while reasonable in itself, was a restriction upon the old freedom of Universities as literary republics. The duties prescribed for the Rector were (1) to make monthly visits to each College, and to honour with his presence, and at the same time criticise, the lectures and exercises; (2) to act as judge in all civil cases that might arise between members of the University, and again to act as assessor to the provost and bailies of the town in trying criminal actions against members of the University; (3) to be a member of the Superintendent's chapter for the election and afterwards the supervision of Principals of Colleges. The Rector's office, in the scheme of the *Book of Discipline*, had no salary attached to it. It was probably meant to be tenable together with some paid appointment in one of the Colleges.[1]

the rest; and it gradually became a privilege, which was conferred by election, to be "Regent" in some department, such as Philosophy or Theology. Thus "Regent" came in Universities to mean pretty much the same as Professor. But when "Regents," that is, University graduates, were employed to teach in Colleges, the word took another sense and became nearly equivalent to what at Oxford and Cambridge is now called a College Tutor. The Regent in a College, instead of confining himself to one subject, as a Professor does, usually had a class of students assigned to him, and this class he carried through all the subjects of their curriculum, from their entrance into the College till he had conducted them to laureation. The term "Regents," as used in the *Book of Discipline*, may be taken indeterminately to mean both the "Readers" in the proposed Colleges and any University teachers outside the Colleges that there might be. The term *Supposita* in Mediæval Latin meant all the subordinate members of a University, including servants as well as students. The *Book of Discipline* proposes that only graduates or senior "Supposts" shall vote for the Rector, thus confining the term to students. It apparently contemplates the vote of the students being given in nations, according to the old custom.

[1] Probably the Commissioner who took most interest in this part of the regulations was John Douglas, Provost of St. Mary's College,

Besides the Superintendent and his "Special Procurator," and the Rector with his two assessors ("a lawyer and a theologian"), there is no mention of any other University officer, except the Bedell, who was to be "subject to serve at all times throughout the whole University, as the Rector and Principal shall command," and to be paid by dues from the students—two shillings from each at entry, and from three to five shillings from each at graduation.

With regard to the privileges of the Universities, the *Book of Discipline* was for taking away from them (very properly) the right which they had hitherto possessed, of having their members tried, even in criminal cases, before no tribunal except their own Rector's court. However, it proposed to give the Rector jurisdiction in every civil suit between two members of his University; and to allow him to claim a seat as assessor in any municipal court where a member of his University fell to be tried criminally. And it proposed, with the defined purpose of leaving their time free for teaching and study, that "the Rector and all inferior members of the University should be exempted from all taxations, imposts, charges of war, or any other charge that may onerate or abstract him or them from the care of their office; such as Tutory, Curatory, Deaconry, or the like."

So much and no more was laid down in the *Book* as to University institutions. And now as to

and at the same time for twenty-three years Rector of the University of St. Andrews.

the Colleges which each University was to contain, and which were to embody its teaching functions, and to define its courses of study. In this respect St. Andrews was to be a complete University, with provision for degrees in the four Faculties of Philosophy, Medicine, Law, and Divinity. Glasgow and Aberdeen were to be incomplete Universities, with no provision for the teaching of medicine. This arrangement was based upon the existence beforehand of three Colleges in the University of St. Andrews (see above, pp. 10-18). These three Colleges were now to be reorganised as follows:—The first College was to provide for degrees in Philosophy and Medicine. The curriculum for Philosophy (or, as we should now say, Arts), was to occupy three years; one year of Dialectic; one year of Mathematics, comprising Arithmetic, Geometry, Cosmography, and Astronomy; and one year of Natural Philosophy. Then, in the same College, a Reader in Medicine was to complete his course in five years, and graduate those who had successfully gone through it.

The second College was to turn out graduates in Law, after a one year's course in Ethics, Economics, and Politics; and a four years' course, under two readers, in Municipal Law and Roman Law.

The third College was for graduation in Divinity; there was to be a one year's course in the Greek and Hebrew languages, and then a five years' course in divinity under two readers, one in the Old Testament and one in the New.

Each College was to have a Principal, who was to manage College property, administer discipline, and supervise teaching, but not himself to teach. In each College there were to be twenty-four bursars, to be admitted by a chapter consisting of the joint Principals and the ministry, the parish ministers being added, as likely to be acquainted with the family circumstances and character of applicants for the bursaries.

The Universities of Glasgow and Aberdeen were to have only two Colleges each, of which one was to be the counterpart of the first College at St. Andrews, *minus* medicine. That is, it was to be a College for Philosophy (or Arts) alone. The second College in Glasgow and Aberdeen was to provide for graduation in both Law and Divinity, and to comprise all the courses of teaching which were to be given in the second and third Colleges of St. Andrews. In both Glasgow and Aberdeen there would thus be saved the cost of buildings for one College, the salary of a Reader in Medicine, and twenty-four bursaries. That would be the only difference between those Universities and that of St. Andrews. The conception of the Commissioners, then, was that the University education of Scotland should be conducted by means of Colleges, with a division of labour between them, each College representing one or more Faculties. The old Colleges of St. Salvator, St. Leonard, St. Mary, and King's College, were no longer to be religious houses, but schools of science. And instead of College tutors, under the name of "Regents," to conduct each his own class through all the different subjects necessary for graduation; there were to be separate Professors or "Readers" for the separate branches. It was only in Medicine that the whole course was to be entrusted to one teacher.

No provision was to be made for any elementary teaching in the Universities, not even of Latin; though, of course, according to the custom of the times, all the lectures in every subject would have been delivered in Latin. But it must be remembered that the University scheme of the *Book of Discipline* was not meant to be taken by itself; it was meant to be the apex of a graded system of national instruction. The Commissioners contemplated that when this system should be in full working no student would come to a University who had not passed through (1) two years of primary instruction, including the catechism; (2) three or four years of grammar, *i.e.* Latin; (3) four years of Greek, Logic, and Rhetoric; altogether nine or ten years, which would bring the Student to the University at the age of sixteen or seventeen. He would have to produce "a testimonial from the master of the school, and the minister of the town where he was instructed in the tongues;" and he would have to pass an entrance examination, in which, if he should be "found to be sufficiently instructed in Dialectic," he would be allowed to proceed at once to mathematics, thus reducing his course in philosophy to two years.[1]

[1] It is to be noticed that the authors of the *Book of Discipline* had

Every Student in the University was to graduate in Philosophy, which he might be expected to do at the age of eighteen or nineteen; after which it would be open to him to enter on a five years' course of Medicine or Law; or a six years' course of Divinity. The Commissioners considered that at the age of twenty-four the Student would have completed his courses, and be prepared to commence serving the Church or Commonwealth in one of the learned professions.

One cannot but be struck by the sternly practical character of the scheme. Mediæval subtleties are pushed aside in it, and equally so humanism; the curriculum of Philosophy was to consist, with the exception of Logic, which might have been got through beforehand, entirely of Mathematics and the Physical Science of the day. Plato was to be read in the Divinity Colleges, but this was the only trace of any encouragement to literature throughout the scheme. In the professional courses Municipal was to be substituted for Canon Law; and a thorough textual knowledge of the Old and New Testament, in the original tongues, for the *Sentences* of Peter Lombard.

In spite of its deficiency in regard of literature this was, on the whole, a high type of University. Slowly and by degrees the Universities of Scotland have subsequently succeeded in realising this type in their professional Faculties, especially that of

no jealousy of University subjects being taught in High Schools. On the contrary, they encouraged it.

Medicine. But, owing to causes to be hereafter brought out, the Faculty of Arts in the Scottish Universities has always failed to attain the high level, above all school teaching, proposed for it on the scheme of the Reformers. That scheme, with every advantage, could not have been worked out in a day; it demanded a complete system of graded education below it, with High Schools equal to the German *Gymnasien* of the present day. With full national unanimity, and cordial, high-minded, co-operation of all ranks, such a system could have been realised under men like Andrew Melville and Alexander Arbuthnot. But how hard, even in the nineteenth century, to find national unanimity and enthusiasm about schemes for the higher education of the country! It is no wonder, then, that in 1560 the scheme of the *Book of Discipline* was still-born; and that of its best recommendations, some were worked out piecemeal long afterwards, and some have never been realised to the present moment.

There is one more point in the unfulfilled proposals of the Commissioners which deserves mention here—namely, their notions as to the stipends of University officers. When they wrote they were in sanguine expectation of obtaining sufficient church property to meet all reasonable demands; therefore they set down simply what they thought would be fair. They were for allowing Principals of Colleges £200 a-year; Readers in Hebrew, Greek, and Divinity £200; Readers in Medicine and Laws £133 : 6 : 8 each. They set the stipend of each

Bursar in Philosophy, Medicine, and Law at £20 per annum, and of each Divinity Bursar at £24; and they estimated the total cost of maintaining the three Universities of Scotland at the modest sum of £9640 Scots[1] per annum. A fund for buildings and repairs was to be provided by dues levied on the Students, according to their social rank and circumstances, at entrance and on graduation.

II. The *Book of Discipline* having been quietly allowed to drop, the Universities remained in the dilapidated condition to which the Reformation had reduced them. In 1563 a petition was addressed to the Queen and the Lords of Articles stating that the patrimony of the Colleges, especially at St. Andrews, was being wasted, and science and tongues imperfectly taught, and praying a remedy. A Committee was then appointed by Parliament (see *Acts* ii. 544), of whom George Buchanan[2] was one, and the report of this Committee contained Buchanan's scheme for the remodelling of the University of St. Andrews, which differed in some respects from that of the *Book of Discipline*.

[1] In 1560 £13 Scots money was equivalent to about £3 English; therefore £9640 Scots = £2224 : 12 : 3¼ English.

[2] Buchanan had returned to Scotland from his long sojourn in France during the summer of 1561. In January 1561-62 Randolph, the English Envoy, wrote to Mr. Secretary Cecil:—"There is with the Queen one called Mr. George Bowhannan, a Scottish man, very well learned, that was schoolmaster to M. de Brissac's son, very godly and honest, whom I have always judged fitter than any one I know." And in April 1562 Randolph again wrote:—"The Queen readeth daily after her dinner, instructed by a learned man, Mr. George Bowhannan, somewhat of Livy."

He proposed that of the three Colleges the first should be entirely devoted to languages; in fact, that it should be a Grammar School, like the great school attached to Calvin's Academy in Geneva.

The second was to be a College of Philosophy and Medicine, with four Regents in Philosophy, and one Reader in Medicine.

The third College was to include Divinity and Law; the Principal was to be Reader in Hebrew, and there was to be one Reader in Law.

This scheme was less complete and less ambitious than the preceding one. All hopes of seeing national education organised, and high schools established in every notable town, had now been frustrated, and Buchanan therefore proposed to provide for the grounding of Students in humanity within the University. But his plan, equally with that of the *Book of Discipline*, fell to the ground, and nothing came of it.

III. It was in Glasgow first that something was accomplished by the Reformers. Mary Queen of Scots, perhaps stimulated thereto by Buchanan, who was still in her confidence, now appears on the scene as the restorer of learning. Being in Glasgow, on the 13th July 1563, she issues a letter to the Lords of Council and Session and the Comptroller, founding five bursaries in the College of Glasgow, in the following terms: "Forasmuch as within the city of Glasgow a College and University was devised to be had, wherein the youth might be brought up in letters and knowledge, the Commonwealth served, and virtue increased; of the which College one part of the schools and chambers being built, the rest thereof, as well dwellings as provision for the poor bursars and masters to teach, ceased,—so that the same appeared rather to be the decay of a University than anywise to be reckoned an established foundation. And we for the zeal we bear to letters," etc. Mary grants the manse and kirk-room (site of the church) of the Preaching Friars, thirteen acres of land lying beside the same city, and various dues on different properties. Ordains the "Master of the said College and University"[1] to take up these emoluments; and expresses a design of endowing, at some future time, the College "with such reasonable living that therein the liberal sciences may be plainly taught, just as the same are in other Colleges of this realm. So that the College shall be reputed Our Foundation in all time coming."

IV. On the 9th February 1566-67 Darnley's murder took place. And it is remarkable that within five weeks of that date Mary signed two charters, which it must have been most unpalatable to her to grant, handing over all the monastic property existing within the burghs of Edinburgh and Glas-

[1] Perhaps this is the first instance on record of a College being identified with a University. The Principal of the College is regarded in the above document as administrative head of the University. This was evidently the idea of the Reformers. University work was to be carried out by Colleges. If, as at Glasgow, there was only one College, then a College with University functions constituted the University.

gow to the Provost, Bailies, Council, and Communities of those burghs respectively, for behoof of Protestant ministers of the Gospel and support of the poor. It is perhaps not unwarrantable to conjecture that these charters were extorted from Queen Mary under stress of the storm of unpopularity which followed upon her husband's murder. However that may be, the charter in favour of the town of Edinburgh was signed 13th March, and that in favour of the town of Glasgow on the 16th March 1566-67. Both charters were signed in Edinburgh in the presence of the same witnesses, and the terms in which they were couched are almost word for word identical. Queen Mary grants to the municipal corporations respectively the lands and buildings of all sorts which had belonged to the Dominicans, Preaching Friars, or Franciscans, " all the gardens, orchards, crofts, annual returns, fruits, dues, profits, emoluments, farms, alms, the daill-silver,[1] obits, and all anniversaries belonging to any altarage, chapelry, or prebend whatsoever," with liberty of turning the buildings into hospitals (*i.e.* alms-houses), under advice of the town ministers, and with obligation to sustain ministers, readers, and other ecclesiastical burdens. The whole of these properties to be united into a general trust, which was to be called

---

[1] " Lie daill-silver " appears to have been money left to Collegiate churches to be "dealt " or divided among the officiating clergy who performed services on the anniversary of the death of the testator. See *Jamieson's Dictionary, sub voce*. The "daill-silver" then was only a special form of the " obits " and " anniversaries " mentioned above.

"Queen Mary's Foundation[1] for the Ministers and Hospitals" of Edinburgh and Glasgow respectively.

These charters were not intended originally for the encouragement of learning or education. They simply granted monastic property for the support of the Reformed clergy and the poor. But they are mentioned here because in each case King James VI. made his mother's gift available for University purposes. In the case of Glasgow it was simply handed over to "our College of Glasgow," and in the case of Edinburgh it was confirmed to the Town Council, with liberty to turn it to educational uses. This, however, was done in the one case ten years, in the other sixteen years, after Mary's grant. And in the meantime but little of the property had been realised by the municipalities, much had been alienated and lost.

It is true that the charters each contained a clause, dictated by Mary's Protestant advisers, animadverting upon the unsettled state of the properties in question, and referring to the fact that prebendaries, chaplains, and friars, had, after the Reformation (post alterationem religionis), fraudulently sold and alienated lands and benefices; and that many private persons had claimed to be rightful owners of lands which their ancestors had mortified to the Church, and had actually gained possession of them through the negligence of the town officials and collusion of the ecclesiastics. The charters annul all these alienations and usurpations; but at

[1] Fundatio nostra Ministerii et Hospitalitatis.

the same time Mary, or her Catholic friends, got another clause inserted to the effect that all existing prebendaries, chaplains, and friars were to retain the liferent of their respective benefices. This last clause must have had an obstructive effect, rendering it hard to realise the properties. And the ultimate result was that from Queen Mary's gift, with its long list of monastic lands, buildings, and sources of annual income, the College of Glasgow only obtained an annual revenue of £300 Scots, and the Town Council of Edinburgh only got sites for their High-School and College, with a revenue for the latter of £200 Scots, from the ground-annuals of the Kirk-of-Field.

V. On the 8th January 1572-73—that is, nearly six years after the date of Queen Mary's charter—the Town Council of Glasgow, who had been made by that charter the nominal inheritors of all monastic property within the burgh, and who had by this time found out how extremely little there was available for the maintenance of the poor and the ministry, threw "Queen Mary's Foundation" overboard, and made a generous present of the whole of it to the Pædagogium, or College of Glasgow. They acted in this matter, as they tell us, under the advice of Master Andrew Hay, Rector of the parish of Renfrew, Vice-Superintendent and Rector, for the time being, of the University of Glasgow. The deed in which they embodied their purpose was the work of some accomplished humanist. Throughout, except in a few strictly business clauses, it is classical and literary, and forms a contrast to the official mediæval Latin of Mary's charter. The style suggests the hand of Buchanan;[1] perhaps he and Andrew Hay concocted the document together. This deed, under the title of the "New Foundation of the College or Pedagogue of Glasgow, by the Town," was ratified by the Parliament of Scotland a few days after it had been signed by the Town Council.

After an eloquent preamble on the decay of learning, the Provost and Bailies make over " to our College of Glasgow" all the church property granted to us by Queen Mary, for the decent support of Regents and Students to the number of fifteen persons—the first to be a Professor of Theology, and to be called the Principal or Provost of the College; then two Regents to teach dialectic, physics, ethics, politics, and, "in short, all philosophy" (*i.e.* Aristotle); then twelve poor Students with an aptitude for letters and philosophy.

The Principal to hold office for life, unless he prove himself unworthy, in which case he may be deposed by the Rector of the University, the Dean of Faculty, the Rector of the parish of Hamilton, and the Rector of the Church of Glasgow.

The Regents to be removable after their sixth year of office, when they shall each have carried two

---

[1] Buchanan evidently took a great interest in the College of Glasgow. He afterwards became one of its benefactors, and presented it with a collection of books.

classes through the curriculum, at the discretion of the Principal, the Rector of the University, and the Dean of Faculty—"especially if they shall have begun to get tired of their work."

The twelve Students to be provided with meat, drink, College chambers, and the usual conveniences (*reliquisque asiamentis*) for three and a half years, that being the period laid down by the statutes of the Faculty of Arts for taking the degree of Master.

The Principal to lecture on Sundays in the College on the Scriptures; and to have the vicarage of Colmonell, with annual teinds to the amount of 40 merks; also 20 merks as a first charge on the income of the College.

The two Regents each to have £20 for dress and expenses. They are to read prayers by turns in the neighbouring church, formerly of the Preaching Friars. The poor students in turn to ring the bell.

The Principal to be bound to live in College. The patronage of his office to belong to the Chancellor of the University (or his Vice), the Rector of the University, the rector of Hamilton, and the Rector of the Church of Glasgow.

The Regents to be appointed by the Rector of the University, the Principal, and the Dean of Faculty.

The twelve poor Students to be presented by the Town-Council, with a right of admission or rejection of the presentees reserved to the Principal and Regents. Sons of burgesses, sufficiently instructed *in re Grammatica* (*i.e.* in Latin), are those for whom the bursaries are intended.

The masters of the College, if they find it necessary, may marry "in the name of the Lord;" but they are not to keep their wives in College. The fifteen persons on the foundation are to eat and sleep in College.

The foundationers, and others who may come to live with them for the sake of study, are to be exempt from ordinary civic jurisdiction, and from all customs, exactions, and payments (*pedagiis*)[1] levied within the city.

The College is to be visited twice a year by the Rector of the University and the Dean of Faculty, together with the town Bailies.

The foregoing statutes, being drawn up under the advice of Andrew Hay, naturally contain no infringement of the rights or prestige of the University of Glasgow. The high University officials are invested with considerable authority over the College, and the studies therein are to be arranged in reference to the regulations of the Faculty of Arts. There is even a renewal of the mediæval idea of "privileges" in the immunity from municipal taxation, and from municipal jurisdiction, granted to the inmates of the College. There was nothing objectionable, from a University point of view, in the ministers of Hamilton and of Glasgow being asso-

---

[1] *Pedagium*, from which *paier* or *payer* (in French) and "payment" (in English) are derived, was originally "foot-money." *Pedagia dicuntur quæ dantur a transeuntibus in locum constitutum a Principe.* It came to be used by the mediæval writers for all kinds of payment.

ciated in the patronage of the principalship; and the Town Council assigned to themselves and their successors very modest functions with reference to the College. They claimed no right of regulating or interfering with the studies of the place, but merely the power of presenting to bursaries, and of visiting the College in conjunction with the Rector of the University and the Dean of Faculty.

This " New Foundation by the Town" of Glasgow consisted then, not in any innovation upon the constitution of the University, but merely in the setting up, or revival, with very slender endowments, of a College in Arts. It was perhaps owing to the want of means that, instead of having separate readers for the different branches of philosophy, as prescribed in the *Book of Discipline*, two Regents were to constitute the teaching staff, and each was to carry his class through the whole course requisite for a degree in Arts. The Principal was only to lecture on the Scriptures, and that, not as preparing for a degree in Theology, but as the Sunday instruction of Arts students.

At this time the Pædagogium, or College, of Glasgow was, and had been for some sixteen years, under the Principalship of John Davidson, a Paris-bred scholar, "modest and candid," says M'Crie, "although not of great learning." In 1557 he had been made " Regens Principalis Pædagogii Glasguensis," and he was the person designated in Mary's letter of 1563 as "Master of the said College and University." It was said to have been entirely through the exertions of Davidson that the College, for a number of years, was preserved in existence. The "New Foundation" of 1572-73 gave it statutes, but not funds; that is to say, only £300 Scots per annum. "There was maintenance for only two Regents, with almost no provision for bursars. The consequence was that the students gradually dispersed, and upon the death of Principal Davidson the classes were completely broken up."[1] The exact date of this occurrence is not, however, known.

VI. Not long after, there came a brilliant sunrise of education for Scotland. In 1574 Andrew Melville, at the age of twenty-nine, full of youthful vigour and ripe learning, arrived in Edinburgh from Geneva, where for five years he had held the Chair of Humanity.[2] Immediately on his arrival he was in great request. The Regent Morton at once offered him a place in his household, to be a stepping-stone to future promotion. This, however, Melville declined, preferring an academical life to the career of a courtier. The Universities of St. Andrews and Glasgow then began to compete for his services. At the General Assembly of August 1574 the Synod of Fife applied to have Melville appointed Provost

[1] M'Crie, *Life of Andrew Melville*, vol. i. p. 71.
[2] That is, of classics, *i.e.* Greek and Latin, not Latin alone. On Melville's arrival in Geneva, "they having need of a Professor of Humanity in the College, put him within two or three days to trial in Virgil and Homer," and then appointed him (see James Melville's *Diary*, Bannatyne Club edition, p. 33. Melville appears to have been classical tutor in the Academy of Geneva.

of St. Mary's College, St. Andrews, in the room of John Douglas,[1] who had just died. But Archbishop Boyd and Andrew Hay, as Superintendent of the West, urged so strongly the ruined condition of the University of Glasgow, that the Assembly recommended Melville's going thither in the capacity of restorer. He accepted the Herculean task; and in October 1574 journeyed to Glasgow from Baldovy, the residence of his elder brother in Angus. On the road he stopped for two days at Stirling, where he saw the young king, aged eight years. "The sweetest sight in Europe that day for strange and extraordinary gifts of ingyne, judgment, memory, and language."[2] He also saw the king's tutor, George Buchanan, then engaged in writing his *History of Scotland;* and took his advice on the plan of education to be followed by him in Glasgow.

As Melville had accepted the Principalship of the College of Glasgow under the "New Foundation," all that he was strictly required to do by the statutes (see above, p. 75) was to supervise discipline and to lecture on the Scriptures every Sunday. But this was far from being his conception of the task before him. He had two objects in view: to introduce new studies into Scotland, and to train up a race of teachers capable of carrying them on. His procedure is graphically described in the *Diary* of

---

[1] See above, p. 57. Douglas in 1571 had been made "tulchan" Archbishop of St. Andrews, but as the Regent Morton took the rents of the See, Douglas naturally held to his appointment as Provost of St. Mary's.
[2] James Melville's *Diary*, p. 38.

his nephew, James Melville, who had accompanied him, and who became a Regent under him after a year's preparation. "He set himself wholely to teach things not heard of in this country before, wherein he laboured exceeding diligently, as his delight was solely therein. So, falling to work with a small number of capable hearers, such as might be instructors of others afterwards, he taught them Greek Grammar; the *Dialectic* of Ramus; the *Rhetoric* of Talæus, with the practice thereof in Greek and Latin authors: namely, Homer, Hesiod, Phocylides, Theognis, Pythagoras, Isocrates, Pindar, Virgil, Horace, Theocritus, etc. From that he entered on the Mathematics, and taught the *Elements* of Euclid; the *Arithmetic* and *Geometry* of Ramus; the *Geography* of Dionysius; the *Tables* of Honter, the *Astrology* of Aratus. From that to the Moral Philosophy: he taught the *Ethics* of Aristotle; the *Offices* of Cicero; Aristotle *De Virtutibus;* Cicero's *Paradoxes* and *Tusculans;* Aristotle's *Politics*, and certain of Plato's *Dialogues*. From that to the Natural Philosophy: he taught the books of the *Physics*; *De Ortu; De Cœlo*, etc. Also of Plato and Fernelius. With this he joined history, with the two lights thereof, Chronology and Chirography,[1]

---

[1] M'Crie, *Life of Melville*, i. p. 73, paraphrases the above passage in the words, "To these he added a view of Universal History, with Chronology and the art of Writing." How the art of writing could be called a "light of History" it is difficult to see. *Chirographum* in mediæval Latin was a deed, diploma, or treaty. If Melville taught his pupils to pay attention to the terms of treaties and other public documents, he certainly had a very advanced idea of the mode of studying history. An examination, however, of the MS. of James

out of Sleidan, Manarthes, and Melanchthon. And all this besides and above his own ordinary province, the holy tongues and Theology. The name of the College within two years was noble throughout all the land and in other countries also. Students who had finished their course in St. Andrews came and entered again as scholars. And I daresay," concludes James Melville, "there was no place in Europe comparable to Glasgow for good letters during these years—for a plentiful and good cheap market of all kinds of languages, arts, and sciences."

The list of subjects and authors, so vigorously taught by Melville, may seem stale and antiquated at the present day. But in reality it was full of the fresh breath of the Renaissance. On the one hand, there was the groundwork of a thorough appreciation of classical antiquity; on the other hand, there was somewhat of the modern spirit and of the revolt against scholasticism. Under Melville, at the College of Glasgow, for the first time at any Scottish University, the Greek authors were studied in their original language. Greek had been taught more than twenty years previously in the school at Montrose; but actually, when Melville returned to Scotland, the Students at St. Andrews did not get any knowledge of it beyond the alphabet and simple declensions.[1] Melville's nephew and pupil, James,

---

Melville's *Diary*, in the Advocates' Library, shows that "Chirography," given by the Bannatyne Club edition, should have been "Chorography," *i.e.* Topography, which is commonly considered to be one of the eyes of History.

[1] James Melville's *Diary*, p. 24.

was the first regent in any Scotch College who took his pupils through the Greek text of the portions of Aristotle which they had to read. We have seen above (p. 65) how much stress the Reformers placed on the study of Greek, and how they designed that every schoolboy should have four years of it before going to any University. But it was in Glasgow College that Greek was first effectively read with University Students; and the example was never lost.

Again, we find in Melville's course a mixture of the study of Aristotle with the revolt against him, as exemplified in the writings of Ramus and Talæus. The modern spirit appears in his lectures on geography and history, with chronology and maps; in the *Arithmetic* and *Geometry* of Ramus; in the *Natural Philosophy* of Fernelius. All these were subjects alien from the genius of a mediæval University. Melville was bringing his pupils up to the newest lights of his age.

What he took them through was evidently a four years' curriculum in Arts. In the first year there was the teaching of Humanity, including both Greek and Latin, with the theory of style as propounded in the *Rhetoric* of Talæus, and this carried out in the study of the Greek and Roman writers. The *Dialectic* of Ramus was also taught, and doubtless made to explain the trains of reasoning in those writers. The second year was devoted to Mathematics, Cosmography, and Astronomy. The third year to the Moral and Political Sciences. The fourth year to Natural Philosophy and History. At the end of this Arts course there was apparently a two years' course in Theology, in which Melville "taught the Hebrew Grammar, first shortly, and afterwards more accurately; thereafter the Chaldaic and Syriac dialects, and the practice thereof in the Psalms, and works of Solomon, David, Ezra, and the Epistle to the Galatians.[1] He went through the whole commonplaces of Theology very exactly and accurately; also through all the Old and New Testament."

While Andrew Melville was thus conducting, in his own person and by means of his varied learning, a course in Arts and Theology such as Scotland had never seen before, he lost no opportunity of conferring with kindred spirits, among the more learned of the Reformers, upon the theory of University education, with a view to improving the existing Universities of the country. Among the chief ornaments of the Scottish Kirk of those days was Alexander Arbuthnot, who had studied at St. Andrews and for five years in Paris, and who, in 1569, had been made Principal of King's College in Aberdeen. Of him it is recorded[2] that he was "pleasant and jocund in conversation, and in all sciences expert; a good poet, mathematician, philosopher, theologue, lawyer, and in medicine skilful, so as in every subject he could promptly discourse, and to good purpose." Arbuthnot was a friend of the Melvilles, and a leader among that small section of the Kirk who believed in the necessity of reform-

---

[1] That is, in the Syriac version.
[2] Archbishop Spottiswood's *History*, vol. ii. p. 319.

ing education as a means of religious reformation. With him, after the General Assembly of 1575, Andrew Melville had a long consultation, during a journey which they made together into Angus, about the studies and discipline of their respective Colleges; " and they agreed, as afterwards was set down in the new reformation of the Colleges of Glasgow and Aberdeen."[1]

VII. The ideas agreed upon between Melville and Arbuthnot found expression in the *Erectio Regia* by James VI., dated 6th September 1577. This deed was probably obtained through the influence of George Buchanan with the Regent Morton, who took for himself and his family a little sop out of the arrangement. It is written in excellent, if rather florid, Latin, worthy of the pen of either Melville or Buchanan. The first thing it does is to provide some addition to the stipends of the College, which indeed was most necessary; though Melville, who had declined the flesh-pots of the Court, showed a noble disinterestedness about such matters.

" Understanding," says the *Erectio Regia*, " that the annual profits and returns of the College and Pædagogium of Glasgow are insufficient to sustain the Principal, Masters, Regents, Bursars, and Officials, with the advice of our dearest cousin, the Regent Morton, we grant to the College the rectory of the parish church of Govan, with all its

[1] James Melville's *Diary*, p. 41.

revenues, lands," etc. Then the deed confirms to the College any Friars' lands which may have been previously granted to it, and gives the College power to collect thirds on those prebends or chaplainries whose incumbents are still alive. "The Principal, Masters, etc., to repay the service of common prayers for our prosperity and that of our successors." "Our erection and foundation is as follows :—James VI., by the grace of God King of Scots, to all Christians greeting. We have set our mind on collecting the remains of the University (Academiæ) of Glasgow, which we found languishing and almost extinguished by poverty." Then follows a repetition of the grant of the rectory of Govan, "We wish twelve persons to reside in our College; namely, a Gymnasiarch, three Regents, an Economus (or Steward), four poor Students, the Gymnasiarch's Servant, a Cook, and a Janitor." These are to live a collegiate life, supported by the revenues of Govan, which amount to 24 chalders.[1] The Gymnasiarch is to be learned in Theology, and especially in the Hebrew and Syriac tongues. He is to lecture at least one hour a day. He is to lecture alternately on Biblical exegesis, and on the languages of the original Scriptures. On Sundays he is to preach at Govan. He is not to go from the College any distance without communication with the Rector of the University, the Dean of the Faculty of Arts, and the Regents, and leave granted. If absent three days without leave, he loses his appointment.

[1] Equal, perhaps, to about £400.

" In case of vacancy, the appointment will rest with Us and Our successors. If We or Our successors fail to appoint within thirty days, the election will rest with the Archbishop (as Chancellor), the Rector, the Dean of Faculty, and the Ministers of Glasgow, Hamilton, Cadder, Monkland, and Renfrew." Notice of the vacancy is to be given in Glasgow, St. Andrews, and Aberdeen.

The honorarium for the Gymnasiarch (or Principal) is to be 200 merks out of the old rental (£300) of the College. For his ministrations at Govan the Principal will receive three chalders (£50); the remaining 21 chalders sufficing for the common table, and expenses of the rest of the College.

The three Regents are to be appointed by the Rector, the Dean of Faculty, and the Principal; two of them are to receive fifty merks and the third £50 per annum from the College rental. The First, or lowest, Regent is to teach Rhetoric out of the most approved authors, and Greek. The Second, Dialectic and Logic, with special reference to the works of Cicero, Plato, and Aristotle, on Morals and Politics. He will add the elements of Arithmetic and Geometry. The Third Regent is to teach all the Physiology and Natural Philosophy of Aristotle, Geography, and Astrology, and Universal Chronology. This Regent is to conclude the philosophical course, and enable the Students to be capped (pileo donari). And he is to take charge of the College in the absence of the Principal.

"We do not wish," proceeds the *Erectio Regia*,

"these three Regents, as is the custom in other Universities of our Kingdom, to change their subjects of teaching every year (professiones quotannis immutare), by which it comes to pass that while they profess many subjects they are found to be versed in few; but we wish them each to stick to one line of subjects, so that the youths, as they gradually rise, may at each step find a teacher qualified to do justice to their zeal and ability. But if it be for the good of the College, one Regent may exchange his province with another, under sanction of the Principal."

Four Bursars are to be supported out of the revenues of Govan. Presentation to the Bursaries to rest with Lord Morton and his heirs. Admission to rest with the Principal, who is to keep out rich and idle persons from the Bursaries. Bursars are to enter on the 1st October, and to remain in College three and a half years.

"We hope that Students will flow in great numbers to our College from all parts of the Kingdom." But no one is to be admitted without making Profession of Faith as approved by Parliament. And each Master and Student is to repeat this Profession at least once a year. Finally, "we wish our College and University of Glasgow to enjoy all immunities and privileges conceded by our ancestors or ourselves to any University in the Kingdom." Among the witnesses to this document appears "Our dear Privy Councillor, George Buchanan, Pensioner of Crossraguel, and Keeper of our privy seal." The date is, "Dalkeith, 13th July 1577."

It will be observed that the *Erectio Regia* eliminates the Town Council of Glasgow from all connection with the College, and takes from them the not excessive powers which they had assumed in their "New Foundation" of 1573. The patronage of the Principalship is transferred to the Crown, and that of the Bursaries to the family of Lord Morton. But the most striking point about the charter is its vagueness and uncertainty in regard to the effect which it is to have upon the constitution of the University of Glasgow. It is called "Erectio Regia," but we are not told of what. The King says that he "wishes to collect the remnants of the University (Academiæ), but the whole deed merely goes to a new setting up of the College. Again the word *Academiæ* is used in one place evidently to mean the University; in another place, in paraphrase with the word *Gymnasium*, to mean the College. And at last it appears that the College is the University, or at all events a University, for the King grants or renews privileges to "Nostrum hoc Collegium et Academiam Glasguensem," "just as securely as if they had accrued to it (acsi illi obvenissent) before the memory of man." The deed does not say "accrued to *them*," as making the College and the University of Glasgow separate institutions, but it says "to *it*," thus identifying the College with the University.

No doubt those who drew this charter thought of the College under Melville as the one living reality, the one centre of teaching, which survived or had sprung up out of the ruins of the University. This was to be fostered, and, in accordance with the ideas of the *Book of Discipline*, to constitute a Faculty of Arts within itself. Implicitly, the *Erectio Regia* gives the College the power of conferring degrees; it says that by the labours of the Third Regent the Students are to be finished and capped; and it lays down three and a half years as the most suitable time, "judging from the practice of the other Universities of our realm," to be given to the course for graduation in philosophy. Thus the rules for graduation are not left to the determination of any external "University of Glasgow." The College itself is *the* University, or *a* University, it matters not which. At the same time, with careless inconsistency, the great officers of the University are recognised, and even have functions in relation to the College assigned to them—the Chancellor, the Rector, and the Dean of the Faculty of Arts. No provision was made for their future election, for the *Erectio Regia* did not legislate for the old University of Glasgow, but only for the College. It left the old University to shift for itself, but put the College in the way of supplanting the University and absorbing all its functions, which in reality it ultimately did. And this charter gave the model after which the other Universities of Scotland were transformed and lost their grandiose mediæval character. Through the loss of church livings which had been held by their officers, they fell into destitution, and then the Reformers brought the Colleges into prominence, and the old University institutions dwindled away, though some of them continued to subsist, or else were revived, as integral parts of the Colleges themselves.

VIII. The conference of Melville with Arbuthnot produced not only the *Erectio Regia* for Glasgow, but also the *Fundatio Nova* of King's College, Aberdeen. This was a scheme drawn up on the same lines as those of the Glasgow charter. It abolished not only the Professor of Canon Law in King's College (which was natural after the Reformation), but also the Reader in Medicine,— thus restricting the teaching in Aberdeen to Arts, Civil Law, and Theology, just as had been planned in the *Book of Discipline.* It also contained the same clause as that in the *Erectio Regia* against Regents taking their pupils through the whole course of philosophy. Cosmo Innes says[1] that "it went to break down all the usages and feelings of a University, setting up a teaching institution in its place." This may be true; but the question is whether, in the general disintegration of the Universities, to set up teaching institutions was not the best thing that the Reformers could do — provided always that the teaching was sufficiently high.

But the "remnants" of the old University were much stronger in Aberdeen than they had been in Glasgow. The *Fundatio Nova* was long and successfully resisted, and Principal Arbuthnot, who died in 1583, never saw it carried out. An Act of

[1] *Sketches of Early Scotch History*, p. 285.

Parliament of 1597 ratifies the document, but at the same time speaks of it as "to be revised." Hence some think that it never became law. But M'Crie says that "though its legal ratification cannot be proved, there is no doubt that it was acted upon for many years."

IX. Another learned and congenial friend of Andrew Melville's was Thomas Smeton, who had been Regent in St. Salvator's; at the Reformation had gone to France and attached himself to the Jesuits; afterwards had been gradually turned to Protestantism by the conversations of persons confined for heresy in the prisons of the Inquisition, and to whom he had access; narrowly escaped the massacre of St. Bartholomew; and got back to Scotland in 1577, where he was made Vicar of Paisley, and soon after Dean of Faculty in the University of Glasgow. "Mr. Andrew and he, marvellously conspiring in purposes and judgments, were the first motioners of an anti-seminary to be erected in St. Andrews, to the Jesuit seminaries, and ceased never at assemblies and Court till that work was begun and set forward."[1]

Thus at last, from the interest felt in a proposal for checkmating the Jesuits, something was done, after sixteen years' delay (see above, p. 68), for the improvement of the University of St. Andrews. A Commission was appointed in 1579, of which Buchanan was a member, to draw up a scheme, which in

[1] James Melville's *Diary*, p. 58.

the same year was presented to Parliament and ratified. This scheme is often called Buchanan's, but it was chiefly the work of Melville. Its main outline is as follows :—

St. Salvator's was to have a Principal and four Regents, for whom the course of teaching prescribed was almost precisely the same as that laid down for three Regents in the *Erectio Regia:* the work of the First Regent at Glasgow being divided between the First and Second Regents in St. Salvator's. The same rule was laid down that each Regent was to retain his own separate department of teaching. But there were to be also in St. Salvator's a Professor of Mathematics and a Professor of Law,[1] each to lecture four days a week. The lectures on Law were to be attended by the Advocates and Writers of the Commissary Court. The peculiarity was added that the Principal of St. Salvator's was to act as Professor of Medicine.

For St. Leonard's College the same arrangements were prescribed as for St. Salvator's, *minus* the lectures in Mathematics and Law, and with the variation that the Principal, instead of teaching Medicine, was to read Plato to the Students.

Thus St. Salvator's was constituted a College in Arts, Law, and Medicine; St. Leonard's a College in Arts alone, with the introduction of Plato as a supplement and a counterpoise to exclusive Aris-

---

[1] The addition of two Professors and a Fourth Regent was doubtless due to the richer endowments of St. Salvator's, as compared with the impoverished condition of the Pædagogium of Glasgow.

totelianism. And now we come to the College of Theology, that "anti-seminary to the Jesuits" in which Melville and his coadjutors were so much interested. St. Mary's, or "New College," was, of course, to be remodelled in this capacity. According to the scheme it was to have five Professors:—

> The first to teach Hebrew, Chaldee, and Syriac in a course of one year.
> The second, the application of these languages in critical explanation of the Historical books of the Old Testament, during one year and a half.
> The third the same, with regard to the Prophetical books, for one year and a half.
> The fourth, throughout the four years of the Students' course, to teach them to compare the Greek Testament with the Syriac version.
> The fifth, who was also to be Principal, to lecture on commonplaces, *i.e.* Systematic Divinity.

One cannot fail to be struck by the thoroughness of the training here laid down. If Protestantism was to be based on the Bible, before all things it was necessary to know what the Bible really said, which knowledge could only be acquired by a scientific linguistic study of the actual texts. And this was what St. Mary's College was to provide. The programme reflected the mind of Melville, who had made profound Oriental studies under Cornelius Bertram, the professor of Hebrew at Geneva, and had learnt from him to compare the New Testament with the Syriac version. We miss, however, one weapon against the Jesuits, with which the projected armoury of St. Mary's should have been supplied—namely, the study of Church history, which seems to have been wholly omitted in the scheme.

But alas! what had been so well planned, though ratified by Parliament, was most imperfectly carried out. The new mode of study was only partially adopted in St. Salvator's and St. Leonard's, and St. Mary's never received the proposed number of Professors. There was steady interested opposition to Melville's enlightened measures; and at last the Scottish Parliament of 1621, on the preamble that "the alteration and change which has been made on the first foundations of the Colleges within the University of St. Andrews have bred uncertainty in professions of sciences," etc., altogether repealed the Ratification of 1579, and restored "the first foundations of the said Colleges."

Thus it was not by the rude nobility of Scotland alone that the best ideas of the Reformers were treated as "devout imaginations;" it was not only the adequate endowment of the Kirk, the setting up high schools throughout the land, and other plans requiring grants of money, that met with opposition. Proposals for the reform of the Universities by the redistribution of existing endowments, and the introduction of higher and more thorough courses of study, were opposed, and successfully opposed, within the Universities themselves. In Aberdeen and St. Andrews the wise counsels of Buchanan, Melville, Arbuthnot, and Smeton, were set at naught.

It is true that, within the College of Glasgow, Andrew Melville had hitherto been able to carry out his ideas; and it seems a misfortune for Scotland, not only in respect of higher learning, but also of Church politics, that he was not allowed to remain at a post where he had been so brilliantly successful. Had he remained for twenty years Principal of the College of Glasgow, he might have consolidated a model school of Arts and Theology, and he might possibly have avoided embittering ecclesiastical controversy in a way which did harm to the country. But the General Assembly would not let him rest. In October 1580, "Mr. Andrew Melville, sore against his will, was decreed and ordained to transport himself from Glasgow to St. Andrews, to begin the work of Theology there, with such as he thought meet to take with him for that effect, conformably to the late reformation of that University; whereupon compulsators of horning[1] passed out against him, and Mr. Thomas Smeton was ordained to be placed in the College of Glasgow in his room."

It is not to our purpose to follow the career of Andrew Melville any farther. He had given in Glasgow practical demonstration of what could be done for Scotland in the way of high teaching; and he had in vain proposed measures by which similar results might have been attained in St. Andrews and Aberdeen. Whether this teaching was to be

---

[1] *i.e.* Orders of the Court of Session under pain of outlawry.

called "College teaching" or "University teaching" matters little, it seems to be a mere affair of words. Some writers blame the legislation of the Reformers for destroying ancient University forms, and thus degrading the Universities themselves; but the real misfortune was that the aspirations of the Reformers as to substantial improvement of teaching, and the introduction of a more solid learning, were not suffered to become effective. As a matter of fact the Reformers did not repeal or destroy any University forms; their *novæ fundationes* consisted in the reorganisation of particular Colleges, while the Universities in which those Colleges existed were left untouched; and, as we have seen, in 1619 and 1621 respectively the *novæ fundationes* for both Aberdeen and St. Andrews were swept away by Parliament, and the original constitutions of the Colleges were restored. But the Universities, as distinct from the Colleges, had no vitality or spring of life in themselves. Therefore, from the Reformation onwards, in St. Andrews, Aberdeen, and Glasgow, the Colleges took the place of the ancient Universities, and the University of Edinburgh was founded, from the outset, in the form of a College.

CHAPTER III.

THE ORIGINS AND OUTSET OF THE UNIVERSITY OF EDINBURGH.

> "Cauld blew the bitter biting North
> Upon thy early, humble birth;
> Yet cheerfully thou glinted forth
> Amid the storm,
> Scarce rear'd above the parent earth
> Thy tender form."

SUFFICIENT obscurity hangs over the steps which led to the origination of the University of Edinburgh to have left room for the play of fancy, and for a sort of kaleidoscopic treatment of the fragments of fact which have come down to us. Thus Bower (*Hist. Ed. Un.* i. 69) gives a consistent and pleasing narrative, to the effect that Reid, Bishop of Orkney, having bequeathed 8000 merks "to the town of Edinburgh for the purpose of erecting a University within the city," the Magistrates, "on the faith of speedily obtaining" this bequest, proposed the foundation of a College in 1561, and "in 1563 purchased part of the ground upon which the College at present stands;" and that "three years afterwards the unfortunate and susceptible Mary, whose generosity was unbounded, her love of learning sincere, and her proficiency considerable, entered warmly into the same views, and endowed with revenues the institution which she was so anxious to patronise."

This account, so consecutively put together, is calculated to lend dignity to the University by representing a Bishop and a Queen as the chief authors of its existence. But unfortunately every clause in the statement is erroneous. Reid had never any idea of founding a University; nor did he leave any money "to the town" of Edinburgh. He bequeathed 8000 merks in trust to three friends of his own, for the purpose of setting up a particular kind of College in Arts and Law, on a site which he specified to the south of Edinburgh. The Town Council had no direct interest in Reid's will, and there is no indication that they were encouraged or influenced in any way by a knowledge of the bequest, or by an expectation of its being paid. On the contrary, all their records seem to show that they acted, in their endeavours to supply the educational wants of Edinburgh, quite irrespectively of Reid and his bequest. Craufurd, who was almost a contemporary writer, and who in his *Memoirs* relates vividly in his own way the origin of the University, says not a word about Reid as being connected with its foundation. Ultimately a fraction of Bishop Reid's bequest came into the hands of the Town Council, after they had got their charter and begun building their College; and it was by them employed in aid of the building. Bishop Reid then, though we cannot recognise him among the Founders of the

University, became, incidentally and *de facto*, its earliest benefactor. As such we shall endeavour in an Appendix to pay him honour due.[1]

Mary Queen of Scots, on the other hand, cannot be acknowledged as either a founder or a benefactor of the University of Edinburgh. Whether the epithets lavished on her by Bower were deserved or not, at all events her charter of March 1566-67, of which some account has previously been given (pp. 70-73) had no reference to any educational purpose. It simply gave the monastic property, under certain restrictions, for the support of the Ministers and the poor of Edinburgh. Nor is there the smallest reason for believing that Mary Stuart felt any desire to see a Protestant College or University created within her Capital.

Dispensing, then, with these great and graceful names, the University of Edinburgh must be content with her actual promoters and founders, the Town Council and the Ministers of the City. So far as the Records inform us, the Town Council appear, from 1561 to 1578, to have made constant efforts for the establishment and endowment of a seat of learning; and after that the Ministry became prominent in a final struggle to get this work accomplished, in spite of obstacles.

On the 23d April 1561 a set of "Articles for the common policy of the Burgh" (probably the work of a committee) was laid before the Town Council, and approved by them. The first of these

[1] Appendix A. ROBERT REID, BISHOP OF ORKNEY.

was a resolution that "the rents, annuals, and other emoluments, which before were paid out of lands and tenements within this Burgh to papists, priests, friars, monks, nuns, and others of that wicked sort, for maintaining of idolatry and vain superstition," should "be applied to more profitable and godly uses, such as for sustaining of the true Ministers of God's Word, founding and building of Hospitals for the poor, and Colleges for learning and upbringing of the youth, and other such godly works."

Following up these views, they resolved a year later (April 1562) to write to Lord James Stuart (afterwards Regent Murray), asking him to use his influence with Queen Mary, "to grant to the Town the place, yards, and annuals of the Friars and altarages of the Kirk, for maintenance of the Grammar School, as also for the Regents of a College to be built within this Burgh."

In August of the same year they explicitly petitioned the Queen to grant them the grounds of the Blackfriars for an almshouse, the yards of the Greyfriars for a burial-ground, and the site of the Kirk-of-Field "to build a School."[1] To this petition the Queen promptly replied: granting them the Greyfriars' yard for the purpose named, and promising that "whenever sufficient provision is made for building the hospital and school, Her Grace shall provide convenient sites for them and

[1] The Town Council were as yet undefined in their educational schemes. They had destined the site of the Kirk-of-Field to educational purposes, but at first only proposed generally to build "a School there."

endowments for their future support." Thus Mary staved off for the time conceding the monastic revenues and the site of Kirk-of-Field.

The Provost of that Collegiate Church, one John Penicuik, was still holding on to the ruined fabric of a once splendid establishment.[1] And he, being minded to save something out of the fire—like those other persons afterwards denounced in Mary's Charter (p. 72) who "fraudulently alienated lands and benefices"—was willing to negotiate for the sale of all the ground, buildings, and revenues of the Kirk-of-Field for the paltry sum of £1000 Scots. The Town Council, in June 1563, agreed to purchase on these terms. This was the transaction referred to by Bower in the passage quoted from him above; but the purchase was by no means settled and concluded. On the one hand, Provost Penicuik was to obtain the Queen's sanction for transferring to the Town all the rights of his Provostry. On the other hand, the Town Council were so short of funds that all they could engage was that, after Penicuik should have fulfilled his part of the agreement, they would find security for the payment, within two years, of the thousand pounds.

Under these circumstances it is no wonder if there was a hitch in the business. Penicuik may have been put off by the Queen in his request for her sanction to the arrangement, or he may have disliked the long term of payment named by the Town Council. At all events, we find from the

---

[1] See Appendix B. KIRK-OF-FIELD.

City Register, under date 9th August 1564, that Provost Penicuik "is taking down the stonework of the Kirk-of-Field, and is of mind to sell the same" to other parties, "which the Council find most necessary to be bought for the good town, either for the Hospital or for a University to be made in the said Kirk-of-Field." The Council at once appointed "their assessor" to make final end with the said parson, touching the whole stones and all other things pertaining to the said parson by reason of his Provostry. And on the 25th of the same month they ratified the Act and Ordinance made between the good town and Provost Penicuik, touching the Kirk-of-Field, and ordained the arrangement to be concluded with all diligence. This is the last that we hear of the matter; the Town Council Records are very capricious and uncertain, yet had there been in 1564 a payment of the thousand pounds stipulated for, and a handing over to the town of buildings and ecclesiastical rights, it seems probable that there would have been some mention of the various business transactions that would have ensued. On the whole, it appears most likely that the Town Council never paid anything to Provost Penicuik for the site of the Kirk-of-Field. One interesting fact emerges from their Minutes on the subject, namely, that in 1564 they had got so far in their ideas as to speak of "making a University." They had, however, to wait for more than nineteen years before this aspiration was in any way realised.

Whether Penicuik had died or resigned his Provostry is not known; but at the date of Darnley's murder, on the 9th February 1566-67, Robert Balfour, brother of the notorious Sir James Balfour of Pettindreich, was Provost of the Kirk-of-Field. Thus the buildings and revenues of the establishment had evidently not been taken over by the Town Council, in consequence of any bargain with Penicuik; and Queen Mary, so far from being zealous to grant the site and what was attached to it, for the erection of a College, had put in a new Provost. But five weeks later—under pressure, as we may surmise—she granted her charter, conveying the Kirk-of-Field and all other monastic property in Edinburgh to the Town Council for the support of Protestant ministers and the poor. Yet still she inserted the clause that present incumbents were to have a liferent of their benefices. And this clause, doubtless, took back half the benefits of the charter, and mocked the honest purpose of the Town Council.

Robert Balfour continued to hold office as Provost of the Kirk-of-Field till November 1579, when he was forfeited by Parliament, along with other persons who had been accessory to the murder of Darnley. Even then the Town Council could not get possession of what the Queen's charter had granted them. For the Provostry, still regarded as a place in the gift of the Crown, though no longer as an ecclesiastical appointment, was bestowed on John Gib, "one of the Valets of His Highness' (the young King's) chamber." And him the Council had subsequently to buy out.

Not only had royal apathy to be contended with, but there were also other opposing influences, making themselves felt at Court and in Parliament. Craufurd opens his vivid *Memoirs* relating to the early history of the University by stating that "after the Reformation of Religion was established in Scotland, the City of Edinburgh and Ministry thereof were very earnest and zealous for the promoting of learning—their great intention being to have an University founded in the city; but the three Universities of St. Andrews, Glasgow, and Old Aberdeen, by the power of the Bishops, still bearing some sway in the Kirk, and more in the State, did let their enterprize." The particular circumstances of this opposition seem now to be lost, but several writers repeat Craufurd's statement that the Bishops who were Chancellors of the three old Universities set themselves against the erection of a rival institution in Edinburgh. And King James I. of England (as he then was) in 1617 corroborated this opinion by saying: "After the founding of it (*i.e.* the College of Edinburgh) had been stopped for sundry years in my minority, so soon as I came to any knowledge I zealously held hand to it."[1] King James thus took the credit to himself of putting an end to the opposition. But it is generally agreed that the temporary fall of Episcopacy in Scotland gave the Town Council and Ministers of Edinburgh the opportunity, which they had so long desired, of founding a seat of learning.

The leading spirit in this movement, and the

[1] See Appendix C. DISPUTATION AT STIRLING.

man to whom, above all others, the foundation of the University of Edinburgh is due, was James Lawson, "who for gifts and estimation was chief among the Ministry"[1] of Scotland. Lawson was a man of culture and experience, as well as of piety and earnestness. He had been educated gratuitously by Andrew Simpson, the celebrated master of the school at Perth; and in 1559 he became the fellow-student of Andrew Melville at St. Andrews. Afterwards he travelled on the Continent as tutor to the young Earl of Crawford. In 1568 he was appointed to teach Hebrew in the New College of St. Andrews; and in 1569, after the "purging" of the University of Aberdeen, he was promoted to be Sub-Principal of King's College under Arbuthnot. In 1572 he received the greatest honour which could then be conferred upon a Minister of the Reformed Church, being called to succeed John Knox as chief Minister of Edinburgh. James Melville speaks of him as "a man of singular learning, zeal, and eloquence, whom I never heard preach but he melted my heart with tears." Such was James Lawson, and with him were associated in his educational schemes Walter Balcanquall,[2] another City Minister; William Little, afterwards Provost; and his brother Clement Little, an Advocate and one of the Commissaries of Edinburgh; also Henry Charteris, a printer of good standing.

[1] James Melville's *Diary*, p. 146.
[2] Father of the more celebrated Dr. Walter Balcanquall, who became Master of the Savoy and Dean of Rochester; and who was George Heriot's Executor.

In the meantime the battle of Bishops or no Bishops for Scotland? was being stoutly waged in the Assembly, with varying issues. In 1576 Bishops were called upon to take pastoral charge of congregations. In 1578 the tide ran against them so hard that they were deprived of their titles of honour.[1] And in that year, perhaps encouraged by the state of public feeling, Lawson pressed on the Town Council till he got them to erect a new building for the High School of Edinburgh in the garden of the Blackfriars, which had come into their possession by Mary's charter. He had "some intention," says Craufurd, "if no more could be obtained, at least to make it *Scholam illustrem*, with Profession of Logic and the parts of Philosophy in private classes."

But he did not rest satisfied with measures for the improvement of the High School, as may be seen from an Act of the Town Council in April 1579, which ordained certain parties "to convene themselves in the Ministers' Lodging,[2] on the morrow, by four o'clock of the afternoon, for taking order concerning the foundation of a University." But it looks as if there had been some wavering at this time in the ideas of Lawson and his coadjutors,

---

[1] The honorary titles of Bishops were regarded with democratic jealousy by the Reformers. One of them wittily said that there were three sorts of Bishops: my Lord Bishop, my Lord's Bishop, and the Lord's Bishop. "My Lord Bishop was in the papistry; my Lord's Bishop is now" (*i.e.* a "tulchan Bishop") "when my Lord gets the benefice, and the Bishop serves for nothing but to make his title sure; and the Lord's Bishop is the true minister of the gospel."—James Melville's *Diary*, p. 25.

[2] The Ministers' Lodging, or quarters, was a building on the site of what is now the Parliament House.

for we find another Act in December 1579, by which the Council appointed the Provost and others "to pass and speak with Mr. Robert King and Mr. James Lawson, Ministers, for their counsel to be had concerning the erection of *a College of Theology*, and report." In the next year, 1580, the anti-episcopal party were still more triumphant; for at the General Assembly held at Dundee, of which Lawson himself was Moderator, "the pretended office of bishop" was declared to be unlawful, and "all such persons as bore the said office were ordered to demit the same." "The time being favourable was well plied by the Ministers and citizens of Edinburgh," says Craufurd, "so that having obtained a gift of a University within the city, in the beginning of this year (1581) they purchased from John Gib and John Fenton, servants to the King, their right of the Kirk-of-Field, to be a place for the situation of the intended College."

These words of Craufurd's have a peculiar significance, and, taken in conjunction with other expressions which occur in the City Records, they suggest a very strange point at the outset of this history, namely, a suspicion that the very document from which the whole narrative should have started—the original charter for the foundation of the College of Edinburgh—has been lost.

This idea, on the first mention of it, will appear to many persons to be, not only a paradox, but an impossibility. We find no reference made to the supposed missing document later than April 1584;

the charter of James VI., dated 14th April, 1582, has always been regarded as the charter of the College, and as such it was apparently ratified by the Act of Parliament of 1621; the question as to the constitution of the College, and the powers of the Town Council in reference to it, has been made the subject of repeated inquiries, and of at least two great lawsuits, but throughout all these it never occurred to any one that there could have been any other charter of foundation beyond that above mentioned; to this alone (with the ratifying Act of 1621) Sir James Stewart, the Lord Advocate in 1703, Mr. Thomas Thomson, the antiquarian lawyer who was counsel to the Senatus Academicus in their lawsuit of 1826, and the great lawyers in the case which went before the House of Lords in 1854— were content to appeal. And the Royal Commissioners, who, in the most searching manner, inquired into the history and affairs of the University from 1826 to 1830, never dreamt that at one time there may have existed a document, now lost, which would have been more valuable and interesting than those presented to them. Neither in the Inventories of Deeds in the City Office, nor in those of the Register House, is there any mention of such a missing charter.

All these things together constitute, it must be admitted, a formidable presumption against the possibility of what has been above suggested. But, on the other hand, there are expressions in the City Records which can only be explained as referring to some document which no longer exists. Craufurd implies that "a gift of a University within the city" was obtained in 1580.[1] No stress need be laid upon the word "University," because Craufurd, *honoris causa*, generally applies this term to the College of Edinburgh; the "gift of a University" therefore corresponds with what the Town Council in their Records call the "gift of erection of a College," that is, the grant under Royal sign-manual of powers to found a College. According to Craufurd, who is trustworthy in such matters, this grant was either made or promised, probably the latter, in 1580.

The next step occurred on the 14th April 1582, when James VI. at Stirling gave his sign-manual for the charter which has subsequently been considered to have been the charter for the foundation of the College of Edinburgh. But it does not naturally answer that description. It is a ratification of Queen Mary's charter (1566) granting to the town the monastic properties, and it allows these to be applied to educational purposes, which Mary's charter had not done. It makes no mention of either "College" or "University," but gives quite general

[1] He says that it was after they had obtained a gift of a University that the Town Council purchased from Gib and Fenton their right to the Kirk-of-Field. But the City Records tell us that it was on the 30th March 1581, that is to say, in the first week of the new year (old style) that the Treasurer was authorised "to content John Gib with 300 merks on condition that he renounces his pretended provostry." And it is mentioned at the same time that the King's sanction to this bargain had previously been obtained. All this would take time, so that it must have been at some period during 1580 (old style) that the Royal consent to the founding of a University or College had been obtained.

powers to the Town Council to build houses for Professors of Languages and Science, and to appoint and remove Professors, and it specially ratifies the purchase by the town of John Gib's right to the Provostry of the Kirk-of-Field. Had this charter stood by itself we should have said that it gave the Town Council surprisingly large powers of founding Colleges, without express authorisation to found a College, and without any definition of the character which any College to be founded by them should assume. But there are indications leading to the belief that there must have been another charter besides this.

On the 18th April 1582 the Town Council "find that the Treasurer had disbursed the necessary expenses of the Lord Provost and others who passed lately to Stirling to the King," *inter alia,* "for obtaining *the signatures passed concerning the foundation of a College.*" Here we have the word "signatures" in the plural. "Signature" was the regular legal term to denote a charter in its first stage, being a vernacular writ with the sign-manual subscribed or superscribed. Having thus received the royal sanction, it became the warrant to the Keeper of the Signet to direct to the Keeper of the Privy Seal a precept (written in Latin and embodying a translation of the "Signature") requiring him to issue a precept in like form to the Keeper of the Great Seal for expeding a charter in terms thereof. This (which was the precept recorded in the Privy Seal Register) became in turn the warrant to the Director of Chancery to extend a charter of the same tenor, in full form, and to complete it by the appending of the Great Seal. What the deputation of the Town Council went to seek at Stirling was charters (not a charter) in their first stage "concerning the foundation of a College." And these we must conjecture to have been *first,* the "gift of erection of a College" promised in 1580; *second,* the charter (which we possess) ratifying to the town Mary's grant of Church property and their own recent purchase of the Provostry of Kirk-of-Field, and also giving large powers of educational administration.

Nearly a year passed away without the Town Council apparently having taken any step towards the foundation of their College, but we learn from the City Records that on the 29th March 1583 "the Provost, Bailies, Council, and Deacons, understanding that if they enter not to work in founding and building of a College for letters in the Kirk-of-Field with diligence, *the gift granted* by the King's Majesty to the good town *will expire the 15th April next;* therefore appoint Andrew Sclater, bailie, and David Kinloch, baxter, to agree with certain workmen for the building of the outer walls thereof," etc.

And on the 28th June 1583 (after mention of an assessment to be made on the town towards payment of the King's debts) it is added: "And so foreseeing that the work of the College at the Kirk-of-Field new begun is liable to leave off and decay, and so *the gift of the erection thereof shall expire by virtue of the clause irritant contained therein,* without the same be supported by the good town by the sums given thereto ; for which causes, to wit, for payment of their part of the said extent (*i.e.* assessment) and support of the said work, they have agreed and consented that a general extent of 3000 merks be set and uplifted from the whole burgh and inhabitants thereof."

From these Minutes we get intimation of certain conditions, of which otherwise we should have known nothing, attached to the grant made to the Town Council of powers to found a College. And we find it expressly recorded in terms which nothing can set aside that there was in "the gift of erection," that is, in the deed conveying these powers, a "clause irritant" or clause of forfeiture, by virtue of which the "gift would expire," and the privilege of founding a College be lost unless a definite condition of time were complied with. The clause irritant declared that the work must be begun by the 15th April 1583, else the gift would lapse. This clearly points back to the 14th April 1582, on which date James VI.'s charter, which we possess, was signed. But in that charter there is no "clause of irritancy," and no restriction of time ; on the contrary, that charter granted liberty in general terms to the Town Council *and their successors*, of building and repairing houses for the reception of Professors, etc. From which it follows that on the same day (14th April 1582) another charter must have been signed, granting the Town Council definite powers of founding a College, provided they began the work within a year.

The reason why the Town Council were backward in commencing the building of their College, after being so urgent in obtaining permission to found it, was evidently the want of funds. The gift of erection which was made, or promised, in 1580 probably contained no provision for endowments of any kind. The deputation of the Lord Provost and Bailies above mentioned went to Stirling to negotiate for concessions which might be subsidiary to the bare privilege of founding a College, and might give means for carrying it out. At this time they urged a claim to be put in place of Bishop Reid's trustees, and this was accorded to them by an Act of the Privy Council on the 12th April 1582 (see Appendix A). They probably also pointed out that under Queen Mary's charter they had no power of using the monastic sites and revenues for educational purposes, and hence James's charter of 14th April 1582 was conceded to them, of which the main point was to give them free use of the site of Kirk-of-Field, but into which also they seem to have adroitly obtained the insertion of clauses giving them unbounded powers over the higher education of Edinburgh. The well-known charter of James VI. was, according to this view, not the Charter of the Foundation of the College, but was subsidiary to it.[1] The Charter of Foundation, with a quite definite

[1] It has been pointed out as an objection to the above hypothesis that it would be unusual for the one charter to be subsidiary to the other, and yet make no reference to the other. This is a difficulty, but it seems impossible to find a theory of this obscure matter that shall be free from difficulties.

scope, and containing, as we have seen, a clause of forfeiture, probably became a "Signature" or charter in its first stage, on the same day as the other, the 14th April 1582.

The deputation then doubtless considered that they had been very successful in what they had achieved at Stirling. None of Reid's money, however, came in for more than a year; it was not till July 1583 that they got an instalment of 700 merks out of his bequest (see Appendix A). The site of the Kirk-of-Field was now quite at their disposal, but for want of funds they were still delaying their building operations, when in March 1583 they were reminded of the clause irritant by which the powers granted to them would lapse in little more than a fortnight unless they set to work. The "Signatures" in the meantime had gone to the Signet Office, and, as often happened, there was great delay in turning them into charters. The Town Council therefore, not having the documents before them, used the phrase "*understanding* that if they enter not to work," etc.—implying that they had received an oral reminder of the terms of the clause irritant. They at once proceeded to take action, and saved themselves from forfeiture by beginning to wall in the buildings in which they proposed to locate their College. And on the 28th June following they resolved to assess the town for 3000 merks, of which a portion (perhaps 1000 merks) was to be available towards going on with the "new begun" College.

Under date the 14th September 1583, we find

another indication of a missing charter, for on that day they contract with Rollock, that "he shall enter to the College newly founded within the said Burgh *for instruction of youth and professing of good learning*, as the erection and foundation bears." This is evidently meant for a quotation from the Charter of Foundation, but no such words occur in the existent charter of James VI.

The Town Council had not as yet paid the fees exigible on the charters which had been granted to them, but on the 4th October 1583 they proceeded to do so; and we find it recorded that "the Treasurer is appointed to deliver the sum of £11 to be given for out-redding of *the two privy seals, one of the letter of the erection of the College, and one of a letter concerning the Provostry of the Kirk-of-field.*" And by the 4th December 1583 all the forms had been gone through, and, as the City Record says: "*Two charters* were produced made to the good town *under the Great Seal, the one of the foundation of the College, the other of the Kirk annuals.*" The whole narrative, then, is coherent; the "Signatures" granted on the 14th April 1582 had now reached the Town Council in the form of two charters under the Great Seal; of these the one which they call the charter "concerning the Provostry of the Kirk-of-field," or the charter "of the Kirk annuals," corresponds very well with the existent charter of James VI. The other charter—that "of the foundation of the College" —has gone amissing.

Once subsequently, and only once, the lost

charter has been referred to; and that was a few months later, in another charter of James VI. (4th April 1584) granting the teinds of Currie towards the maintenance of the College of Edinburgh. Whereof the preamble is: "Some time since we gave and conceded to the said Provost, Bailies, Councillors, and the Community, the liberty of erecting a College within the said Burgh, in which learning may be increased, and the liberal sciences, laws, philosophy, and other honest and liberal sciences and disciplines taught, to the great advantage of our whole Kingdom, and especially of the inhabitants of the said Burgh; and to this effect, with the advice of the Lords of our Privy Council, we annexed to the said College the acres, places, and tenements, belonging to the Kirk-of-field, situated within the liberty of the said Burgh, as is more widely contained *in the said annexation.*" In this narrative we see *first* a reference to the terms of the lost charter, which evidently defined the scope of the College to be founded by the Town Council; *secondly*, we see that James's existent charter of 14th April 1582 is designated as "the annexation" of the acres, etc., of the Kirk-of-Field to the said College. The designation is loose, as it corresponds rather with the general design than with the particular terms of the charter in question. But the whole of the passage just quoted is quite in accordance with the facts previously related, and with the interpretation put upon them.

It may now be asked, How is it possible that so

important a document as the charter under the Great Seal for the foundation of the College of Edinburgh should have disappeared, and that no mention of it, if it ever existed, should appear in the Register of the Great Seal charters? The latter circumstance, however, is easily explained:— Though it was intended that every charter, when completed, should also be recorded in the Office of Chancery, the regulations as to sealing and recording for a long period left this to the discretion of the grantee, who, having obtained his charter, was often insensible to the importance of having it put on record, or grudged to pay the fees, and thus the Register continued to be a most imperfect record of the charters which passed the Seal, until, in the year 1672, an Act was passed ordaining that every charter should be recorded before it was sealed and given out. The College charter then very likely came to the Town Council unrecorded, and when they had got it, they had no reason for carefully preserving it; on the contrary, it may have suited them better that it should be suppressed. For the charter probably conveyed to them no privilege beyond the right to found a College, which right was exhausted when the College had been founded. On the other hand, the charter may very likely have imposed duties upon them, such as an obligation to keep up the buildings and provide for the teaching of the College. The Town Council had no interest in preserving the Charter of Foundation, because if it were destroyed their rights of government over the College would come under the terms of the other, and still existing, charter, which, without imposing any responsibilities upon them, gave them, in the widest terms, absolute power over all professorial teaching within the burgh of Edinburgh. Clearly, then, it would be for the advantage of the Town Council that the Charter of Foundation should disappear.

And it is not beyond the bounds of possibility that the King himself may have had motives for preferring to have the Charter of Foundation suppressed. We are on very speculative ground now, and can only advance what seem not impossible solutions. But it is not incredible, and there are some reasons for believing, that James VI., after he had come of age, took a different view of the College from that which had been taken by the Crown officers who drew up the Charter of Foundation. That charter must surely have granted to the College the power of conferring degrees, and one great argument for such a charter having existed is, that otherwise the Town Council would hardly have assumed, as they did, a degree-giving power for their College from its very commencement. Well, we may suppose, from the words above quoted from the charter of April 1584, that the Charter of Foundation defined the object of the College to be— to teach and give degrees in "the liberal sciences, *laws*, philosophy," and so forth. But James may have changed his mind with regard to this, and may have wished to have the province of the College more limited. In particular, he may have objected, and we shall subsequently show reasons for thinking that he did object, to the foundation of a Faculty of Laws in Edinburgh. And it is a remarkable circumstance that the Act of 1621 "ratifies and approves the erection of the said great lodging, manse, and house of the Kirk-of-field into a College for the profession of Theology, Philosophy, and Humanity;" and further encourages the "placing therein sufficient Professors for teaching of all liberal sciences," without any mention of Laws, though "Laws" were mentioned as distinct from "Liberal Sciences" in the charters both of 1582 and 1584. If James VI. had come to the conclusion, perhaps in the year 1590, that it would be better to confine the College of Edinburgh to being a College of Arts and Theology, he may have thought it expedient to cancel the Charter of Foundation, which perhaps constituted it, too definitely for his views, a College of all the Faculties.

A little collusion on such a matter between the Crown and the Town Council would have been quite in accordance with the spirit of these times. If the King suggested the quiet suppression of the Charter of Foundation, the Town Council would have no cause to object to such a step, which, as we have seen, would place them in the possession of unlimited powers over the College, in lieu of a position, which, perhaps, was to some extent defined in the Charter of Foundation. The Ministers of Edinburgh, if they were privy to the transaction, would have no reason to resist it, as the remaining charter of 1582 associated them with the Town Council in the appointment and dismissal of all future Professors. And, moreover, we shall show that it was not unlikely that the Ministers themselves originated the opposition to a Law Faculty. Even Rollock himself would, from his own way of looking at things, be rather glad than otherwise to have his College restricted to Arts and Theology. Thus the only section of any importance in Edinburgh that would have had cause to feel aggrieved at the suppression of the Charter of Foundation was the College of Justice. But in the sixteenth century the King of Scots, with the Ministry on his side, would be too strong for the College of Justice, even if that body were aware of what was being done. But all this is speculation; *valeat quantum.* A grain of fact, if now ascertainable, might supersede it all.

It is difficult for the historian to suppress a sigh of baffled curiosity over the charter too apparently lost. If we had it, it could not fail to tell us the ideas which regulated the foundation of the College. Possibly it defined the position of the Town Council as Patrons and Trustees, and thus to some extent gave a constitution to the seat of learning which was being created. If so, the preservation of the document would have altered the course of subsequent events. It might have obviated a thousand heartburnings and long litigations of which we shall have to tell. It might even have been of advantage to the successive generations of the Town Council, to be placed under definite responsibility, instead of having entrusted to them the indefinite powers given by the existing charter of 1582, and confirmed by the Act of 1621. It was, however, only as time went on that the loss of the charter became of moment; during the first half-century of the existence of the College, in its "day of small things," probably matters would have proceeded very much in the same way with the charter as they did without it.

But to return to the region of solid fact: we have before us King James's charter of 14th April 1582, and, as it could not have been inconsistent with any other collateral document, we may proceed to consider it as it stands, and just as if no other charter of the College had ever existed. We see how totally dissimilar it is to the Bulls constituting the Universities of St. Andrews, Glasgow, and Aberdeen. We miss the preamble with reasons why a University should be founded; the *instituimus et fundamus Studium Generale;* the concession of privileges; and all mention of Faculties, Degrees, Chancellor, Rector, Masters, Regents, and Supposts.

We find that it starts with a summary and then a citation in full of the charter and infeftment granted by "our dearest mother" to the Town Council and community of Edinburgh; and thence proceeds to ratify, at first generally, and afterwards more particularly, the grants and concessions of Church property made by Queen Mary. Its further contents are as follows:—

I. Mary's charter had only specified the Ministry and the poor as the objects to which this Church property was to be applied. King James's charter enlarged the scope by adding on[1] the promotion of education and learning. It granted the monastic revenues to the Town Council, "to be applied by them for ever to the sustentation of the ministry, the assistance of the poor, the repair of schools, and the propagation of letters and sciences, as may seem good to them and their successors."

II. It gave power to the Town Council of accepting endowments which any persons in future time, moved by good zeal, and of their own free will, may give and bestow "for the aliment of ministers of the gospel, the assistance of the poor, and the sustentation of schools (*gymnasiorum*) for the advancement of sciences and learning."

III. It confirmed "the renunciation and demission made by our servant John Gib of all right and title, which by virtue of our gift he could claim, to the Provostry of the Church of St. Mary of the Fields" (*vulgo* "Kirk-of-Field"), "with all its lands, revenues, etc.," in favour of the said Town Council, and in behoof of the Ministry and the poor.

IV. It gave the Town Council power to build Schools and Colleges on the sites and grounds of the religious houses in the following terms:—"And whereas there are now within the privileges and

[1] In the parallel case of Glasgow King James had not merely enlarged the scope of his mother's charter, but had simply handed over all the monastic property specified in that charter to "our College of Glasgow" (see above, p. 85).

liberty of our said burgh diverse void and spacious (*vasta et spatiosa*) places which in time past belonged to the Provost, Prebendaries, Priests, and Friars, especially fit and convenient for the construction of houses and buildings where Professors of good sciences and letters and students of the same might reside, and hold their full course of study (*diuturnam exercitationem habere*), beside other places suitable for almshouses ;—therefore We, strenuously desiring that for the honour of God and the common good of our realm literature should day by day be increased, will and concede that it shall be lawful to the aforesaid Provost, Councillors, and their successors to build and repair sufficient houses and places for the reception, residence, and entertainment of teachers (*professorum*) of grammar schools, of humanity and the tongues, of philosophy, theology, medicine, and laws, or of other liberal sciences whatsoever. Which we declare shall be no infringement of the purposes for which the aforesaid property was devised (*prædictæ mortificationis*)."

V. Finally, it gave full liberty to the Town Council and their successors, "with advice, however, of the ministers," to choose persons most suitable for teaching the said branches ; with power of inducting and removing them according as may be expedient; and of prohibiting all others from professing or teaching the said sciences within the boundaries of the burgh, except with the permission of the Town Council.

Obviously this is no charter founding a University;

and several writers have been careless in speaking of it as "the Charter of the University of Edinburgh."[1] The document is, under the circumstances, peculiar; for if, as Craufurd says, the Town Council had obtained "the gift of a University"—that is, the promise of one—it would have been natural for the King, as other kings had done before him, and as he alone could now do in Scotland (the power of the Pope being extinct), to issue a charter founding a University, with such privileges as might be deemed fit, and endowing it with certain definite grants of the monastic property. But he did nothing of the kind; he confirmed Queen Mary's gift of monastic lands and revenues, made this applicable to educational as well as other purposes, and gave the Town Council large and exclusive powers of creating and regulating establishments of higher education in Edinburgh, at their own pleasure, "with, however, the advice of the ministers." It is true that the charter not only permits, but seems to invite, the erection of a College in the Kirk-of-Field; this being in accordance with former petitions of the Town Council, and doubtless with recent negotiations on the subject. Yet still, had the Town Council and Ministers changed their mind after the

[1] If any definition of the scope of James VI.'s charter of 1582 were required, it is to be found plainly given in Charles I.'s charter of 1636, which, after citing it, says: "By which our dearest father gave and conceded to the Town Council the liberty of erecting a college—building houses for Professors of Humanity, the Tongues, etc., and choosing adequate Professors. And to this effect he gave and conceded to them and their successors the Provostry of the Kirk-of-Field, with its lands, tenements, revenues, and appurtenances."

granting of the charter, there was nothing in the charter itself to bind them to this particular course; they were left at liberty to choose their own line of action in reference to educational measures. The charter, while speaking of *scholæ* and *gymnasia*, seems carefully to avoid making mention of either a College or a University. The subjects which it specifies as lawful to be professed are indeed co-extensive with those of any *Studium Generale*, but there is no authority given to found a *Studium Generale*.

We may safely conclude that all this was not fortuitous, but that all the terms of the charter were the result of careful consideration on the part of the King's advisers. In King James's charter to the College of Glasgow in 1577 the old University of Glasgow had not been abrogated, but simply ignored. When it came to the question in 1582 whether the King should found a University in Edinburgh, it is extremely likely that cautious counsellors represented that it might be more safe not to do so. In the early days of the Reformation there was on both sides a certain jealousy of Universities, on account of their independence, and their natural tendency to deal with theological questions. Thus we learn that in 1594 the Magistrates of Geneva having sent a deputation to the King of France, to obtain from him the rights of a University for the Academy of Geneva, the King refused, declaring that he had made the same answer to the States of the Low Countries, " because Universities are hotbeds of heresy."[1] And we have seen throughout the last chapter how the Reformers in Scotland, from 1560 to 1579, took no measure for founding any new University, or for strengthening the old Universities as such, but gave all their attention to promoting the higher education of the country by means of Colleges. The same policy was apparently kept in view in 1582 with regard to the movement in Edinburgh. A compromise was agreed upon, which was probably quite acceptable to Lawson, Balcanquall, and the Littles, as well as to the Town Council. The King was not to found a University, but was to give full powers to the Town Council, " with the advice of the Ministers," to found a College, or Colleges, for the higher studies. And the municipal authorities and clergy of Edinburgh were entrusted for ever with the absolute control of higher education within the burgh.

At first sight, and in contrast with mediæval notions, this may seem to have been a strange and novel arrangement; but there was precedent for it, and reflection shows that it was of the nature of a copy. The precedent and the model in this matter was Geneva—Geneva, to which the Scottish Kirk looked as the fountain-head of its doctrine and discipline—Geneva, which had been the asylum for refugee Scottish Reformers from 1554 till 1560. In the republic of Geneva the Municipal Council was of course supreme; and in 1559, while the place

---

[1] "Parce que les universités sont des pepinieres d'héresie." Senebier, *Histoire Litteraire de Geneve* (1786), vol. i. p. 55.

was still full of Scotchmen, that Council had, by the advice of Calvin, opened their Academy.[1] The Academy of Geneva failed, as we have seen, to obtain recognition as a University from the King of France. But it at once rose to be a distinguished seat of learning; Melville had been Professor there from 1569 to 1574, and it is not to be supposed that Melville had not his say upon the question of founding a College or University in Edinburgh. The result, probably of much consultation, was that the King should not found a University, but that he should put the Town Council of Edinburgh in the same position as the Municipal Council of Geneva, and enable them, "with the advice of the ministers," to found a College just as the Municipal Council of Geneva, with the advice of "the Venerable Company of Pastors," had established their Academy. The magistrates and clergy who accepted this arrangement may have been secretly pleased with its democratic aspect; but they forgot that the Municipal Council of Geneva were the rulers of the entire republic, and therefore had powers for carrying out what was best, which were wanting to the Town Council of Edinburgh. And, on the other hand, the young King's flatterers would tell him, or he would be astute enough to reflect, that Town Councils would be his creatures, and that he could appoint and remove them at pleasure; therefore that the educational powers granted to the Town Council could still be wielded by himself. And we

[1] See Appendix D. ACADEMY OF GENEVA.

find him very soon afterwards acting upon these principles.

The Town Council of Edinburgh then had full liberty given them to found a College, but they were far from being in a position to emulate Bishop Kennedy or Bishop Elphinston by erecting a structure of architectural grace and dignity. It was quite understood that what they had to do was to adapt the buildings which had appertained to the Kirk-of-Field for collegiate purposes. But even for this they lacked funds :[1] we have seen how they hung back, till, having been threatened with the loss of their privilege, they set to work at the beginning of April 1583, and began to wall in the buildings which they considered suitable.

Of these the chief was "Hamilton House," also called "The Duke's Lodging," which they destined to be the main building of their College. This mansion had been erected by the Duke of Chatelherault, upon the site of an hospital belonging to the Collegiate Church of Kirk-of-Field, and which had been burned down by the English some time during the invasions of 1544-47. The site was purchased by the Duke in 1555; it ran from north to south, commencing at the centre of the north side of the present University quadrangle. The large house which the Duke built upon it was confiscated on the

[1] In June 1583, as we have seen, they levied an assessment on the city, part of which went to the College buildings. This has been erroneously represented by Bower to have been a loan for the purpose. In the next month 700 merks of Reid's legacy came in. In January 1583-84 they raised another assessment of 2000 merks on the town, 1100 of which were to go to the College buildings.

forfeiture of the Hamiltons, and was bestowed upon some courtiers, and by them sold to the Town Council of Edinburgh. Thus the chief site and fabric for the accommodation of their College did not come to the Town Council by virtue of Queen Mary's charter or James's confirmation, but by a private purchase, the validity of which was afterwards successfully disputed,[1] so that the subjects had to be paid for over again. The interior of Hamilton House was adjusted so as to furnish class-rooms and a tolerably large hall, with three "chambers" or sleeping apartments for Students. To this "great lodging" the Town Council either adapted, or built, a sort of wing running east from its northern end, and containing fourteen "chambers." Hamilton House and its wing constituted the whole of the buildings hastily prepared and partially walled in during the summer of 1583 for the reception of the Town's College.

And now the Town Council began to look out for the man who should be entrusted with the headship of it. A contemporary writer, Henry Charteris, wishing to uphold the dignity of the nascent institution, and availing himself of the ambiguity of certain Latin

[1] In 1586 Lord John Hamilton, on the removal of the attainder from his family, "laid claim to the lodging in the Kirk-of-field, which had been converted and employed for the schools of Philosophy." He was persuaded to waive this claim, but his son, the second Marquis of Hamilton, twenty-six years afterwards revived it, and "by the aid of Lord Binning and other strong friends on the Session" made it good, and compelled the Town Council to pay him £3000 as compensation, which, as if in mere despite and scorn, he handed over as a gift to a dissipated follower. See Craufurd, p. 78.

terms, says that "they began to deliberate on a Rector to preside over the Academy."[1] *Academia* was the word which the Humanists had introduced to mean "University," because they disliked the mediæval terms *Studium Generale* and *Universitas;* on the other hand it was sometimes used to denote a College, and the "Academy" of Geneva was distinctly declared not to be a University. *Rector* was the title of a high University officer, but it was also given in early times to the head-master of a municipal school.[2] Thus Charteris could not have been called to account for the terms he used, for they admitted of a double sense. But it is certain that he meant them to be taken in their more dignified import. And his words are here quoted as the first instance of what often occurred afterwards, namely, that all who wrote on the history of the University of Edinburgh—Charteris himself, Craufurd, Dalzel, and Bower—claimed for it from the commencement the high titles and functions belonging to a mediæval University, whereas it is plain that the Town Council considered that they were only founding a College. In the City Records the "Town's College," as they generally call it, is never once designated as a University till near the end of the seventeenth century, when the reader of these records meets all of a sudden, under date 24th

---

[1] Consultare de Rectore qui Academiæ præesset. H. Charteris, *Vitæ et Obitus D. Roberti Rolloci, Scoti, Narratio*, p. 42.

[2] The title of "Rector" came into Scotland long before there was a University in the country, for in 1233 the schools of St. Andrews were under charge of a "Rector."

March 1685, with the admission that the College had, by James VI.'s charter, been "erected as a University." This remarkable entry will be commented on in the next chapter.

James VI., at the Stirling disputation, was explicit in saying: "I will be godfather to the *College* of Edinburgh, and will have it called the College of King James." And accordingly the institution in question got the official title of *Academia Jacobi Sexti* now engraved over its portal, which title of *Academia*, being conveniently ambiguous, suits its present fortunes, as well as the more restricted views of its founders.

The Town Council, in seeking a head for this College, did not turn their eyes towards Montague College,[1] or the Scots College in Paris, in search of some Scot perfected abroad in scholarship and philosophy—like Bishop Kennedy, who fetched home John Athelmar to be Provost of St. Salvator's, or Bishop Elphinston, who recalled Hector Boece to be Principal of King's College. Home-bred learning had now become respectable in Scotland; and, on the other hand, in the then earnest mood of the national mind, personal religion, as well as a correct theology, would be thought of as primary requisites in one who was to be made the guide of youth. Between Paris and Scotland the Reformation had set a gulf. The Town Council might have looked to Geneva for aid, but James Lawson thought that he knew, "from the report of many," a man who

[1] See Appendix E. MONTAGUE COLLEGE AND THE SCOTS COLLEGE.

was possessed in eminent degree of all the needful qualifications.

This was Robert Rollock, son of the laird of Powis, near Stirling, who had never been out of Scotland, but had been educated, first at the school of Stirling under Thomas Buchanan (nephew of the great George), and afterwards at St. Salvator's, where in 1580 he had been made Regent of Philosophy. This young man, now in his thirty-third year, had, during his short career as a teacher, made a reputation, not only for his competence in philosophy, but also for the piety which he instilled into the minds of his pupils.

To him Lawson wrote a letter, making overtures, which being favourably answered, a deputation was sent over to St. Andrews by the Town Council of Edinburgh to confer with Rollock, and honourably invite him to accept the newly-created charge. Rollock then came to Edinburgh and had an interview with his future patrons, the result of which was that on the 14th September 1583 a contract was concluded between the Magistrates and himself to the following effect :—

I. "The said Master Robert shall enter the College newly founded within the said Burgh for the instruction of the youth, and professing of good learning (as the erection and foundation bears) the fourteenth day of October next, without further delay, and shall exercise the office of the Regent of the said College, in instruction, government, and correction of the youth and persons which shall be committed

ROBERT ROLLOCK
Principal of the College of Edinburgh.

to his charge, during the space of one year immediately following his said entry, and further, so long as the said Mr. Robert uses himself faithfully therein, according to the rules and injunctions which shall be given to him by the Provost, Baillies, and Council of the said burgh."

II. The Council engage to pay him the sum of £40 Scots, in two equal portions, at Candlemas and Lammas; and also to "sustain him and one servant in their ordinary expenses."

He is also to have as fees "from the bairns inhabitants of the said burgh forty shillings, and from the bairns of others not inhabitants therein, £3 or more, as the bairns' parents may please to bestow of their liberality." And if at the end of the year the said Mr. Robert finds himself "not sufficiently satisfied" with his said yearly fee and casualties, he is to have an augmentation, not, however, exceeding the amount of 40 merks.

III. The Council bind themselves that "as it shall happen their College in policy and learning to increase, the said Mr. Robert, upon his good merit, shall be advanced to the most honourable place that shall be vacant therein" (*i.e.* to the highest post or title which should be created).

This document had many characteristic features. We note in it the straitened circumstances of the Town Council, which obliged them—after all the fine phrases in King James's charter about Professors of all the liberal sciences—to content themselves with starting a College to be furnished with only one

Regent or tutor. We note their caution in engaging Rollock as Regent for only one year certain. We note also their Scottish homeliness in designating the future Students as "bairns." Nor can we fail to observe the tight hold and absolute control which they reserve to themselves over this future seat of "good learning," in which the Regent is only to hold office so long as he faithfully obeys the "rules and injunctions" of the Provost and Bailies. We cannot but reflect upon the humble and abject start into existence made by the University of Edinburgh, as compared with the free and honourable position conferred by Papal Bulls upon the older Universities of Scotland.

There is, however, no just ground of complaint against the Town Council of 1583. In asserting their powers they only did what was natural in the situation in which, by the King's charter, they had been placed. Rollock seems to have had no difficulties placed in his way after he had assumed rule. He at once inspired confidence, and was consulted in everything. The emoluments covenanted to him seem paltry, but the extreme poverty of the municipality is to be borne in mind. To illustrate the pecuniary arrangement made with Rollock we may recall some of the payments for literary offices made or proposed in Scotland during the sixteenth century. In 1500 Boece came to be Principal of King's College on a salary of 40 merks; he, however, had free board in addition, and he obtained the rectory of Fyvie, and a pension from the King of £50 per annum. In 1541 Bishop Reid gave Ferrerius, a foreign scholar, for instructing the monks of Kinloss, £40 a year, and maintenance for himself, a servant, and two horses. In 1560 the *Book of Discipline* proposed that Principals of Colleges should have £200 per annum each, and Professors from £200 to £100. In 1573 the Town Council of Glasgow, having hardly anything to give, gave the Principal of the College of Glasgow 60 merks (or £40) per annum, with free board. In 1577 the *Erectio Regia*, drawn up under Melville's inspiration, allotted to the same Principal 200 merks and 3 chalders (equal perhaps to £50 sterling), and board at the common table of the College. Rollock was to have £40, or 60 merks, per annum, fees from each Student of 40s., with £3, or more, according to the liberality of parents, from Students coming from outside the town; and if the aggregate of salary and fees should prove insufficient, he was to have an augmentation not exceeding 40 merks. In computing what this would actually come to, we find that Rollock's class, during his first four years as Regent of Philosophy, was probably not over sixty in number. In 1587 he graduated forty-eight Students, apparently the whole number with him, but some may have dropped off during the course. Taking sixty as a liberal estimate of the average number, we get 180 merks fees per annum, plus 60 merks salary, and perhaps 40 merks augmentation; total 280 merks, or £187 Scots. As the Scots currency was debased in 1585 from one-sixth to one-eighth of the value of the English currency, Rollock's emoluments would be equal to about £23:7:6 sterling of that day. In addition to this he was to have free board and lodging for himself and one servant.[1] After four years a new arrangement was made, and his salary was consolidated at 400 merks, the same sum which in 1560 had been settled as the stipend of John Knox. Rollock, doubtless, was provided with all the necessaries for a simple, frugal life; and he not only married, but he was even able to exercise a certain amount of hospitality; for it is recorded that "he never suffered his old teacher, Thomas Buchanan, when he happened to come to Edinburgh, to live in any house but his."

The standard of teaching in the College of Edinburgh was from the outset fixed at University level, according to the ideas of these times. The line of demarcation consisted, in the first place, in this— that Latin was to be the language of the classes; not only was the Regent to lecture upon all his subjects in Latin, but all intercourse, all question and answer, between him and the Students was to be conducted in the same language. Hence arose the necessity of the first act of the College, namely, to hold an Entrance Examination, in order to prevent Students being admitted to the classes who, from their want of sufficient familiarity with Latin, would not be able to follow the teaching. Rollock

---

[1] The allowance for the board of Rollock and his servant was fixed at half a merk per day, equal to £120 Scots, or about £20 sterling per annum in 1583.

having come to Edinburgh delivered an address, which has not been preserved, in the hall of Hamilton House on the 1st October 1583. A crowd of youths —*magna multitudo*, says the somewhat florid biographer—applied for admission ; but they were directed to enrol their names before one of the Bailies, and to appear for a testing examination on the 11th of the same month. Rollock in the meantime worked paternally with the young men, assisting them to bring their Latin up to the mark. But on the day of trial a considerable proportion failed.[1] By the advice of Rollock these persons were not absolutely excluded from the College, but a tutor was provided for them, "to furnish them more thoroughly with Latinity against the following year." On the 8th November Mr. Duncan Nairn was appointed to this office, and thus became "Second Master" of the College. He had been a pupil of Andrew Melville's at Glasgow, and graduated there in 1580; he was said to be a young man "of remarkable scholarship and great refinement." The class now entrusted to him, though attached to the College, held an infra-Academical position ; for the year passed by them in

[1] This was probably due in a great measure to the High School having been hampered for more than twenty years with a head-master —one Robertoun—who held his appointment from a former Abbot of Holyrood, and who was not only "an obstinate Papist," but also an incompetent scholar. The Town Council tried to get rid of him, and in 1562 had summarily dismissed him. But Queen Mary, interfering on behalf of her co-religionist, had arbitrarily ordered him to be restored to his office. As, by a charter of James V., dated 1529, the "principal Grammar School" of Edinburgh had a monopoly of teaching classics within the burgh, the incompetency of this head-master was very serious.

preparation did not reckon as part of their four years' curriculum for graduation.

The "Town's College" of Edinburgh was opened, probably on the 14th October 1583 (that being the day named in Rollock's commission), under two Masters, and with an attendance of eighty or ninety Students, of whom between fifty and sixty were in Rollock's class, commencing their first year's course for a degree, and the rest in a preparatory or tutorial class under Nairn. It was evidently the idea of the Town Council and Ministers not to have Students merely attendant on classes, as in a modern Scottish University, but to institute a College wherein the main body of the Students should reside. Thus, on the 8th November 1583, they resolved "that all the students of the Town's College shall nightly lie and remain in their chambers within the same, and that they all shall have and wear gowns daily; and such as want gowns and will not lie therein to be put forth thereof." This quaintly-worded order shows a true collegiate spirit. But unfortunately the Town Council were set to make bricks without straw. They had not the means of providing adequate lodging for the scholars. Craufurd speaks of two apartments, which in his time (1626-1662) were class-rooms, having been originally employed for chambers, "there being none else beside, except the fourteen little chambers (now called the Reid Chambers[1]) on the north side of the little close."

---

[1] Probably because fitted up with the 700 merks of the Bishop Reid's bequest, which fell in in 1583.

There can hardly then have been accommodation for all the Students, though the Town Council ordered "that they be two in each bed, and pay of chamber rent 40s. each person; and if any will have a bed to himself to pay £4 of chamber rent."

But for collegiate life not only lodgings but also a common table would have been requisite. The founders of the College of Edinburgh manifestly aimed at this, and lost no opportunity of realising their idea.[1] We are told that in 1584 "the Abbey of Paisley, by the forfeiture first of the Hamiltons and afterwards of the Erskines, being vacant at the King's donation, was bestowed upon the town of Edinburgh, who intended to employ a part thereof for an economy to be kept in the College, but the revolutions of State which shortly followed quashed that design" (Craufurd, p. 26). It is certain, however, that a portion of the Students resided within the College walls, and Craufurd, speaking of a period about forty years after the first start, implies that more would have done so had there been room for them. He says that then twenty-three chambers were the total number available—"a number improportional to the number of students, which in many years exceeded sixteen score." But if in those early days of the College forty or fifty Students slept

[1] As late as 1646 we find that they had not abandoned this aspiration. The Regents having complained of the inadequacy of their salaries, the Town Council granted them an augmentation "during the not-establishing of an economy (*i.e.* provision for household expenses) within the said College."

within its walls, the question arises, how did they breakfast and dine? And it is most curious that neither the City Records, nor any other source of information, throws any light on this problem. There seems no resource but to conclude that the "in-college" Students catered for themselves. Under date 1628 we find an order of the Town Council containing "Laws to be observed by the Scholars in the said College," and also a statement of "The form of discipline usually observed in the said College." The curious thing about these documents is that no distinction is made in them between in-College and out-College Students. Though the latter class— those living in the town—must have formed two-thirds of the whole body, yet the regulations almost entirely apply to those resident in College chambers. Thus: none are to "go out of the gate after it is once locked by the Janitor, without leave of one of the Regents." They are all to "speak Latin," both in the schools, in the close, in the fields, and in all other places where they are together; and "none is to be found speaking Scotch." The following passage, however, would seem applicable to out-Students: "After their dismissal (from classes) at all times in the day, especially in the evening, they are to go directly to their lodgings, and not to be found assembling in companies either in the gaitt (*i.e.* the road or street) or elsewhere, and in like manner at the time of their coming again to the schools." The order that "none go to taverns" seems hard on the resident Scholars, if they had to provide their own eating and drinking. But as to this point the otherwise minute Regulations of the Town Council say not a word. The law about wearing gowns, so stringently laid down in 1583, is not repeated in the later code, and in all probability it was a dead letter from the first. Perhaps it was disliked and resisted by influential parents, and was dropped in consequence. Thus from the outset the Edinburgh Students presented rather a citizen-like than an Academic appearance.

In some of the domestic arrangements of the "Town's College" the Council imitated the usage of the mediæval Colleges, for they exacted a certain amount of menial service from beneficed Students.[1] The bursars in turns, two each week, were to have charge of ringing the bell[2] to summon classes, at five o'clock in summer and six in winter; then again at ten o'clock and at half-past one. They were also to "paidell" (*i.e.* scour with brushes attached to the feet) the stairs and entrances to the schools. The Janitor, who had a paid office, was at first always a Student of the fourth year, or else a graduate who was studying theology. He was to keep the main gate of the College; unlock it in the morning, and lock up at ten at night. Also to keep the keys of the schools, or class-rooms; to place

[1] This practice, however, does not date from the first opening, for there were then no Bursaries. We shall see in the next chapter that six Bursaries were established in 1597, by the College of Justice and the Town Council jointly.

[2] On the 6th December 1583 the Town Council ordered their "Master of work in the Town's College to buy the skellet bell for the said College, and to hang up the same by the advice of the Bailies."

candles in them at night, and sweep them out thrice a week. And he was to have an eye to the buildings in general, and report when repairs were necessary. He was to ring the bell for dismissal of classes, probably because the bursars, who were otherwise the bell-ringers, would be themselves in class.[1]

Both in-College and out-College Students had to assemble early in the morning, and they had a long day's work every day throughout ten or eleven months of the year. Even on "play-days" they were only allowed to go for two hours to the fields —that is, to a part of the "Muir lands" (answering to what is now "Warrender Park"), where they had a playground assigned to them, and where they used to practise archery. Each Regent had constant tutorial supervision of his class, and when they were not attending lectures he was perpetually "conferring" with them and examining them. Under Rollock a religious character so far pervaded the institution that he may almost be said to have presided over a Protestant religious house in the Kirk-of-Field. Every evening the Principal conducted family worship with the Students. Every Wednesday he instructed all the Scholars "in the knowledge of God and of their duties." On Sundays all the Students assembled for morning lessons, and then were taken

[1] This shows that the Janitor would have his studies interfered with by the duties imposed upon him. And in 1635 Principal Adamson recommended the Town Council to confer the office of Janitor upon some one who was not a Student, "especially upon a bookbinder, who might employ himself at work within the gate of the College, in a room fit for this purpose." Whereupon one "David Smith, bookbinder, was elected porter," and others of his craft succeeded him.

to church for the morning and afternoon sermons; after which they had to return to the College and give an account of the sermons. At first they appear to have gone to the "High Church" (St. Giles'), but in 1600 the Town Council allotted the east loft of Trinity College Church for the use of the Students.

The foregoing particulars serve to give us a tolerably clear picture of the general life of the College of Edinburgh, as shaped out by Rollock during the first years of its existence—all except the arrangements for meals, on which we find no information. And in all those particulars we see that it was as yet no University, but an essentially collegiate and domestic institution. On the other hand, its founders assumed for it from the outset the power of conferring degrees. This power before the Reformation had been derived solely and directly from popes or kings. Whence, then, did the College of Edinburgh obtain it? There seem to be only two alternative answers to this question. Either the privilege was conveyed in a lost charter of the foundation of the College, or else, after negotiation on the subject, it was orally conceded by the State authorities that the Town Council should imitate the Municipal Council of Geneva (see Appendix D), and assume a degree-giving power for their College. It is true that the Geneva degrees were disallowed by other Universities, or only recognised as a matter of courtesy. But it never happened to the Edinburgh degrees to be questioned, as we shall see below, till 1709, and that was far too late, for the Act of 1621 had fully ratified the degree-conferring powers of the College of Edinburgh.

On the 16th October 1583 the magistrates appointed a committee, of which William Little— one of the chief promoters of the University, and afterwards Provost—was a leading member, " to devise the order of teaching to be kept in the College now erected." Of course this was done in consultation with Rollock. The scheme adopted was one for a course of strictly University study. A curriculum for the attainment of the Master of Arts degree was laid down on the lines of what had been in use in the older Universities, with some modern improvements based on the practice of Andrew Melville or the ideas of the post-Reformation educationists.[1] The curriculum was divided into four sessions or classes ; and the old University nomenclature for these classes was retained. The first or lowest was styled the " Bajan " class, as consisting of the *Bajani* or " Freshmen." The mode of spelling this term adopted in Scotland has been misleading, and hence Principal Lee[2] says, " There is no doubt that the word is derived from the Latin *Pagani*, rustics requiring to be civilised or humanised though enlisted among the *cives academici;* in the same manner as the name *pagani* was anciently given to the Roman conscripts or raw recruits." But the word, as an Academic term, came from the University

---

[1] George Buchanan did not live to see the opening of the College of Edinburgh, or to give his advice as to its regulation. He had died in September 1582.   [2] *Academic Annual*, p. 27.

of Paris, where the form was always, not *Bajanus*, but *Bejanus* or *Beanus*;[1] while the entrance fee paid by a new Student to his "nation" was called *Bejaunium seu jucundus adventus*—money to furnish a feast in celebration of his arrival. In the forms *Bejanus* and *Bejaunium* we find the two syllables *Bec-jaune* clearly retained; and Ducange says: "Vox Gallica *Bejaune*, quasi *Bec-jaune*, ut sunt aviculæ quæ nondum e nido evolarunt." The "Bajan" class, then, was for the *Gelbschnabel*, or callow bird of Universities. The second class in the College of Edinburgh were called "Semies," *i.e.* "Semi-Bajans," or "Semi-Bachelors." In the third year the Students were called "Bachelors," or "Determinands;" because at the end of that year they might "determinate," that is, finish their course with the imperfect degree of Bachelor (*bas chevalier*). The fourth year's class consisted of "Magistrands," or Students about to be made *Magistri*. Of course when the College was opened in October 1583 it could only have a class of first-year men, or "Bajans." These were under Rollock, while there was a tutorial or preparatory class of unmatriculated Students under Nairn. In October 1584 Rollock's class became "Semies" or second-year men, while Nairn's class were promoted to be "Bajans." In May 1585 the plague broke out in Edinburgh, and the College was disbanded till February 1586. Thus the second

---

[1] Ducange quotes from Lambecius a piece of mediæval wit on this word: "Beani definitio latitat in ipsa nominis sui acrostichide—Beanus Est Animal Nesciens Vitam Studiosorum."

and third sessions of the College lasted only seven months each, instead of eleven, which was the full Academical year originally prescribed. And, from the same cause, it was not till October 1586 that a third Bajan class was started, and a third Regent, Alexander Scrimger, added to the staff of the College. Nairn had died in February 1586, and Adam Colt had been appointed to take his class. Thus in the session of 1586-87 the classes were:—

> Magistrands under Rollock;
> Bachelors under Colt;
> Semies—none;
> Bajans under Scrimger.

At the end of this session Rollock's class laureated with the M.A. degree; and had he been an ordinary Regent he would have begun again at the bottom with a new class of entrants. But as he was "Principal" (this title having been conferred upon him in February 1585-86), it was thought proper that he should be removed from the drudgery of Regenting, and he was made Professor of Theology, Philip Hislop being appointed to the vacant Regentship. Thus in 1587-88 the classes were:—

> Magistrands under Colt;
> Bachelors—none;
> Semies under Scrimger;
> Bajans under Hislop.

And in 1588-89:—

> Magistrands—none (therefore there was no graduation this session);
> Bachelors under Scrimger;
> Semies under Hislop;
> Bajans under Colt.

At the beginning of the session 1589-90 a fourth class was for the first time added to the College; Charles Ferme being appointed fourth Regent, and placed in charge of a new Bajan class.

The above details exhibit the working of the rotation system among the Regents. This system had been commonly in use in mediæval Colleges; it was a tutorial as distinguished from a Professorial system. For, while the Professor or Reader has his particular subject to teach to all pupils who may come to him, the rotating Regent or Tutor has his particular pupils to instruct in all the subjects of a prescribed curriculum. We have seen that the authors of the *Book of Discipline* proposed to abolish the rotation of Regents, and to substitute Readers of each separate subject. Andrew Melville actually introduced this change in the College of Glasgow. And the rotation of Regents was forbidden in all the *Novæ Fundationes* of the Colleges in Scotland. But all those Colleges either did not entirely relinquish, or soon returned to, the old plan, which Melville and the most enlightened Reformers had denounced. And the teaching of the College of Edinburgh was established from the outset on the old plan, which continued in vogue in all the Universities of Scotland till the beginning of the eighteenth century.

There was one cogent argument in favour of the system which probably decided the Town Council of Edinburgh to adopt it, and that was its economy. It would be cheaper to get the whole work of preparing the Students for graduation done by four

Regents than to appoint separate Readers or Professors for each of the subjects to be taught. The Regents in the College of Edinburgh under Rollock got a salary of only £100 Scots [1] each, or about £11 : 10s. sterling, without any provision for board. They might earn perhaps £80 Scots additional by class fees, but the appointments were altogether meagre, and were looked on as stepping-stones to other preferments. The persons appointed to be Regents were almost always young men who had recently graduated ; and they were chosen after public trial,[2] in the shape of Latin disputations held before competent judges, who acted on the part of the Town Council. The procedure was analogous in some respects to the election, after a competitive examination, of young graduates to be Fellows and Tutors of Colleges at Oxford and Cambridge.

The four Regents of Philosophy each carried on his own class from entrance to laureation, and then began again from the bottom with a fresh class of "Bajans." What the course in Philosophy was we find completely drawn out in the City Records some years later. The work for the four successive years was, in brief, as follows :—

The Bajan year was mainly taken up with Latin and Greek scholarship—the books to be read being works of Cicero, the Greek Grammar of Clenardus, some of the New Testament, Isocrates, Homer, Hesiod, and Phocyllides. Large portions of these books had to be committed to memory, and constant

---

[1] See Craufurd's *Memoirs*, p. 41.   [2] See *Ib.* p. 30.

"versions" or translations into the vernacular, and *vice versa*, had to be made. During the last four or five months of the year the *Dialectics* of Ramus were gone through.

In the Semi-Bajan year the first month was occupied with repetition and revisal of last year's work. For the next two months the class had to study Rhetoric out of the works of Talæus, Cassander, and Aphthonius. The remainder of the session was devoted to the *Organon* of Aristotle, the greater part of which was read. Towards the close of the session a compendium of Arithmetic was given to the Students.

In the Bachelor year the Regent, after examinations, first read Hebrew Grammar with the Students. Then he exercised them in Dialectical Analysis and Rhetoric, and read through the *Posterior Analytics* which had before been omitted. At the close of the session he gave them a description of the Anatomy of the human body. On Saturdays throughout the year there were disputations.

In the Magistrand year, after a repetition of all before gone through, the *De Cœlo* of Aristotle and the *Sphere* of Johannes de Sacrobosco were read, and demonstrations of Practical Astronomy were given. Then the Students read the *De Ortu*, the *Meteorologica*, and the *De Anima*,[1] and also *Hunteri Cosmographia* (a work on Geography). And they were constantly exercised in disputations.

---

[1] The *Ethics* of Aristotle must also have been read at this time, as they are included in the subjects enumerated for examination.

In comparing the course thus laid down for the College of Edinburgh with its antecedents the following contrasts arise :—It differed from the mediæval degree system in Scotland—(1) By making Greek an indispensable part of University study; whereas, before the Reformation, Aristotle had been studied in Latin translations, and the Greek Testament had not been read. (2) By the spirit of humanism which it exhibited, great attention being paid to purity of style both in Greek and Latin. (3) By its modernising tendency, in the admission of Ramus, and Talæus, and Hunter's Cosmography, and descriptive Anatomy.

It differed from the scheme of the *Book of Discipline* in being not exclusively a scientific course, but giving up the first year to scholarship and literature. It was evidently moulded, to a great extent, upon Andrew Melville's course, but it omitted two of the most important features of that course, namely, Geometry and History.[1] Probably the Edinburgh curriculum was drawn up in accordance with what Rollock, who was far less widely accomplished than Melville, was prepared to teach.

One great merit of the system was that it was calculated to keep the Students' minds in a constant state of activity. The classes were at first small, averaging about thirty Students each;[2] thus there

---

[1] It is remarkable that the study of Universal History, thus omitted in the first programme of the University of Edinburgh, has been strangely neglected in all the Universities of Scotland ever since.

[2] We infer this from the numbers laureated each year. In 1587,

was constant tutorial supervision. There was no mere passive note-taking allowed, but frequent examinations, translations, themes, and disputations ensured assimilation of the text-books read, and gave to each Student a certain command of thought and language. On the whole, the education which the College of Edinburgh gave at the end of the sixteenth century was, for those times, quite as good and useful as that which many modern Universities up to very recent times have given.

The system of examinations for degrees in Edinburgh as settled in those early times has been minutely recorded by Craufurd, and deserves attention. The only degree which the College then and for long afterwards conferred being that of Master of Arts. The first batch of Magistrands to be laureated was Rollock's class in 1587. These he carefully examined himself, and then gave them their degrees. Afterwards, when the College staff was complete, this simple procedure was superseded by minutely-prescribed arrangements. The first principle of these arrangements appears to have been that no Regent should be allowed to examine the class which he had himself taught. The Regent of the Magistrand class was thus excluded from their final examination for degree, and as he had had the sole training of them since their matriculation they would now have to be examined by persons who had

48; in 1588, 30; in 1590, 13 (after an outbreak of the plague); in 1592, 28; in 1593, 19, and another class 20; in 1595, 29; in 1596, 24; in 1597, 34; in 1598, 32. See Craufurd's *Memoirs*. He does not give the number for 1591.

taken no part in their teaching. This was devised to exclude all suspicion of favouritism. As all the Regents were supposed to be thoroughly acquainted with the whole curriculum, it was assumed that one could examine as well as another.

At the final examination in July the Magistrands came before the Regents of the Bachelor, Semi-Bajan, and Bajan classes, and the Regent of Humanity.[1] The first examined them in the early books of the *Organon;* the second in the *Analytics;* the third in the *Topics* and *Sophistics*, and in Ramus; the fourth in the *Ethics.*

Then again :—The first examined them in the *Acroamatics;* the second in the *De Cœlo* and in Astronomy; the third in the *De Ortu* and the *Meteorologica;* the Humanist in the *De Anima.*

The results of all these examinations were severally reported to the Principal, and at the same time the five Regents each laid before him a report on the conduct and "carriage" of every Student. And the Principal, considering the conduct as well as the ability of each, proceeded to draw up what we should call a class-list of the Students to be graduated "according to their deservings."

What we term "classes" of honours they called "circles," and the fixing of the class-list was called "circulation." The list as adjusted by the Principal contained the names of :—(1) *Exortes*, those who were above the circles; (2) Those who were in the

[1] The nature of this office, created ten years later than the graduation of Rollock's class, will be fully explained in the next chapter.

first circle; (3) Those who were annexed to or approached the first circle; (4) Those who were in the second circle; (5) "The remainder in a line, whose names were thought fittest to be spared in public calling upon them."[1]

The honour system in Edinburgh in those days was more complete and stimulating than anything of the kind now existing in any University of Scotland. But it is curious to find that its very thoroughness brought it into disfavour. "Diverse of good note," says Craufurd, "being dissatisfied with the public notice of their children's weakness, procured the laying aside of the Circulation from the year 1631 to the year 1643, at which time it was revived in part,"—the names being called in ranks, not at the public disputation, but the night before, in the presence of only the Town Council, the Ministers, and the Masters of the College.

There are two points which strike one in the examination system above detailed:—*first*, that it does not comprise all the studies of the four years' course, Greek and Latin Scholarship, Arithmetic, Hebrew Grammar, Anatomy, and Geography being omitted. Thus the examination was entirely in Aristotle, with the items of the *Dialectics* of Ramus and Astronomy added on. Probably scholarship was considered to have been sufficiently tested in previous College examinations, while Hebrew Grammar,

[1] Craufurd, p. 51. This last division is analogous to what in Oxford is called "the Gulf," consisting of the names of those who, having sought honours, fail to obtain them, but still are admitted to bare graduation.

Anatomy, Arithmetic, and Geography were regarded as *hors d'œuvre*—useful in themselves, but not essential parts of the qualification for a degree in Philosophy. And this shows that the Town Council and Ministers of Edinburgh had not as yet shaken off mediævalism. *Second*, we note the thoroughly collegiate and domestic character of that part of the system which made the conduct and carriage of a Student to form an element in determining his position in the class-list for graduation.

On the night before the ceremonial of laureation the successful Students "convened before the Principal and whole Regents, when they first subscribed the Confession of Faith, and next a solemn engagement to be dutiful to the College where they had got their breeding." Next day came the "Act," which consisted of public disputations. This was invariably held on a Monday, in order that the Lord Chancellor of Scotland, "and other Privy Councillors, the Treasurer and Lords of Exchequer, with the Lords of Session, Advocates, and Writers, having no meeting on that day, might attend; which they used to do with great frequency." A Thesis had been drawn up by the Regent of the Magistrand class, and subscribed by all the candidates for laureation; and they were now, in presence of a dignified assembly, in the Church of Trinity College, or the Greyfriars', or in the College hall, severally bound to defend every proposition in it against all impugners. Probably some of the class may have been told off to impugn, in default of external controversialists; but the audience, containing numerous ministers and lawyers who had been trained in foreign Universities, would in the sixteenth century furnish many veterans able and willing to show their skill in such combats of words. The disputations were conducted in Latin, and lasted all day, till six in the evening ; but, as the graduation-list had been settled before, they had no influence upon the fate of the candidates. They were a mere exhibition of the Students' expertness in a kind of exercise which still pleased the taste of the day.

The disputations ended, the candidates were by public proclamation called up according to the distinct ranks which had been assigned them ; and the Principal, after a short exhortation to a virtuous and pious life, performed the ceremony of laureation "by the imposition of a bonnet (the badge of manumission) upon the head of each of the candidates ; and then one of their number, in a brief speech, gave thanks to the assembly, and dismissed them."

We have now seen clearly the arrangements made for education in the College of Edinburgh as a College for graduation in Philosophy or Arts. But very soon arrangements for education in Theology (without graduation) were added. It came about in this wise: In February 1585-86 Rollock received the title of "Principal or First Master."[1] This was

[1] Bower most erroneously supposes that this was done by the Town Council "with a view of raising their infant institution to the rank of a University," whereas the office of Principal is not a University office at all. It, properly speaking, has no place in the System of a University ; a "Principal" is simply Head Tutor of a College ; he is, in

simply in fulfilment of the Town Council's pledge to him (above, p. 133) that they would advance him to the highest post vacant in their College. They could not have made him Principal to start with, as that would have been a contradiction in terms so long as he was sole Regent; as soon as there were Regents under him he was made First Regent or Principal. When thus dignified with the title of Head, Rollock did not immediately give up his Regenting, but carried through his class to laureation in August 1587. And it was only on his obligations to his class having been discharged that he retired from the teaching of Philosophy. And in the following November he was appointed by the Town Council, with the consent of the Presbytery of Edinburgh, to be Professor of Theology in the College. This reference to the Presbytery was an acknowledgment of the right of the Kirk of Scotland to control in spiritual matters all Universities and Colleges,—a right asserted down to 1858. The combination in Rollock's person of the offices of Principal and Professor of Theology was in accordance with the ideas of Melville, as expressed in the *Erectio Regia* (above, p. 85).

By this appointment a school was created for those

short, what is called in Oxford or Cambridge "Head of a House." At St. Andrews we see two Principals, because there are two separate Colleges. The University of Glasgow only got a Principal because the Pædagogium or College of Glasgow usurped the place of the University, and thus the first officer of the College came to be considered the first officer of the University. But modern usage in Scotland has completely adopted the misnomer of "Principal of a University."

graduates in Arts who proposed to enter the office of the Ministry. Of Rollock's work as Professor of Theology his biographer says: "I can scarcely describe the assiduity, the watchfulness, the laboriousness, with which he set about training in Divinity such of his former pupils as applied their minds to this study. Sometimes he dictated a logical analysis of one of the Epistles of St. Paul, or of some other book of Scripture; sometimes he handled general topics; sometimes he examined into the points of controversy with Popery; and in these pursuits he suffered no hour of the day to pass unemployed." Craufurd says of him: "He had incredible dexterity in framing the spirits of the young divines to the pastoral charge, and had for the space of eleven years the most flourishing seminary of that kind which was known in that age." Without quite endorsing Craufurd's retrospective eulogy, and his claim for Rollock's school of Theology to have been the first of those days, we cannot fail to recognise that Rollock personally did a noble work. Though, on the other hand, looking at the matter, not from a spiritual, but from a scientific point of view, we see that his conception of theological teaching was inferior to that of Andrew Melville. But reserving a more particular account of Rollock as a Divine for a later page, we only note here that in 1587 the College of Edinburgh was complete in its first stage of development as a College of Arts and Theology. There were four Regents, each of whom in turn every fourth year brought up his class to be graduated, and there was a Principal, who was also Professor of Theology, and who laboriously taught such of the Masters of Arts as chose to stay on at College, not, however, with a view to a degree in Divinity, but as a preparation for the Ministry.

In this simple form the College, owing chiefly to the zeal and wisdom of Rollock, and the beauty of his character, took firm root. It did not, like the older Universities, commence with a blaze of success and then collapse. It started from a very humble beginning and steadily expanded into greater things. External circumstances, both in nature and in politics, were at the outset very unpropitious to it. In its second session it had to be disbanded, owing to an invasion of the Plague. In the year after its opening its chief promoter, and best and wisest friend, James Lawson, was banished from Scotland by the influence of the Earl of Arran, and shortly afterwards "died at London, to the great grief of all the godly." And Principal Lee seems to think that it was a disadvantage to the College that in 1584 James VI. arbitrarily deposed the Town Council—at the head of whom was Alexander Clark, laird of Balbirnie, who had been Provost for six years, during all the efforts to get a University established—and forced upon the Town a Council of his own nomination, with that same "profligate Earl of Arran" as Chief Magistrate. However this may be, the King did some good turns to the College; first in granting it the teinds of Currie, and secondly in sending some of the young nobility of Scotland to be Rollock's pupils. And there is pleasing evidence that Lord Arran's Council did not neglect to exercise a paternal supervision over the College. For the Records tell us that on the 23d December 1584 they authorised payment to a "walx-maker" (*i.e.* a wax-chandler) "for two torches bought and received from him for the convoy of the Provost and Bailies from the College at the lessons made there." With the eye of fancy we can see the little band of civic authorities trudging back, in the winter evening, with torches to guide them through the unlighted lanes down into the Cowgate and up again, after hearing Rollock teaching Rhetoric to the "Semi" class, and Nairn classics to the "Bajans."

APPENDIX A. ROBERT REID, BISHOP OF ORKNEY.

FROM amongst the old Catholic hierarchy of Scotland the figure of Bishop Reid shines out, second only to that of Bishop Elphinston, in the combination of goodness with magnificence.

Robert Reid, son of a gentleman who fell at Flodden, had the usual education of those times. He entered St. Salvator's (St. Andrews) in 1511, and, having graduated there, finished his education at Paris. Returning a cultured and engaging man, he soon became a favourite of James V., and had an extraordinary succession of high appointments and offices in Church and State. From Sub-Dean of Moray he became, in 1526, Abbot of Kinloss; in addition to this, in 1532, he was made one of the Senators of the College of Justice, then being established. Next, he was employed on several embassies: four times to the Papal Court, three times to the Court of Francis I., and three times to that of Henry VIII. In 1541 he was recommended by James V. to the Pope for the See of Orkney, as one "well fitted to repair the evil condition of those polar islands, in which the Catholic faith and even the laws of Scotland were but little observed." But, as the King suggested, he was to retain his other benefices, the Abbey of Kinloss, and the Priory of Beauly (which he held *in commendam*), that out of their revenues he might provide a pension of 800 merks for His Majesty's natural son, John Stewart! Notwithstanding the spiritual destitution of the northern islands, which had now become his diocese, Reid was by no means permitted to devote himself entirely to their care. Both in 1541 and 1542 he was at the Court of Henry VIII.; after the death of James V., in 1542, he was appointed one of the Privy Council of the Regent Arran; in 1548, on the death of Abbot Myln, he was made Lord President of the College of Justice; in 1551 he was a Commissioner for settling the peace between Scotland and England; in 1554 he was appointed one of the Curators of the youthful Queen; in the same year he was at Paris with reference to the affairs of the Duke of Chastelherault; in 1555 he was appointed a Commissioner for the introduction of a universal standard of weights and measures; in 1556 he was at Carlisle for settling the disputes of the Border; and in 1558 he was sent to Paris by the Estates as one of their Commissioners to sign the marriage-contract and witness the nuptials of Mary Queen of Scots with the Dauphin of France.

Such were some of the external facts of the life of Reid, showing the multifarious functions performed in the sixteenth century by a high ecclesiastic, who could be at the same time an Abbot and a Bishop, and the head of the judicial establishment of Scotland, and yet also have the most important special commissions entrusted to him from time to time. Of Bishop Reid's personal character two pictures have come down to us; the one drawn by the pen of a powerful detractor; the other to be found in the eulogies of perhaps too appreciative dependants. Between these two representations of him the court of posterity has to decide; and certainly the evidence of his recorded actions seems greatly to preponderate in his favour.

Reid's last mission was in every way disastrous. On his voyage to France he was shipwrecked near Boulogne, and losing his rich equipage, was with difficulty saved, together with the Earl of Rothes, in the ship's boat. At the ceremony of Mary

Stuart's marriage the Scotch Commissioners were invited by the Guises to give their consent to a clause in the contract, securing the "crown matrimonial" to the Dauphin, that is, making him King of Scotland, if he should be predeceased by his wife. This they all refused to sign, as being beyond their instructions, and it was commonly supposed that, in revenge for this patriotic firmness, the Commissioners were poisoned at Dieppe, by the order either of Catherine de Medicis or one of the Guise family. John Knox relates the story with malignant pleasantry; he says: "The most part of the Lords that were in France at the Queen's marriage, though they got their congè from the Court, *yet they forgot to return to Scotland.* For whether it was by an Italian posset, or by the French figs, or by the potage of their potinger (he was a Frenchman), there departed from this life the Earl of Cassilis, the Earl of Rothes, Lord Fleming, and the Bishop of Orkney, whose end was even according to his life."[1] It so happened that out of the number of the Commissioners two great Lords of Congregation, Lord James Stuart, afterwards the Regent Murray, and Sir John Erskine of Dun, escaped the effects of the alleged poison, and together with Beatoun, Archbishop of Glasgow, and Lord Seton, Provost of Edinburgh, got safe home. Knox therefore could afford to make merry over the fate of the rest. For the murder of a Catholic Bishop he was not likely to express either pity or reprobation. It would be out of the question to expect that Knox, in his stern controversial writing, lit up by flashes of grim humour, should stop to do justice to all the good that there was in a man like Reid. It would be like expecting appreciation to be shown in the fiercest article of a party newspaper towards one of the chiefs of the opposite side in politics.

Knox had one grievous charge to bring against Reid, namely, that he had sat with other Bishops and Lords on the trial of the unfortunate Adam Wallace, who was burned for heresy on the Castlehill of Edinburgh in 1550; and that Reid did not support the protest uttered on that occasion by the Earl of Glencairn against the cruel sentence.[2] All that we can now say is, that such were those times. The gentlest spirits on both sides of the religious controversy were ready to condemn their opponents to martyrdom.

When Knox said that Bishop Reid's "end was even according

[1] Laing's edition of *Knox*, vol. i. p. 263.   [2] *Ibid.*, i. p. 240.

to his life," he probably alluded to his declining to listen to the "exhortations" of Lord James Stuart, who visited him when he was dying. "Nay, my Lord," said Reid, "let me alone; for you and I never agreed in our life, and I think that we shall not agree now at my death; and therefore let me alone."[1] But Knox added another gossiping touch to his account of Reid's death, which he may also have had in view when he said that his "end was even according to his life." He tells us that Reid, when his illness came on, "caused his bed to be made betwixt his two coffers. Such was his god; the gold that therein was inclosed, that he would not depart from, so long as memory would serve him." If the fact, as stated, be true, the simple interpretation of it would seem to be, that a sick man may naturally feel anxious about the money which he has with him in a foreign town. But at all events it appears a most extraordinary thing, in the face of all that is recorded about Bishop Reid, to charge him with avarice.

In turning to the opposite view of Reid's character, we may notice in passing the more generous view taken by George Buchanan (in relating the Dieppe affair) of the four Commissioners who died. He says that they were "omnes summa virtute et caritate in patriam."

Many details of the life of Reid have been recorded for us by Joannes Ferrerius, a Piedmontese scholar, whom in 1528 Reid, when returning from an embassy to Rome, brought back with him to Scotland. For three years the Abbot (as he then was) kept Ferrerius as a companion at the Scottish Court in Edinburgh, and then sent him down to Kinloss to instruct the

[1] This shows that personally Reid remained satisfied with his own religion. Principal Lee (*Inaugural Addresses*, p. 69) expressed the opinion that Reid was "not unfriendly" to Reforming principles. But there is no evidence of this. Among Reid's books, marked with his book-plate, was one which came into possession of the late Dr. John Stuart, Secretary of the Society of Antiquaries of Scotland, and with this book Reid may possibly have sympathised. It was a volume of the works of Wicelius, a German divine, who first joined Luther, and afterwards, becoming disgusted, went back to his old Church, for which Luther persecuted him and had him imprisoned. "The writings of Wicelius," says Stuart, "seem to have commended themselves to those of the Reformers who were desirous of some comprehensive scheme which should keep in communion the members of the Roman and Protestant Churches." See Stuart's *Records of the Monastery of Kinloss*, Preface, p. liv.

monks.[1] Ferrerius, with an interval of two years, remained in Bishop Reid's service at Kinloss till 1545—altogether fifteen years; and he tells us a good deal about Reid's enlightened splendour, of which, in answer to Knox, we will here collect a few instances. In all the places with which he was ecclesiastically connected—Kinloss, Beauly, and Kirkwall—Reid left memorials of himself in the shape of architectural buildings for pious uses. At Kinloss he built a spacious fire-proof library, and added several other buildings to the monastery. At Beauly he built a nave for the church, and restored the bell-tower; he also erected "a noble, spacious house" for the Prior, in place of one that was ruinous. At Kirkwall he enlarged the Cathedral Church, and added to it a fine porch. He built St. Olave's Church in Kirkwall, and also a large College for instructing the youth of Orkney in Grammar, Philosophy, and Mathematics. And he added a stately tower to his episcopal palace there, on which a half-effaced effigy of himself is still to be seen. Besides these creations in stone and lime he settled two considerable funds to be given yearly: the one for the maintenance of gentlemen's sons at the Universities of Aberdeen, St. Andrews, and Glasgow, "that had good spirits, but had not whereupon to prosecute their studies";[2] the other for providing "dowries for young women of humble fortune, that they might be settled in honourable mar-

---

[1] The list of Lectures given by Ferrerius in the Chapter-house of Kinloss is very interesting (see Stuart's *Records*, p. 54). It was quite a University course; he taught no Greek, but the best Latin authors, and the greater part of Aristotle in Latin translations. He used Melanchthon's works on Grammar and Rhetoric, and compendiums of Arithmetic and Logic written by himself. In Theology he taught St. Jerome's *Letter to Paulinus*, the First Psalm, the Fourth Book of the *Sentences*, and the mystical writings of St. Dionysius. It is observable here that "the First Psalm" was the only part of Scripture on which Ferrerius then lectured, but in 1537 he returned for a time to Paris; and he thence reported to his patron a change which he observed in the teaching of the University. "The Old and New Testament," he says, "after mature consultation of theologians and of the supreme Senate, are now everywhere in men's hands, and are daily lectured on in the public schools of theologians, to the great increase of true piety." Ferrerius, after two years, returned to his post of instructor of the monks of Kinloss. And in the list of his Lectures during this second period we observe that he lectured on St. Paul's *Epistle to the Romans*. This shows that a study of the Scriptures had been forced by Luther upon the Catholics in self-defence.

[2] Mackenzie: *Lives of Scottish Writers*, vol. iii. p. 47.

riage." And it was said that he died "to the great regret of many learned men whom his munificence was supporting at the Universities of France." Two minor instances of Reid's μεγαλοπρέπεια may be added from the records of Ferrerius. In 1538 he brought to Kinloss a famous painter, named Andrew Bairhum, who painted altar-pieces for three Chapels in the Church; those of the Magdalen, St. John the Evangelist, and St. Thomas

BISHOP REID'S TOWER AT KIRKWALL.

of Canterbury. And about the same time he imported another artist in a different department, one William Lubias, a gardener from Dieppe, who was skilful in the planting and grafting of fruit trees, and who "left tokens of his method in the improvement of the gardens, not only round the Abbey, but also throughout the whole of Moray." This rich catalogue of life-works—so well calculated to promote the welfare and education of individuals and communities, and the civilisation of the country—would appear to vindicate Reid against the spiteful aspersions of John Knox; while at the same time it presents a contrast to the somewhat narrow and jejune earnestness of the Reformers.

But Reid's complete panegyric occurs in one of the *Chapter Discourses* of Adam Elder, Monk of Kinloss, printed at Paris in 1558, perhaps during Reid's stay there during his last fatal embassy. Reid, as we have seen, continued to be Abbot of Kinloss after being raised to the See of Orkney. But in 1553 he procured one of those family arrangements which were common at the time by getting his own nephew, Walter Reid, still a mere boy, appointed Abbot. This was probably only to secure to him the succession, while Reid himself would retain the revenues and a supervision of the Abbey. To this boy-Abbot Adam Elder addressed an exhortation in excellent Latin, which was delivered before the brotherhood in their chapter-house,[1] and which we can still read. He sets before him the examples of St. Benedict and St. Bernard, and still more urgently invites him to follow in the steps of his uncle, whom he sets up "not as a perfect character, but as a living and actual example of what is good and what is possible." He then draws the portrait of Robert Reid, which, though composed in the lifetime of that prelate, and intended to come to his notice, has still an air of sincerity about it. He reminds his auditors how the good Bishop gladly lived in retirement when he could be free from the State offices imposed upon him; how he enjoyed the reading of the Scriptures, realising in daily meditation the sweetness of the Lord, and "making his breast a library of Christ," so as to be stored with the food which he might impart to his sheep. How, possessed of the honours and riches of this world, he used them all as one who had to give account; he was neither puffed up by them nor did he set his heart upon them.[2] He recalls to their minds, from the experience of many years, the Bishop's fatherly care and tenderness towards the stranger and the desolate; and addressing the young Abbot, he asks, What is all this but to be a true monk—to be one who lives in the world and yet renounces it? Then, after alluding to the Bishop's works of charity and benevolence, he descants upon his love of literature. He says: "All riches he cares not for in comparison with his beloved libraries. Neither castles, nor palaces, nor buildings of

[1] See Stuart's *Records*, pp. 79-84.
[2] "Divitiis affluentibus animum non apponit"—the direct contradictory of the calumny of Knox.

fair architecture, nor gold, nor silver, nor lands, nor horses, nor raiment, nor gems, does he prefer to good books." Truly we may say that if all the praises of Reid which this discourse contains were not literally deserved (though we have no reason for thinking that they were not), still the very fact of such an ideal of life being entertained by a monk of Kinloss in the sixteenth century is a strong testimony in favour of him who, as Abbot, had given its tone to the fraternity.

Among his exhortations to Walter Reid to follow the example of his uncle, Elder uses one or two phrases which now, for a reason connected with our history, have a peculiar significance. He says: "At all events, do not let his magnificence be tarnished by your indolence and sloth." And he adds the warning: "If you disregard my words, as I hope you will not, you will not only bring yourself and your flock into peril, but you will stamp upon yourself a mark of perpetual disgrace and ignominy." Unfortunately, in the matter of Reid's bequest for a College in Edinburgh, his nephew Walter did really "tarnish his magnificence" by want of diligence in carrying out the provisions of the will. What hindrances there may have been we know not, but at all events five-and-twenty years elapsed after Reid's death before any part of this particular legacy was paid. And thus a certain "stamp of disgrace" has come to be affixed to the name of Walter, Abbot of Kinloss.[1]

Bishop Reid had resided a good deal in Edinburgh, either in attendance on King James V. or in performance of his duties, first as Senator and afterwards as President of the College of Justice, and as he had benefited and connected his name with all the seats of his ecclesiastical offices, so he appears to have determined not to depart from this life without benefiting Edinburgh, the place where his high secular functions had been performed, and leaving a memorial of himself here. His will was

[1] It is stated in the *History of the Earldom of Sutherland* (p. 137) that Reid "left a great sum of money for building the (*sic*) College of Edinburgh, which the Earl of Morton converted to his own use and profit, by punishing the Executors of Bishop Reid for supposed crimes." But there is no record of Abbot Walter Reid having been punished. He was one of those dignitaries of the Old Church who signed the first Covenant in 1560. He alienated a great part of the Abbey lands of Kinloss. Being a reformed Abbot he married Margaret Collace, by whom he had several children. See Stuart's *Records*, p. 56.

signed in Edinburgh in February 1557. In it he bequeathed his library to the Abbey of Kinloss, and left the sum of 8000 merks,[1] "for founding a College in the burgh of Edinburgh, for exercise of learning therein."

This sum he devised "to buy the tenement, with the yards and appurtenances, of the late Sir John Ramsay, Knight, lying on the south side of the burgh of Edinburgh, in order to build a College, in which were to be three schools—one for the bairns in Grammar; another for those learning Poetry and Oratory, with chambers for the Regents, a Hall and other necessary buildings; and the third school for the teaching of the Civil and Canon Laws."[2] And this was appointed to be carried out under the advice of James Makgill of Rankelour Nether, Clerk of Register; Thomas Makcalyean of Clifton Hall, one of the Judges of the Court of Session; and Abraham Crichton, Provost of Dunglas.

Reid, not being Bishop of Edinburgh, would probably never think of founding a University there; such a thing would not occur to him as possible. Therefore he did not apply to the Pope for a Bull, or to the Regent for a charter. What he purposed to do was simply to leave money for founding one of those schools of "Arts and Jure" contemplated by the Act of James V. (see above, p. 27). It was to be a College for the study of Latin Literature, and Civil and Canon Law, with a High School department for preparing the Students in Latin as their first stage. Such would in itself, and in default of a University, have been a very useful institution in Edinburgh. Reid evidently did not intend his College to have degree-giving powers. He speaks of "the Regents," but only in the sense of "College Tutors." He probably expected that Graduates from St. Andrews would be engaged to teach in his College.

But his ideas and wishes were all completely frustrated. Eighteen years after Reid's death, in 1576, "letters were raised" before the Privy Council sitting at Holyrood House, under the Presidency of Regent Morton, to compel his executors to do

[1] "The sum of four thousand merks which he had in wadset (*i.e.* mortgage) on the lands of Strathnaver, when it should be recovered, and also other four thousand merks of his goods and gear."

[2] See the *Register of the Privy Council of Scotland*, edited by John Hill Burton, LL.D. (1878), vol. ii. p. 528; from which the above is modernised.

their duty—the King's Advocate moving the petition. After hearing of the case the Council cite John Reid of Aikenhead, Walter, Abbot of Kinloss; and Sir John Anderson—the only three surviving executors—to produce the said sum of 8000 merks. Reid of Aikenhead and Sir J. Anderson appear by procurators, and declare that they had never accepted or acted in the office of executors. The whole responsibility then rested with the Abbot of Kinloss; and, "the said Abbot being oftentimes called and not appearing, my Lord Regent's Grace, with advice of the said Lords, decerns the said Walter, Abbot of Kinloss, to exhibit, deposit, and consign into the hands of such person as His Grace shall appoint, the said sum of 8000 merks, to be employed to the effect above written, according to the will of the Deed, or otherwise *ad pios usus.*"

All in vain; six years more passed away, and then, on the 11th April 1582 the Privy Council, sitting at Stirling under the Presidency of the young King himself, heard a petition from the Town Council of Edinburgh which set forth the legacy; its non-payment; the "letters directed" under Morton's regency; that the money was still unpaid; and that all the persons under whose advice the College was to have been erected were dead. "Which being read, heard, and considered by the King's Majesty and the said Lords, and His Highness willing to have the will of the Deed, tending to so godly use, fulfilled, and to hold hand thereto, so far as in him lies," His Majesty therefore gives full powers to the Town Council; places them in the same position of authority in respect of the College which Reid's will had assigned to Makgill, Makcalyean, and Crichton; and enjoins them to pursue and recover the money and bestow it according to the will of the Deed, within the space of one year, without further delay."[1]

It will be observed that this order enjoined the Town Council to carry out Bishop Reid's wishes without giving them any latitude, and had they in 1582 received full payment of the legacy they might have held themselves constrained to do so. But it would appear that after the Stirling decree, "at the request of our Sovereign Lord, and for other good and weighty considera-

[1] *Register of the Privy Council*, edited by David Masson, LL.D., Professor of Rhetoric and English Literature in the University of Edinburgh (1880), vol. iii. pp. 472-74. The above is modernised.

tions," they compromised matters with Abbot Walter Reid for the sum of 2500 merks out of 4000 merks of the legacy, the other 4000 being apparently not realisable. And this amount of 2500 merks was paid to the Town Council in instalments, 700 merks in 1583, and 1800 merks in 1587. They had probably obtained leave to apply these minor sums, as they fell in, to the uses of the Town's College. And so it came to pass that the only memorial of Bishop Reid's munificent purpose to endow a College "of Arts and Jure" in Edinburgh, existed for some time (though it has long since passed away) in the name given to "fourteen little chambers," which formed part of the original College buildings, and which were called "the old Reid chambers."

APPENDIX B. KIRK-OF-FIELD.

THE town of Edinburgh was for many centuries a mere strip, running along the ridge of a height from the Castle down towards Holyrood. It was defended on the north side by the piece of water called "the Nor' Loch," which lay where now are the Princes Street Gardens. Along the south side was "the Cowgate Loch," all the hollow of the Cowgate being filled with water, which served instead of a wall to the town.

On the rising ground to the south of the Cowgate there were three religious establishments; the Monastery of the Black Friars to the east, occupying, to speak roughly, the site of the old Royal Infirmary down to the Cowgate; the Monastery of the Grey Friars on the site of the present Greyfriars' Church and Churchyard; and the Collegiate Church of "St. Mary in the Fields," occupying most of the space between the other two, and extending from where Drummond Street is now diagonally to what is now the middle of Chambers Street. After the battle of Flodden it was thought necessary, for the safety of these religious houses, "to have the town wall drawn about without them;[1] and so, drying the Cowgate Loch, they enlarged the town on the south side." It was only a year previous to this (in 1512) that "the Church of the Blessed Mary in the Fields"—so called from having been originally planted outside the town's defences, and

[1] Craufurd's *Memoirs*.

in the country—became a Collegiate Church, with a Provost and Prebendaries. The date of its original foundation is not known, but its name is said[1] to occur in documents of the thirteenth century. In 1512 the church obtained, through private benefactions, a great extension of site, houses for the Provost and Chaplains, and a full collegiate establishment. David Vocat, the celebrated Master of the Grammar School of Edinburgh, was one of its benefactors, and became a Prebendary of the church.

But its glory was short-lived. The "Flodden Wall" did not suffice to protect the religious houses. "The Duke of Somerset and his heretical host, fresh from their victory at Pinkie Cleuch (1547), made an end of the Monastery of Blackfriars and its pleasure grounds; and the Kirk-of-Field, too, suffered wofully in the cruel raids of 1544 and 1547."[2]

In 1555, during the Provostship of Alexander Forrest (who was only fourth Provost of the Kirk-of-Field) he and his Prebendaries "considering that their houses, especially the Hospital annexed and incorporated with their College, were burnt down and destroyed by their auld enemies of England, so that nothing of their said Hospital was left, but they (*sic*) are altogether waste and utterly destroyed; wherethrough the Divine worship is not a little decreased in the College; and because they were unable to rebuild the said Hospital;" therefore they granted in feu to James, Duke of Chastelherault, "the tenement or hospital with the yards and pertinents thereof, for the purpose of erecting a mansion-house there for his own use."

We have already related (above, pp. 128-29) the subsequent history of "Hamilton House," as it was called, which the Duke built upon this site: how on the forfeiture of the Hamilton family it was purchased by the Town Council, and so came to be the main building of the College of Edinburgh, in which were located the public *auditorium*, and the class-rooms of Philosophy; and how, being claimed back by the Marquis of Hamilton, in 1612, it had to be paid for a second time.

The Hospital having been burned down, and many of the old

---

[1] See David Laing's *Collegiate Churches of Mid-Lothian* (published by the Bannatyne Club), from which most of the above particulars have been gathered.
[2] *Reminiscences of Old Edinburgh*, by Daniel Wilson (1878), vol. ii. p. 293.

PRINCIPAL ROBERTSON'S HOUSE, WITH THE GUARD-HALL
AND TEVIOT CHAMBERS (1789).

THE GUARD-HALL AND TEVIOT CHAMBERS LEFT STANDING (1831).

buildings ruined, the great Church of Kirk-of-Field still stood; but in 1558 the Earl of Argyll, with a band of the "Congregation," threw down its altars and burned the images. Then came the Reformation, and laws making the Mass illegal. And it was in this state of things that John Penicuik, fifth Provost, negotiated in 1563 with the Town Council for selling them the whole buildings, ground, and revenues of the Kirk-of-Field for £1000 Scots. This transaction was apparently never carried out; and in 1564 we read that Penicuik was "taking down the stonework of the Kirk-of-Field," and was "minded to sell it." Most probably this process was continued by the succeeding Provosts, Robert Balfour (during whose Provostship Darnley was blown up in an outbuilding of the Kirk-of-Field) and John Gib, the King's valet, who had the Provostry bestowed upon him in 1579. So that when the Town Council in 1582 got possession of the site they would not have much of the central church to clear away. It was very likely all gone by that time. Its original position had been about the centre of the present University quadrangle.

The Provost's lodging corresponded with the east corner of the present library. There Balfour lived, and Gib feued the house to one John Fenton, an office clerk, who held it for many years after the College had been opened. When the Town Council got possession of it it was made the Principal's lodging, and continued to be so till the beginning of the present century. Some have supposed that it was in this house that Darnley's murder took place. But Craufurd, who must have known, says distinctly that it was "to the east from thence, in the Prebendaries' chambers," that is, on the site corresponding with the present north-west corner of Drummond Street.

APPENDIX C. DISPUTATION AT STIRLING.

(*Extracted from Craufurd's Memoirs*, pp. 81-87.)

"THE King's Majesty had ane earnest desire to honour the Colledge with his presence, and hearing an publick disputation in Philosophy; but the multitude of business distracting him all the time he was at Holyroodhouse, it pleased his Majesty to appoint the Maisters of the Colledge to attend him at Sterling, the 29th day of July, where, in the Royal Chapel, his Majesty, with the flower of the nobility, and many of the most learned men of both nations, were present a little before five of the clock, and continued with much cheerfullness above three hours. Mr. Henry Charteris (then Principal of the Colledge) being naturally averse from publick showes, and Professor of Divinity, moved that Mr. John Adamson (then minister at Libberton) should preside in the disputation. Mr. James Fairly was chosen to draw and defend the theses; Mr. Patrick Sands (sometime Regent, but at that time attending the Tolbooth), Mr. Andrew Young, Mr. James Reid, and Mr. William King, the other three Regents professing Philosophy for the time, were appoynted to impugne. They divided the theses, each of them chusing three; but they insisted only upon such purposes as was conceived would be most acceptable to the King's Majesty and the auditory.

"The speciall purposes agitate were, first, the theses, That Sheriffs and other inferior Magistrates ought not to be hereditary; oppugned by Mr. Sands, with many pretty arguments.

"The King was so well pleased with the answers, that, after he himself had pressed some arguments to the contrary, and the defender had directed his answers to Mr. Sands, his Majesty, turning to the Marques of Hamilton, who was standing behind his chair, and at that time was Heritable Sheriff of Clydesdale, 'James (said he), you see your cause lost, and all that can be said for it clearly satisfied and answered.'

"Mr. Young who disputed next, insisted upon the Nature of Local Motion, pressing many things by clear testimonies of Aristotle's text. To which, when the defender made his answers and cleared the purpose, the King said to some English Doctors which were near to him, 'These men know Aristotle's mind as well as himself did while he lived.'

"Mr. Reid disputed third, anent the Original of Fountains. The King being much taken with his last argument, notwithstanding the time allotted (three quarters of an houre) was spent, caused him prosecute the purpose. His Majesty himself sometime speaking for the impugner, and sometime for the defender, in good Latin, and with much knowledge of the secrets of Philosophy.

"Mr. King, who disputed last, had his dissertation, De Spontaneo et Invito. In the which, and in all the rest, the King let no argument nor answer passe without taking notice thereof, and speaking to the purpose, with much understanding and good language.

"After the disputation, his Majesty went to supper, and after a very little time commanded the Maisters of the Colledge of Edinburgh to be brought before him. In their presence he discoursed very learnedly of all the purposes which had been agitated.

"Then he fell to speak of the actors. 'Methinks (said he), these gentlemen, by their very names, have been destinated for the acts which they have had in hand to-day. Adam was father of all; and very fitly Adamson had the first part of this act. The defender is justly called Fairly: his theses had some fair lies, and he sustained them very fairly, and with many fair lies given to the oppugners. And why should not Mr. Sands be the first to enter the sands; but now I clearly see that all sands are not barren, for certainly he hath shewen a fertile wit. Mr. Young is very old in Aristotle. Mr. Reid need not be red with blushing for his acting to-day. Mr. King disputed very kingly, and of a kingly purpose, anent the royal supremacy of reason over anger and all passions. I am so well satisfied with this day's exercise, that I will be godfather to the Colledge of Edinburgh, and have it called the Colledge of King James; for after the founding of it had been stopped for sundry years in my minority, so soon as I came to any knowledge, I zealously held hand to it, and caused it to be established; and although I see many look upon it with an evil eye, yet I will have them to know that, having given it this name, I have espoused its quarell.'

"One who stood by, told his Majesty that there was one of the company of whome he had taken no notice, Mr. Henry Charteris, Principal of the Colledge (who sate upon the President's right hand), a man of exquisite and universal learning, although not so forward to speak in publick in so august an assembly. 'Well,' answered the King, 'his name agreeth very well to his nature, for charters contain much matter, yet say nothing, but put great purposes in men's mouths.' These who stood by the King's chair, commended his Majestie's witty allusions to the actor's names; whereupon his Majesty pressed that the same should be turned into verse, wherein his Majesty both delighted much and had an singular faculty. Some of these versions (both in English and Latin verses) were written by such as heard them, and thereafter printed.

"One of the English Doctors, wondering at his Majesty's readiness and eligancy in the Latin style, 'All the world (said he), knows that my maister, Mr. George Buchanan, was a great maister in that faculty. I follow his pronounciation both of the Latin and Greek, and am sorrie that my people of England doe not the like: For certainly their pronounciation utterly spoils the grace of these two learned languages; but ye see all the University and learned men of Scotland express the true and native pronounciation of both.' His Majesty continued his discourse anent the purposes of the dispute till ten o'clock at night, and professed that he was exceedingly satisfied therewith, and promised, that as he had given the Colledge a name, he would also, in time convenient, give to it a Royall God-bairne gift (as we say), for enlarging the patrimony thereof. He took occasion of the purposes ventilate that day, to speak of diverse poynts of philosophy, with much subtilitie and variety of knowledge, to the admiration of the understanding hearers; and being on his return to England, wrote back a letter to the Honourable Council of the Good Town, wherein he both renewed his Royall pleasure for calling the Colledge after his name, King James his Colledge, and his promise of a Royall God-bairne gift, which, it is hoped, that his Royall Grandchild, King Charles the Second,[1] will, in time convenient, royally perform."

Craufurd's simple aspiration shows that James VI. never fulfilled his fine promises of a royal gift to his god-child, the College. Nor were those promises redeemed, or likely to be redeemed, by Charles II. James VI., immediately after the opening of the College of Edinburgh, had granted towards its maintenance the revenues of the Vicarage of Currie. Beyond this he did no more for the College than his grandson, Charles

---

[1] The concluding words of the graphic record show that Craufurd, who died in 1662, must have been engaged shortly after the Restoration in putting together his *Memoirs*, the materials for which, doubtless, existed in contemporary notes jotted down from year to year.

II., did for the Royal Society—that is, he gave it a name. "Very different," says Principal Lee,[1] "was the conduct of James towards Universities in other parts of his dominions. Not to mention what he did for Oxford, it is stated by Mr. Taylor, in his late *History of the University of Dublin*, that King James settled on Trinity College, which is ten years junior to ours, a pension payable out of the Exchequer, and also endowed it with large estates in the province of Ulster."

Though the King, no doubt, felt a lively pleasure in hearing the theses of the Regents, and in showing off his own erudition at the Stirling Disputation, he was too volatile and selfish to entertain any settled purpose of promoting the development of the College of Edinburgh as a seat of learning. He had many spiteful feelings towards Scotland,[2] recalling the severities and the masterful attitude of Buchanan, the indignities which he had sustained at the hands of Scottish subjects, and the way in which he had been lectured and preached at by the Ministers. He was not likely to be zealous about the aggrandisement of a College, the foundation of which had been so greatly due to the Ministers of Edinburgh, and in the government of which they were associated. If any impulse or opportunity to endow the College arose, there would be a counter-instinct that it would be better to keep it in a humble and dependent position.

With regard to other relations of King James VI. to the College of Edinburgh, we shall in the next chapter show reason for conjecturing that he interfered in 1590 so as to frustrate the intentions of the College of Justice and the Town Council with regard to the foundation of a Professorship of Laws. He certainly interfered in a most arbitrary manner thirty-two years later. The office of Principal being then vacant, the Town Council bethought

[1] *Inaugural Addresses in the University of Edinburgh* (1861), p. 75.

[2] James VI., in a speech at Whitehall, 31st March 1607, showed the cynical shrewdness of his thoughts about Scotland, and complete absence of any favour or affection for the land of his birth. He said: "Consider therefore well if the minds of Scotland had not need to be well prepared to persuade their mutual consent, seeing you here have all the great advantage of the Union. Is not here the personal residence of the King, his court and family? Is not here the seat of justice and the fountain of government? Must they not be subjected to the laws of England, and so with time become but as Cumberland and Northumberland, and those other remote and northern shires?"

themselves of securing for the place Robert Boyd of Trochrig, who was at the time Principal of the College of Glasgow. Boyd was an accomplished man, author of a Commentary on the *Ephesians*, and of some Latin poems; he was son of the Archbishop of Glasgow, and had considerable private fortune. He liked the offers of the Town Council of Edinburgh, and in 1622 came over to hold the joint-offices of Principal of the College and City Minister, on a salary of 1400 merks. But his appointment was distasteful to the King. Boyd in early life had been Professor of Divinity at Saumur, and among the French Protestants had imbibed their antipathy to ceremonies. In 1618 he opposed the Articles of Perth, and refused to conform to them. In December 1622, as soon as Boyd had been appointed to Edinburgh, there came a letter from James VI. remonstrating with the Town Council, and commanding them to urge Boyd to conform, or else to remove him. The Council deprecated this proceeding, urging the "gifts and peaceable disposition" of Mr. Robert. On the 31st January 1623 the King's answer was received: "On the contrary, we think his biding there will do much evil; and therefore, as ye will answer to us on your obedience, we command you to put him not only from his office, but out of your town, at the sight hereof, unless he conform totally. And when ye have so done, think not this sufficient to satisfy our wrath for disobedience to our former letter." This being intimated to Boyd, he resigned, and was afterwards confined within the bounds of Carrick.

Appendix D. Academy of Geneva.

IF the peculiar constitution and government of the College or Edinburgh was not suggested by what Scotchmen knew of the Academy of Geneva, there was at all events a coincidence of ideas entertained by the founders of the two institutions. A few particulars will illustrate this point.

In 1541 Calvin began to give lectures on Theology in Geneva which attracted many Students. In 1542 he proposed to the Municipal Council to form an Academy where the citizens and strangers might make solid and complete studies. After many years, and repeated representations, the Council in 1558 determined on building a College. This was done by means of an appeal to the citizens for subscriptions. The virtuous Bonnivard, the "Prisoner of Chillon," in a will, dated 1558, left all his property for maintenance of the new College.

In 1559, when Geneva was full of Scotchmen, the regulations of the Academy were published in the Church of St. Peter before a crowd of citizens and strangers, on which occasion Calvin made an harangue. All appointments to office in the Academy were to be made by the Venerable Company of Pastors, subject to the confirmation of the Municipal Council. And this arrangement resembles that afterwards made in Edinburgh, where the Town Council were to have the appointment of all Professors and Teachers, but were to act with the advice of the Ministers.

The chief Magistrate read the Confession of Faith to be subscribed by Professors, Regents, and Students, and declared the names of office-bearers.

Theodore Beza had been elected Rector by the Pastors, and his election had been confirmed. Calvin had been elected Professor of Theology.[1] Then there was a Professor of Hebrew, one of Greek, and one of Philosophy or Arts, who appears to have taught Latin, and to have resembled the Regent of Humanity in the College of Edinburgh. Then there were seven Regents, of whom the highest was called Principal of the College, and who was to regulate its internal discipline, in concert with and under orders from the Rector. The chief Magistrate was to hold the title of Archigrammateus, or Chancellor.

Many of these arrangements found their counterpart in the College of Edinburgh. There also a Rector was, for a time at least, appointed to supervise the Principal, and this Rector was, as at Geneva, distinct from the chief Magistrate, who had powers analogous to those of Chancellor, till an ambitious Lord Provost absorbed both offices in his own person. We may notice that in Edinburgh, so long as a separate Rector was allowed to exist, it was part of his duties to keep the matriculation roll; and this in Geneva was called the "livre du Recteur."

It was Calvin's idea to establish a seminary of Ministers for Geneva and Dauphiné, with a good school attached. And the

---

[1] He taught in this capacity, but declined the title of Professor.

seven Regents were in fact teachers of the seven classes in this school which was called *Schola Privata*, while the Academy proper, taught by Professors, was called *Schola Publica*. The High School in Edinburgh may be said to have filled the place of the *Schola Privata* at Geneva.

Two Professors of Law, of whom Henry Scrimger was one, were soon added to the Academy of Geneva. And that institution, like the College of Edinburgh, seems without any authorisation to have assumed the power of giving degrees. For we learn that in 1591 the Universities of the United Provinces agreed to recognise the Doctors of Divinity, Law, and Medicine, of Geneva, as holding degrees equally valid with those of other Universities. We have seen above (p. 125) that the Academy of Geneva failed to obtain recognition as a University from the King of France.[1]

On the whole, it may be said that the founders and administrators of the Academy of Geneva set an example of confounding the functions and titles of a University with those proper to a College—which example the post-Reformation educationists of Scotland persistently followed.

APPENDIX E. MONTAGUE COLLEGE AND THE SCOTS COLLEGE.

DURING the fourteenth and fifteenth, and the early part of the sixteenth century, these two Colleges were resorted to by a great number of Scotsmen seeking the instruction of the University of Paris. Thus, one or other of these Colleges had a hand in the training of most of the eminent Ecclesiastics, Lawyers, University Professors, and Heads of Colleges in Scotland down to the time of the Reformation.

Strictly speaking, Montague College was the older of the two, having been founded in 1314 by the distinguished French family of Aicelin de Montaigu. It was originally called the "College des Aicelins," but its name was Latinised into *Collegium Montis Acuti*. Its attraction, however, for Scotch Students, and its connection with Scotland, do not date from the early period of

[1] The facts mentioned in this Appendix have been derived from Senebier, *Histoire Littéraire de Genève* (1786), and Mark Pattison's *Isaac Casaubon* (1875).

its history, which seems to have been by no means distinguished, and to have terminated in degradation towards the close of the fifteenth century, when it is described as having its titles lost, its buildings in ruins, no Students in attendance, and a total revenue of sixteen shillings per annum.[1] But in 1483 the chapter of Notre Dame appointed John Standonc, a poor Flemish priest, who by great struggles had raised himself out of a menial position, to be its Principal. And then immediately under him a great revival of the College took place. His ideal was learned poverty and asceticism; and he had already acquired sufficient reputation and influence to enable him to enlist the assistance of exalted and wealthy persons in carrying out his views. Having obtained the institution of many bursaries, he drew up the severest regulations for those who were to benefit by them. The Bursars were to do all the domestic work of the house, to wear a mean garb, and to subsist on a meagre diet, in which fish was the chief item, and from which meat was excluded. For himself, he elected to be styled "Minister" or "Father" of the poor, rather than "Principal" or "Master;" he was to get no salary, and to share the humble attire and hard diet of his scholars. His ardour, and the attraction of self-sacrifice to other ardent natures, drew eighty-four bursars round him; for whom he made his College a school of Grammar, Philosophy, and Theology.

Two of these bursars at the beginning of the sixteenth century were men of very different minds: one, Ignatius Loyola, probably derived from Standonc the first germs of that enthusiasm which prompted him to found the Jesuit fraternity; the other, Erasmus, who always had a peculiar dislike to fish, looked back with repugnance to the asceticism of Montague College, which in one of his *Colloquies* he satirises under the name of *Collegium Montis Aceti*.

But the rigours of the system did not deter the hardy Scotch, and after Standonc's revival of it many of them flocked to Montague College. Bishop Elphinston is supposed to have had part of his education there. And there were four Scotsmen, members of the College, who were Professors of Philosophy in the University of Paris: John Mair, Hector Boece, George Lockhart, and William Gregory.

[1] Crevier, *Histoire de l'Université de Paris*, vol. v. pp. 20-29.

The history of the "Scots College" in Paris is not without a certain element of romance. Its origin was connected with the renewal of the "Ancient League" between France and Scotland. In 1326 Robert the Bruce had sent over the Earl of Moray to the Court of Charles le Bel to conclude a treaty of "confederacy." The Earl was accompanied by his kinsman, the Bishop of Moray; and the good Bishop took advantage of his position to do a service to his countrymen. He bought up the lands of Grisy, a village near Paris, and settled the revenues as a maintenance for Scotch Students of his own diocese attending the University of Paris. Thus was founded the "College de Grisy," or "Scots College." Subsequently the Bishops of Moray, retaining the patronage of offices in the College, appear to have opened the bursaries to persons from all parts of Scotland. In 1526 George Buchanan entered this College, having been, as is supposed, placed there by the bounty of John Mair. But a host of other Scotsmen, in the intervening two hundred years, must have benefited by the Scots College. After the disestablishment of the Roman Catholic Church in Scotland the Scots College in Paris was looked to by Catholics in this country as a place of education in the old faith. And Mary Queen of Scots is said to have sent contributions for it from her place of captivity.

The Scots College became the receptacle of archives conveyed out of Scotland at the time of the Reformation. It had appropriate buildings and a chapel erected for it in the Rue des Fosses de S. Victor as late as 1662. In 1736 it possessed "a large MS. volume, called *Acta Scotorum in Universitate Parisiensi*,[1] compiled by its Principal, Louis Innes, brother to the famous Father Innes, the first critical historian of Scotland. But all these priceless treasures were lost in the French Revolution of 1792, when the Scots College was sacked by the mob.

[1] Bishop Nicolson: *Scottish Historical Library*.

CHAPTER IV.

HISTORY OF THE UNIVERSITY OF EDINBURGH UNDER ITS FIRST FORM AS A DEGREE-GIVING COLLEGE, 1583-1708.

"Parva metu primo mox sese attollit in auras."

By many persons the terms "College" and "University" appear to be regarded as synonymous. And this is no wonder, because the mediæval University system has been subjected to manifold change, and its clear outlines have been confused. Where Colleges existed within Universities they have frequently grown into greater importance than the Universities to which they were subsidiary. And elsewhere institutions have arisen partaking of the nature both of College and of University, so that it would be hard to say to which class they would most properly be assigned. Of old the distinction was obvious; the University was an unlimited corporation, comprising sometimes as many as twelve or fifteen thousand persons, within a certain city or town, but not necessarily attached to any special buildings or local centre. This community had its organised constitution, and even its own courts of civil and criminal jurisdiction. The College, on the other hand, was essentially a house;[1] it was a home provided for a small definite number of poor Scholars wishing to partake of the advantages of the University, and for Masters to supervise and teach them. The inmates of a College thus constituted a family, and were generally under a prescribed rule of life. The arrangements of the College were domestic, though outsiders were frequently admitted to the benefit of the lessons taught in it. Its teaching was for the most part of a tutorial character, though sometimes, as in Elphinston's College at Aberdeen (p. 37), specialists or Professors of separate subjects were added to the tutors who prepared the scholars for obtaining the University degree. The practice of employing Regents to take their respective classes through the whole curriculum of philosophy was undoubtedly a collegiate idea. Of course there were often many Colleges within one University. In some cases (pp. 12-16) the power of conferring degrees was granted by the Pope to a College, but even had this power been exercised it would not have made the College into a University;[2] it would have still remained a domestic institution, within the greater corporation, and lacking

[1] Owing to this primary association it seems natural now to speak of the buildings of a University as "the College."

[2] A new-fangled and very restricted type of a University has been set up in quite modern times, with the solitary function of examining and conferring degrees. The London University was perhaps the first example of this type, which has also been reproduced in the Universities of British India.

the (at all events nominal) freedom and dignity of a University.

After the Reformation Colleges were erected in many places where there had been previously no University. If a College thus standing by itself had degree-giving powers assigned to it, it would obviously partake of the character of a University, and by expansion it might come more and more to do so, though still retaining traces of its collegiate origin. The question then would arise at what point the University characteristics would so far predominate in the supposed institution as to make it inappropriate to style it "a College" any more.

This was precisely the case with regard to the College of Edinburgh. It was strictly a College to begin with, not because its founders always called it "the Town's College," but because, as we have seen (p. 141), they gave it a thoroughly domestic character. At the same time they started it with a University standard of instruction in Philosophy, and with the power of conferring the degree of Master of Arts. As time went on the College of Edinburgh showed itself equal in its teaching to the old-established Universities of Scotland; Professors of various subjects were added to its staff, and the domestic side of the institution dwindled away as Students gradually ceased to reside within its walls. It could never become a University in the mediæval sense, because it lacked a charter as such, and all the forms of a mediæval University. But it did grow into a University in one of the modern senses of the term, that is to say, an institution for specialised teaching in many subjects, and for conferring degrees in four Faculties. The point at which it would seem most proper to drop the designation of "College," and to begin to speak of "the University of Edinburgh," will be from that date when its patrons abolished the tutorial system and substituted Professors of special subjects for the Regents of Philosophy. During all the period to be described in this chapter the domestic and collegiate practice of "regenting" was continued. Thenceforward the College of Edinburgh became virtually a University, and might properly, by courtesy, be styled so. But, with all its progress, it had acquired, as will be seen, no legal rights as a University, and had no defined constitution.

But to take up the thread of its history. The original staff of the College having been completed with a Principal, who was also Professor of Theology, and four Regents under him, the first addition to this was accompanied by mysterious circumstances, which even conjecture cannot satisfactorily explain. The simple facts as recorded were these:—In February 1590, after much "communing betwixt the Lords of Session and Town Council," a contract was concluded, according to which the Lords of Session, the Advocates and Writers to the Signet, and the Council, as three parties, each provided the sum of £1000; and the Town Council obliged themselves to pay £300 a year interest upon the total stock of £3000, towards the maintenance of "a Professor of the Laws." "Notwithstanding, Mr. Adam Newton, advocate, who was first called to that place, and Sir Adrian Damman, who was second in that charge, did only profess Humanity publicly in the College, without any mention of the Laws."[1]

From this statement we see clearly that the College of Justice took a kindly interest in the newborn "Town's College," and that they liberally contributed in order to have the teaching of Law added to that of Philosophy and Theology within its walls. This being so, the question arises—Why was their design frustrated? Why did the two persons who were successively first appointed to be "Professor of the Laws" only lecture on Greek and Latin scholarship "without any mention of the Laws"? The former of these was an advocate, which, according to the practice of those days, he could not have been without going through a course of legal study in some foreign University. He therefore was doubtless qualified to lecture on Roman and Municipal Law. But neither he nor his successor did so.

Another curious fact was this: "Mr. Adam Newton (who first had that charge) albeit the son of a burgess, yet neglected the Town Council in his entry; for which cause, in January 1594, he was discharged to teach in the College." By the terms "neglected the Town Council in his entry" must be implied that Newton, having received his appointment from some source other than the Town Council, did not obtain

[1] Craufurd, p. 35.

confirmation of it from the Town Council, which, in terms of King James's charter (giving them the exclusive right of appointing Professors), would be necessary. But, in the first place, why did he, the son of a burgess, neglect this formality? And secondly, why did the Town Council condone his neglect for four years, and at the end of that time dismiss him from his Professorship on account of it?

One way there is of accounting for these anomalies, and that is, to attribute them to the arbitrary interference of the King—the only obstacle to this method of explanation being that James VI. sailed for Norway on the 22d October 1589, and did not return with his Queen till the 2d May 1590. The first appointment, therefore, may have been made in his absence. But Craufurd does not say that it was: he only says that in February 1590 the contract between the Lords of Session and the Town Council was concluded. Both parties may have considered it respectful to the King to delay appointing the first Professor of Laws till his return. If they did so all becomes simple, on the theory that the King, when the matter was brought before him, took the appointment out of their hands and bestowed it upon a favourite of his own, Adam Newton, an accomplished man, whom he afterwards made tutor to Prince Henry. If this happened, Newton would very naturally accept his appointment at the King's hands without going through the ceremony of confirmation by the Town Council. The King no doubt regarded the Town Council as his creatures, and the College as his own property, and if he had not previously interfered in the selection of Regents, it was perhaps because they had ill-paid appointments. When a new Professorship was created three times more valuable than an ordinary Regentship, it would be worth while for a courtier to apply for it, and for the King to exercise his patronage.

This view would account for the Town Council putting up with the slight which they had received from Newton's entering upon his Professorship without their sanction. And it may easily be imagined that after four years the King, wishing to gratify another favourite, and meaning to provide otherwise for Newton, graciously signified to the Town Council that they were now at liberty to discharge Newton;[1] which having been done, the King appointed Sir Adrian Damman[2] in his place.

On our hypothesis all would be clear about the two first appointments to the chair of "Laws." But the difficulty still remains—why, from the outset, did Newton never lecture upon Law? Here, again, we must suppose that the King's authority inter-

[1] It is one of the peculiarities of this affair that the City Records make no mention of Newton's appointment or dismissal, or of Damman's appointment.

[2] Sir Adrian Damman seems to have been a diplomatic adventurer. He was a native of Ghent, and being an excellent Latin scholar, was chosen by the Court of Denmark to accompany King James and his Queen on the voyage to Scotland, and talk Latin to the King. On arrival here Damman published some Latin poems, called *Schediasmata*, in honour of Scotland and its King. He was made Consul for the Netherlands; and in 1594 he had the so-called "Professorship of Laws" given to him, which he held for three years, and then went off to something better on the Continent.

vened, for nothing short of this could have set aside the joint purpose of the Lords of Session and the Town Council. But why should the King have interfered to stop the teaching of Law in the College ? He may have been personally jealous (in spite of the fine phrases in his charter) of the development of a Law Faculty in the College. But another conjectural explanation is also possible. It may have been that the Ministers of Edinburgh urged the King to stop the movement which had been made. If they did so they were only following the example of the Venerable Company of Pastors in Geneva, who had made a strong remonstrance against the introduction of a Law Faculty into the Academy of Geneva; and who, among other objections, had alleged that "those who apply themselves to this Faculty are for the most part of dissolute habits, being young men of quality, whose humour would not admit of their being subject to the discipline of the Church."[1]

The foregoing hypothesis of the King's interference in College matters is, of course, a mere shot in the dark; but in our ignorance of the actual facts it seems to afford the only possible explanation of the extraordinary circumstance that the Judges and the Town Council having, after much deliberation and conference, founded a Chair of Law, they suffered the first two incumbents of that Chair to teach nothing but classics. It is not possible for us to conceive, as some have done, that Newton found

[1] Mark Pattison's *Isaac Casaubon*, p. 37.

the Students too backward in Latin to follow his lectures on Law, and therefore took to giving them Latin lessons. Newton would find four classes in the College following the Latin lectures of their Regents in Philosophy, and therefore able to follow him. And indeed he was, in all probability, intended to lecture on Law to Students who had already graduated—those graduates, in short, who, not wishing to enter the Ministry, did not join Rollock's class in Theology. If there was any such action on the part of the Ministers, as we have before surmised, it is quite possible that Rollock took part in it, not wishing to see a rival school of Law started which might draw off Students from the school of Divinity, to which his whole heart was given.

But we may now leave the field of conjecture, and note the actual result to the College of this curious episode. On Damman's resignation in 1597 the Town Council and the College of Justice again met together to consider what they should do under the circumstances. And they now resolved, without reason recorded, to give up altogether, even in name, the Professorship of Laws which they had endowed. Neither party withdrew their contribution; the £3000 was to remain in the hands of the Town Council, but the interest thereon (calculated at ten per cent) was to be differently applied. The scheme now adopted was that, instead of paying £300 for a Professor of Laws, £200 per annum should be employed in providing six bursaries of 50 merks each, and £100 (Scots) should be allotted "for the ordinary stipend of a private Professor of Humanity." An addition was thus made to the College staff, but not of the sort which careless historians suppose. Dalzel, who in speaking of these times perpetually indulges in syncretism, or a mixing up of the old and new, calls the four Regents and their Principal the "Senatus Academicus," and tells us that "the first Professor of Humanity" was now appointed, suggesting that the office created in 1597 was the same as that which goes by the same name at the present day.

This, however, was far from being the case. It must be observed that what was then created was a "private Professorship of Humanity;" and this word "private" so far qualifies the term "Professorship" to which it was attached, that it reduces it from meaning what we understand by a Professorship to mean a mere tutorship. In the Academic language of those days "private" was applied to school teaching, or infra-University teaching, "public" to teaching which was up to the University standard. Thus the Academy of Geneva had two departments; one called *Schola Privata*, which was, in short, a good grammar school; the other called *Schola Publica*, which was to all intents and purposes a University. We have seen before that Newton and Damman "professed Humanity publicly," that is, they did not teach it tutorially, or like schoolmasters, but lectured on it like University Professors. Quite in accordance with this mode of speaking the Town Council in 1597 instituted a "private Professor of Humanity," that is, an infra-Academical teacher of the subject.

In short, they revived and made permanent the office which Nairn had held (see above, p. 137) during the first session of the College; they provided a tutor to assist those who on coming to the College were found unfit to enter the Bajan class. The *Regens humaniorum literarum*, or Humanist, as this tutor was called, was not confined to teaching Latin (which is another note of difference from the " Professor of Humanity " of the eighteenth and nineteenth centuries). Teaching Latin was indeed his chief function, but he was also directed to teach his pupils the Greek grammar. To be drilled in this latter branch of study his class had to remain in College during the month of September, when all the other classes were away for their vacation. At the beginning of November they were examined by the other Regents and Principal for admission to the Bajan class. The Humanity class, till a much later period, was not matriculated, and was thus extra-Academical, as well as infra-Academical; but those attending it were doubtless subject to College discipline.

The Regent of Humanity himself had not only a month's more work than the other four Regents, to whom he served as a subsidiary, preparing students for them in Latin and in the rudiments of Greek, but he was considered to hold a distinctly inferior office to them. A dispute on this point having arisen, the Town Council in 1625 decisively "ordained that the whole four Regents of Philosophy shall have place and precedency before the Regent of Humanity in all time coming." The Regent of Humanity was considered to be entitled to the first vacancy that might occur among the Regents of Philosophy. He was almost invariably a person quite equal in accomplishments to the other Regents, and he had to take an important part (see above, p. 151) in the examinations for degrees. But, owing to his position and small emoluments, it frequently happened that the Regent of Humanity resigned his position and went off to be Rector (or Principal, as it was then called) of the High School, as being a place of superior emolument.[1] And in some cases it happened that the same person returned from the Headship of the High School to fill the place of a Regent of Philosophy within the College.

Widely different as is the Professor of Humanity (*i.e.* Latin) of the present day, both in position and functions, from the Regent of Humanity, as first instituted at the end of the sixteenth century, he is still his lineal successor; and evidence to this is borne by the mode of his election. In 1597 it was agreed that the private Professor of Humanity should be chosen by "six Commissioners, whereof two for the Lords of Session, two for the Town Council, one for the Advocates, and one for the Writers to the Signet, using the advice of the Principal." And the

[1] The salary of the Regent of Humanity was £100 Scots, that of the Principal of the High School 200 merks, besides a fee of 20 shillings from each scholar in his class, and a "quarterly duty" of 40 pence from every boy in the school. In 1636 Alexander Gibson, being Regent of Humanity, surprised his friends by accepting the Headmastership of the Canongate Grammar School, which was of course inferior to the Edinburgh High School.

board of electors for the Professorship of Humanity remains constituted in precisely the same way, except that by the Universities (Scotland) Act of 1858 the University Curators, instead of the Town Council, nominate two electors.

A knowledge of Latin had always been taken for granted in the mediæval Universities. And it has been said that the appointment of persons within the Scottish Universities to teach Latin as a separate subject argues a decline in the schoolteaching of Latin after the Reformation.[1] This may be so; but it also points to a higher standard of Latin introduced by the Renaissance. In the mediæval Universities the Latin was monastic, and often slovenly to the last degree; but at the end of the sixteenth century such a jargon could not be tolerated. And in Edinburgh a tutorial class in the College was necessitated by another reason, namely, by the tendency now showing itself in the citizens to send their sons to the College when they would have been better kept at school. The Town Council were masters of the position, and it rested with them to check or encourage this tendency as they saw fit. Unfortunately, they rather encouraged than checked it. They always took care that the High School should not encroach on the College, but they did not prevent the College encroaching on the High School. Thus in 1584, when they were for the

---

[1] Professor Veitch, in *Mind*, No. V. Chairs of Latin were founded—at St. Andrews in 1620; in Glasgow in 1637; in Aberdeen not till 1839.

first time in full command of their School, with a suitable building in the garden of Blackfriars, and an accomplished Headmaster of their own choosing, they appointed a committee to draw up the order of School studies, with special injunctions that it should be kept separate from the College course. In 1597—the same year that the private class of Humanity was established in the College—the School course was revised; and we may say briefly that the work now prescribed for the senior class in the High School bore about the same relation to the work of the Humanity class in the College as is borne by the Fifth Form to the Sixth Form in an English public school. The Town Council, who by King James's charter had been constituted Supreme Ministers of Public Instruction in Edinburgh, would have better discharged their functions if, instead of introducing a tutorial class into the University, they had added on an advanced class at the top of the High School, so as to relegate to the High School all preparation for the course of Philosophy within the College. Had this been done, an example would have been set to the whole of Scotland, and the degradation of the Scottish Universities, which has since ensued, would have been avoided.

Some thought of this kind appears, many years later, to have been entertained by the Town Council; for we read that in 1656 they appointed two of their number to wait on the Judges, Advocates, and Writers, and lay before them a proposal for abolishing the Humanity Class, "as prejudicial not only to the Grammar School, but to the College itself." But the College of Justice did not concur with the Town Council in this opinion. The high educational ideas of the *Book of Discipline* had by this time died out of the land. And so the staff of the College was allowed to retain the appendage of a classical tutor below the Principal and four Regents. And this was the College staff as constituted in 1597.

The next changes that were made in this establishment appear to have been partly the results of a very questionable transaction on the part of the Town Council, partly to be due to the influence of the Ministers of Edinburgh, who in the early part of the seventeenth century acquired a greatly-increased authority over the affairs of the College. By King James's charter the Town Council were required to act "with the advice of the Ministers" in the election of Professors, but they seem to have generally ignored this injunction. In 1608 the Clergy of Edinburgh bought a distinct acknowledgment of their rights in the following way:—Walter Balcanquall (see above, p. 105) and John Hall, "considering that the late pestilence and other causes had diminished the city's revenue," and prevented the Magistrates from setting the College on a proper footing, persuaded the Kirk-Session to make over to the Town Council a sum of £8100, on condition that the Council should engage to pay to the College, for augmentation of the salaries of the Masters, in all time coming, 1000[1] merks per annum, and should grant to the Kirk-Session that the Ministers of Edinburgh should for the future have joint voice with the Town Council in electing the Principal, Masters, and Regents of the College.

The Ministry of Edinburgh at that period comprised some very able and energetic men, and during the seventeenth century clerical control[2] over the "Town's College" was very distinctly and on the whole beneficially exercised. This influence appears afterwards to have gradually died out in the course of years, without ever having been directly abrogated. In 1620 the Kirk-Session gave countenance to a cabal, by means of which an influential Councilman was enabled to exercise a shameless piece of nepotism, and the Ministry got one of their own body put into a position of high authority in relation to the College.

---

[1] This was nearly 8½ per cent. Eighteen years previously the Town Council had granted a rate of 10 per cent on the sum lodged with them for endowing a Professor of Laws.

[2] A striking instance of this occurred in 1626-27, in the case of their treatment of James Reid. One of the Ministers, William Struthers, who was Moderator of the Presbytery, had in a public address spoken of Philosophy as "the dish-clout of Divinity." Reid, who had been Regent of the College since 1603, and was a distinguished man in his vocation, answered this remark in a thesis, which he propounded at a graduation ceremony, and in which he reminded his hearers that "Aristippus said he would rather be a Christian philosopher, than an unphilosophical divine." Struthers, highly offended at the retort, got all the Ministers of the city to join him in a complaint to the Town Council, and the result was that "though Reid was very well beloved in the Council, and in the whole city," and though he obtained a mandate from the Privy Council ordering the Patrons to retain him in his office, he was forced to resign his position in the College, receiving from the City Treasurer £1000 (Scots) as an honorary recompense for his faithful service of twenty-four years. And all this for a smart answer to the foolish saying of a Minister.

The circumstances were these : Henry Charteris, who by Rollock's dying advice had been appointed second Principal of the College, was a learned man, but of a too humble and retiring disposition for the conflicts of life, and was accordingly undervalued by the Town Council. A former colleague of his among the Regents, Patrick Sands, who had left the College to be travelling tutor to Lord Newbattle, now returned to Edinburgh ; and as he was unsuccessful at the bar, his brother-in-law, who was Dean of Guild, "having great power in the Council, began to project a way to get him made Primar of the College." Charteris gave an opening to the schemers by applying to have his salary, which was only £500 (Scots), raised to an equality with that of the City Ministers, as indeed had been promised him. He was told that the present state of the College funds would not admit of his request being complied with,[1] and that he would do well (being a preacher) to accept some call to the ministry elsewhere. Charteris, taking the hint, early in 1620 accepted a call from the parish of North Leith ; resigned his Principalship, after twenty years' tenure of office, and departed.

The resignation of Charteris was received at a meeting of the Town Council, conjoined with representatives of the Kirk-Session, and these two parties now proceeded to divide the spoil. The offices which had been united in the persons of Rollock and

[1] How false was this excuse will be shown in an Appendix to Vol. II. on the financial history of the College.

Charteris were separated, and "Mr. Andrew Ramsay, Minister," was appointed "Professor of Divinity in their College during the Town's will," and also "Rector of the said College for the year to come," while Patrick Sands was "elected and chosen Principal of their College during the Council's will."

These are the terms under which the appointments are designated in the City Records of 20th March 1620. Craufurd, however, with his usual desire to attribute the forms of a University to the College of Edinburgh, puts a false colour on the transaction, saying: "The Primar's charge (who before had been Rector and Professor of Divinity) was divided; the Council and Ministers choosing Mr. Andrew Ramsay, Minister, to be *Rector of the University*, and Professor of Theology; and Mr. Patrick Sands, *Primar of the Philosophy College.*" This represents the arrangement as if it recognised a University outside of and including the College, and as if the College was now to be designated as "the Philosophy College," implying the existence, actual or potential, of other Colleges within the University. All which, as their words demonstrate, was utterly remote from the ideas of the Town Council and Ministers.

Edinburgh was not like Paris, Oxford, Cambridge, St. Andrews, Glasgow, or Aberdeen, in each of which a University had existed previous to the existence of any Colleges or College. In Edinburgh, while there was no University, a College had been created, standing by itself; the University function of conferring degrees had indeed been assumed for this College, yet still it was regarded by its patrons, with all simplicity as "the Town's College," and nothing more. In 1586 Rollock had received the titles of "Principal and Rector" of the College, and to these titles Charteris had succeeded. While the offices implied by these names were held by the same person they were indistinguishable, merely comprising all the functions of Headship, subject to the control of the Town Council. When the offices were separated the Principal was left to carry on the discipline, religious and moral control, and administration of the College; the Rector was constituted a Supervisor[1] or Inspector, "the eye of the Council of the Town" (as he is defined in an order of 1640) "for universal inspection, and as the mouth of the College for delivering such overtures to the Council as himself and his assessors shall find convenient." These functions, however, were not defined so clearly as this till twenty years after Ramsay's appointment. The peculiarity of Ramsay's position was that he should hold the Rectorship, which implied supervision of the College from with-

[1] It is curious to observe that as early as February 1587 the Town Council had appointed an external supervisor to the College, without giving him the title of Rector, which was then borne by Rollock. This was John Johnston, brother to the Laird of Elphinston, who was appointed "to have the oversight and government of the affairs of the College lately founded and erected by the good Town in the Kirk of Field, and of the place, Masters, and Students thereof." We have no subsequent mention in the City Records of Mr. John Johnston in this capacity. Probably nothing came of the appointment. But this creation of an office without a name is an instance of the homely, unacademic way in which the Town Council went to work.

out, while he was himself a member of the College, as being at the same time Professor of Divinity. But when at the end of six years Ramsay[1] laid down his two offices, he acknowledged that his Rectorship had been a merely nominal title, as he had never exercised any functions in connection with it.

As Sands was not a Divine, but an unsuccessful Advocate, his jobbed appointment to be Principal of the College necessitated an increase in the staff by the appointment of a Professor of Divinity in addition to the Principal. And this separate Professorship, which had come into existence quasi-fortuitously, was made a permanence. The Principalship of Sands, who completely failed in the discharge of his duties,[2] only lasted one year and a half; and he then retired with "a gratification of 1000 merks." After him a succession of Principals were appointed who were all Divines, and they reassumed Rollock's title of "Professor of Theology."[3] They relinquished, however, to the "Professor of Divinity" the duties which Rollock had performed in the way

[1] Andrew Ramsay, younger son of the Laird of Balmain, and whose elder brother was one of the first batch of baronets, was an accomplished man. He wrote Latin poems in the style of Ovid, on the *Creation, Fall of Man*, and *Redemption*, and dedicated them to Charles I. He was a Calvinist, but attached to the Episcopal form of Church Government.

[2] Curiously enough, Sands, though a layman, seems as Principal to have been put in charge of Greyfriars' Church. Perhaps it was in this capacity that he gave dissatisfaction.

[3] Thus Principal Andrew Cant's inaugural address, published 1676, bears on the title-page: "De Concordia Theologorum et Discordia. Oratio habita ab Andrea Cantæo in Acroaterio publico Academiæ Edinburgenæ ad diem 15 Novemb. Anni 1675, dum Primariatum, eique annexam SS. Theologiæ professionem auspicaretur."

of training graduates for the office of the Ministry. In short, the Principal henceforth had no concern with the systematic teaching of Theology; he conducted family worship with the Students, and after Rollock's plan gave them every Wednesday a discourse, "to instruct them in the knowledge of God and of their duties."

Except under the circumstances of a layman being made Principal, it appears difficult to see what was the necessity of separating the office of Professor of Divinity from that of Principal. The conjoint duties of these appointments had been discharged successfully by Rollock, and probably also by Charteris.[1] In the Code of Regulations for the College drawn up by the Town Council in 1628 the work prescribed for the Professor of Divinity does not look very severe; it was:—

1st. To give two "public" lectures on Divinity each week, before the Principal and Regents, the two highest classes of the Philosophy Students, and the Students of Divinity.

2d. To make the Divinity Students "dispute" once a week.

3d. To give them private exercises in Latin.

4th. To hold "public" disputations (*i.e.* before the whole College) once a month.

---

[1] On the resignation of Ramsay in 1526 Charteris was brought back to the College from North Leith, to be Professor of Divinity with a salary of 1000 merks. He was not made Rector, and it is evident that the Town Council regarded him as a good and learned teacher, but unfit to govern.

5th. To "read a lesson" to the Divinity Students in the Hebrew language once a week.

This scheme for the Theological studies of the College of Edinburgh in the seventeenth century appears very slight. It immeasurably falls short of Andrew Melville's ideas of what a Theological course should be (see above, p. 93), and even of Rollock's programme of teaching, as Professor of Divinity. We might almost say, as the Ministers of Edinburgh were probably more responsible than the Town Council for the above list of duties, that it indicates a decadence in the learning and intellect of the Kirk of Scotland in the sixty-eight years which had elapsed since the Reformation. The duties of the Professor of Divinity were, at all events, light enough to admit of his undertaking, in addition, the work of a City Minister; and this in two cases, if not more, was done; *a fortiori* then he might have performed the duties of Principal, and there was no necessity for separating the offices.

And yet it is curious to note that the establishment and endowment of a separate Chair of Divinity became quite a popular object, perhaps owing to the influence of the Ministers, for private donations and bequests. From 1618 to 1634 the Town Council received from ten different donors or testators the aggregate sum of 8475 merks for this purpose. And in 1639 they had entrusted to them by Mr. Somerville of Sauchton Hall the munificent gift of 26,000 merks (£1444 sterling), of which 20,000 were for the endowment of a Professor of Divinity and

6000 for building him a house. These facts testify to the interest felt by the middle classes of Edinburgh in the improvement of their College, and also to the religious feeling which made them regard with especial favour the promotion of Theological studies.

The institution of the new Professorship made at first no difference in the educational system of the College. There was no thought, as yet, of graduation in Theology. But still the addition of this new Chair was a step, taken unconsciously, towards the formation of a Theological Faculty, and thus towards the expansion of the College into a University.

At the same time (in 1620) other steps were taken in the same direction. For the senior Regent in the College was made "public Professor of Mathematics," and the second Regent "public Professor of Metaphysics." This was a slight movement towards the specialisation of teaching and the introduction of a Professorial system; but for the time no change was made in the course for graduation. The two senior Regents, who had received these appointments, remained rotating Regents as before, and all that was required of them in their new offices was to give a couple of lectures per week, each in their respective subjects, before the two highest classes. These lectures no doubt supplemented and improved certain parts of the course of Philosophy. But in its essential features the degree system remained unaltered. The staff of the College had merely been increased from six to seven, and it stood as follows :—

> Rector of the College and Professor of Divinity.
> Principal of the College.
> Senior Regent and Professor of Mathematics.
> Second Regent and Professor of Metaphysics.
> Two Junior Regents of Philosophy.
> Regent of Humanity.

The institution being arrived at this stage of its development, there came next year (1621) an Act of the Parliament of Scotland confirming its privileges, such as they were; ordaining "the said College in all time coming to be called King James's College," and granting "in favour of the Burgh of Edinburgh, Patron of the said College, and of the said College, and of the Rectors, Regents, Bursars, and Students within the same, all liberties, freedoms, and immunities, and privileges appertaining to a free College, and that in as ample form and large manner as any College has or bruiks (*i.e.* enjoys) within His Majesty's realm." The real importance of this Act was that it set the College of Edinburgh upon the same footing as Earl Marischall's College in Aberdeen,[1] which had been founded as a degree-giving College in 1593, and had received ratification of its powers from Parliament. The degrees conferred by the College of Edinburgh now accordingly received Parliamentary sanction, and were placed above dispute. Other privileges and immunities the

---

[1] See Appendix F. · MARISCHALL COLLEGE.

College enjoyed none. It is curious to note that the Act speaks of "Rectors" in the plural number, apparently indicating under this designation the Rector and the Principal, lately constituted as separate officers.

Another great peculiarity has been already referred to (p. 119), namely, that the Act ratifies "the erection of the said great lodging, manse, and house of the Kirk of Field into a College for profession of Theology, Philosophy, and Humanity;" and in another place speaks of the Town Council "placing therein sufficient Professors for the teaching of all Liberal Sciences," without following the charter of 14th April 1582 (which it quotes and ratifies) into the mention of Medicine and Laws. "Liberal Sciences" in those days meant "Arts," as distinguished from Laws. Therefore the Act of 1621, whether intentionally or by accident, restricted the College of Edinburgh to be a College of Arts and Theology. This, however, was never noticed, and therefore not acted on.

It has been seen that Andrew Ramsay, first Rector of the College, treated his office, which he held from 1620 to 1626, as a merely nominal one. The same course was adopted by Lord Prestongrange (a Lord of Session), who was elected Rector in 1627, and gave the oath *de fideli administratione*, but did nothing farther. He died in 1631; and the office of Rector remained in abeyance for nine years, when the Town Council resolved to revive it. They ordained in 1640 that a Rector of the College should be appointed annually, with six Assessors, to be chosen from the Council, the Ministers, and the Masters of the College. An elaborate table of his duties was drawn up :—

1st. (As above quoted) he was to be "the eye of the Town Council," and the medium of communication between the College and them.

2d. He was to see that the Principal and Regents fulfilled their duties. Otherwise, he was to report them to the Town Council.

3d. He was to arbitrate (under privilege of appeal to the Town Council) upon all disputes arising between members of the College which did not naturally fall to be decided by civil or ecclesiastical courts.

4th. He was to keep the Matriculation Roll, and administer the *Sponsio Academica* to entrants, and also the Confession of Faith to persons about to graduate.

5th. He was to keep a list and honourable record of benefactors.

6th. He was to advise the Town Council as to the College finances.

7th. He was to preside at all ceremonials of the College.

A certain amount of pomp was to be attached to his person: a silver mace[1] was provided to be carried before him; and one of the Students was appointed to be his bedell, or macer, with a stipend of £20 (Scots) per annum.

[1] See Appendix G. HISTORY OF THE UNIVERSITY MACE.

ALEXANDER HENDERSON.

From a Scarce Print by Hollar.

In January 1640 Alexander Henderson, "Minister of the Great Kirk of Edinburgh," and the most eminent of the Presbyterian Ministers of that day, was appointed to the office of Rector of the College,[1] under the above mentioned regulations. He held office for five and a half years; and during that time, though constantly occupied by Church politics, he did great service to the College. Immediately after his appointment, and probably by his advice (in accordance with the sixth article of his duties), a separate Treasurer was appointed to manage the College rents, as distinct from the other City revenues. In the same year (1640) he succeeded in raising a loan of £21,777 (Scots) on the security of the Town, and handed it over to be applied to College purposes. In 1641 Henderson preached before Charles I. at Holyrood, and was made Dean of the Chapel-Royal. We may ascribe it to his influence that in that year the Scottish Parliament assigned some remnants of the rents of the Deanery of Edinburgh and of the Bishopric of Orkney to the College of Edinburgh. In 1641 the General Assembly agreed to overtures concerning Universities and Colleges to be laid before the King and Parliament. In 1642 they passed a resolution "that in respect of the present scarcity of Professors of Divinity, it were good for the Universities to send abroad for able and approved men." In the same

---

[1] Henderson's Rectorial gown was long preserved in a chest in the University Library. It is now in the Museum of the Society of Antiquaries. It appears, however, to be an ordinary "Geneva gown."

year, "by the advice of the Rector and his Assessors," John Fleming, merchant, bestowed 4000 merks for College buildings. In 1643 "Circling" was restored (see above, p. 152) after thirteen years' intermission, and not without much opposition. In 1644 a new library was commenced to be built for the College; a chamber was erected over the north gate of the College, opposite College Wynd; and other chambers were built by the liberality of Town Councillors and other citizens. In 1645 "Overtures for advancement of learning and good order in Grammar Schools and Colleges" were carried in the General Assembly; these consisted of nine articles, enjoining: visitation of Grammar Schools; greater attention to Latin poetry; monopoly of Greek and Logic for the Colleges; Entrance Examinations in Latin; non-promotion to higher classes of those not sufficiently prepared; careful examination for degrees; non-reception from one College to another without certificate; correspondence and uniformity between the Universities. In 1646 a sum of 7000 merks, which by the Rector's advice David Graham, merchant, had bequeathed to the College, was received and applied to carrying on the building of the new library. In the autumn of the same year Henderson died, worn out, having been engaged during the last months of his life in a celebrated controversy with Charles I., at Newcastle, on the respective claims of Episcopacy and Presbyterianism.

In the brief period of his Rectorship Henderson gave an immense stimulus to the College of Edinburgh. He was the ablest educationist and the man of clearest insight of all who had had to do with the College since its foundation. He saw what was wanted, and had the energy and the tact necessary for securing it. It would have been an inestimable advantage for the Universities of Scotland if his life could have been prolonged for twenty years. In all the movements for University and College reform just mentioned we trace his hand; and with one exception—that of giving a monopoly of Greek and Logic to the Colleges—they were all in the right direction.

After the death of Henderson the Town Council, resolving to continue the office of Rector, re-appointed to it, for one year, Andrew Ramsay, now in charge of the parish of Greyfriars, and the oldest Minister of the City. And in this capacity he appears as a Commissioner to represent the "University" of Edinburgh (formally recognised as such) in an inter-University conference, held in accordance with the 9th article of the General Assembly's enactment of 1645. By that Commission it was concluded, *inter alia:* "To communicate to the General Assembly no more of our University affairs but such as concern religion, or have some evident ecclesiastic relation;" that the "*Leges Scholæ et Academiæ Edinburgenæ* be now given or sent to the other three Universities, to be thought upon;"[1]

[1] This means that the Town Council's regulations for the High School and College of Edinburgh were to be proposed as a model to the other Universities. This is certainly a feather in the cap of the Town Council.

and that "it is found necessary that there be a *Cursus Philosophicus* drawn up by the four Universities; that St. Andrews take the Metaphysics, Glasgow the Logics, Aberdeen the Ethics and Mathematics, and Edinburgh the Physics." This idea of a dogmatic, cut-and-dry system of Philosophy, to be provided by a division of labour among the Universities, was of course absurd, and said little for the mental grasp of those who proposed it. But it occupied the attention of various subsequent University Commissions for some time to come.

Ramsay was again appointed Rector next year, but in 1648 the General Assembly deposed him, in his old age, from the office of the Ministry, on the charge of favouring the Duke of Hamilton's "Engagement" with Charles I. And so the Rectorship of the College of Edinburgh (which by delegates of the three older Universities had been recognised as a University) again became vacant. At the beginning of 1649 Mr. Robert Douglas, who was now eminent in the City Ministry, was appointed to the post, with six Assessors, as had become the rule. But the sole recorded outcome of his tenure of office is, that shortly after his appointment he held a meeting with his Assessors in College, and recommended the observance of certain regulations relative to the hours of meeting.

The Town Council had made excellent choice of Rectors for their College in the persons of Ramsay, Henderson, and Douglas; it would probably have been a good thing if they had steadily gone on putting the most able Minister of the day, or occasionally a Lord of Session, into the office. But it was characteristic of the relations of the Town Council to the College, during 275 years, that, while almost always actuated by the best intentions, they were subject from time to time, at long intervals, to impulses of self-assertion. One of these moods seems to have come upon them on the 10th November 1665, when they agreed "that Mr. William Colvill, Principal, should be sent for to the Council, and gently reproved for having given greater importance to the Commissioners from the College of Justice, at the choice of a Regent of Humanity, than to the Town Council;" and at the same meeting resolved "that the Lord Provost, present and to come, should be always Rector and Governor of the College."[1]

This terminates the history of the Rectorship of the College of Edinburgh, as distinguished from the Rectorship of the University, which was instituted for the first time by the Universities (Scotland) Act of 1858. By the arrangement, which made the Lord Provost Rector, the Town Council lost their "eye" and the College its mouthpiece. Remonstrances were subsequently made by the College on the abolition of a "useful office;" but without

[1] Bower declares that this assumption of the Rectorship was a piece of spite and revenge on the part of the then Lord Provost, because his son had been chastised by one of the Regents. However this may have been, the person in question must have been a very potent Lord Provost, who probably had things all his own way, for he appears to have held office no less than fifteen years. He was Sir Andrew Ramsay; it is a pity that, with so much influence, he had not greater wisdom.

effect. By the Lord Provost's assuming the title of Rector he was not enabled to be of any more use to the College than he had been before, nor did he gain any accession of authority. His position in this respect was reduced to the ludicrous at the trial of certain Students in 1838, "on the charge of mobbing, rioting, and assault" in a snow-bicker with the citizens. The then Lord Provost, who had appeared on the scene, being cross-examined by the celebrated " Peter Robertson," and asked : " You are Rector of the University ?" replied, " No ; I may be, but I am not aware of it."[1]

In following up the Rector of the College till his last public appearance in 1838, we have a little stepped out of the chronology of Academic development. We must now go back to 1642, when, during Henderson's Rectorship, and no doubt by his advice, an addition was made to the staff of the College of Edinburgh, by the appointment for the first time of a Professor of Hebrew. The wonder is that this should never have been done before. From the first the training of Ministers had always been a chief function of the College; during the first ten years of its existence out of 259 graduates, 103, or 38·6 per cent, became Ministers. This proportion afterwards fell off, but down to 1642, that is, for the first sixty years of the history of the College, above 20 per cent of its graduates entered the Ministry.[2]

[1] The students, who were acquitted, afterwards produced a caricature of " The man who doesn't know he's Rector.

[2] These statistics are obtained from the early Graduation Lists, which, from 1587 to 1657 inclusive, show brief notes, indicating the

We have seen also that the endowment of the teaching of Divinity was a popular object with the citizens of Edinburgh. Under these circumstances it was hardly creditable to the Ministers and the Town Council to have made no provision during sixty years for the systematic teaching of Hebrew to the Divinity Students. In the College courses, as originally laid down, the Regent of the Bachelor class had been required to give his pupils a smattering of Hebrew grammar during the early part of one session (see above, p. 149). In the description by Charteris of Rollock's work with the Divinity class there is no mention of his teaching Hebrew. He must have done so to some extent, but evidently with no thoroughness, else Charteris, his pupil, would have mentioned it. When, in 1620, a separate Professor of Divinity was appointed, he was required in the formal list of his duties to "read one lesson in the Hebrew language" with the Divinity Students each week. All which was perfunctory in the extreme, and contrasts lamentably with Melville's studies at Geneva, with his practice in the College of Glasgow, and with his ideal scheme for "New College" at St. Andrews.

But now under Henderson's auspices a change was to be made. The General Assembly of 1642, in which he was a leading spirit, had resolved that "it were good for the Universities to send abroad

career of some of the Graduates in each year, and especially marking "Minister Verbi" against the name of each person who entered the Ministry. The annotator may very likely have been Thomas Craufurd, who died in 1662.

for able and approved men" to be Professors of Divinity. The reason was added, "that our Ministers may be kept in their pastoral charge as much as may be;" but probably the real reason for the "overture" was that Henderson had observed the streams of home learning to be running low, and saw that they must be replenished, as in old times, from the Continent. In the same year the Town Council of Edinburgh (presumably by his advice) determined to introduce the special teaching of Hebrew into their College, and for this purpose to engage a learned foreigner. The City Record on the subject is, as usual, laconic; it states that "the Council, considering that they had caused bring home Julius Conradus Otto to be a Professor of the Hebrew and Oriental[1] Tongues," therefore they appoint him on one year's trial, with a salary of 1200 merks. Otto was said to have been a Jew; nothing else is known of his history or nationality. Nor are any particulars of his teaching in Edinburgh recorded, except that he held the Chair till 1656.

By this time Henderson was dead, and perhaps

[1] This title, which the Professor of Hebrew has borne ever since, gave rise to some dispute in 1869, when the Professor of Sanskrit wished to open a class for teaching Hindustani, which is one of the modern dialectical corruptions of Sanskrit, with a large infusion of Arabic words. But the then Professor of Hebrew remonstrated, on the ground that his Commission gave him the sole right of teaching "Oriental languages." Perhaps he should have protested earlier against the foundation of a Chair of Sanskrit at all. Henderson and the Town Council probably never thought of either Sanskrit or any of the dialects of India. They doubtless meant to imply under the term "Oriental languages," Chaldee and Syriac, and perhaps Arabic; in short, the Semitic languages and dialects which are cognate with Hebrew.

there was no one after him with sufficient insight and influence to keep the Town Council up to the mark in maintaining a proper standard of the higher learning. Various local Ministers were successively put into the Chair of Hebrew; once "a Student of Divinity," who was kinsman to the Principal. A Florentine, named Amedeus, was tried, but he seems not to have given satisfaction, and only held the professorship for a year. The salary fluctuated during the remainder of the seventeenth century, but was never so large as what had been allowed to Otto. From 1200 merks it was reduced to 900; then to 600; then raised to 1000; finally, at the end of the century it appears at the wretched sum of 500 merks, or less than £30 sterling. At the same time we find the Professor of Hebrew enjoined "to give lessons on Mondays and Fridays." The old perfunctory notions of the way in which most deeply important subjects could be taught had resumed their sway. Scotland had relapsed into a Dark Age of its own. But the revival of intellect was at hand, and a streak of dawn might have been observed in 1674, when the first of a family of geniuses was introduced into the College of Edinburgh. It is not the object of this chapter to depict the qualifications of distinguished Professors of the past. That topic is deferred, and we are at present only concerned with the development, treated impersonally, of Academic offices, studies, and constitution. But it is permissible here to mention the name of the first James Gregory, because by his appointment in 1674, not only was a man of genius attached to the College, but also a separate Professor of Mathematics, exclusively devoted to his subject, and not called upon to go through the drudgery of regenting, was inaugurated. It is true that Gregory was only required to give two public lectures a week to such Students as wished to attend, and his career in the College was unhappily cut short within a year after his appointment. But the idea of having a distinct teacher of Mathematics was never afterwards relinquished. A tutor of the subject held office for ten years, and then there followed, as Professors of Mathematics in the College of Edinburgh, the brilliant succession of the two other Gregorys and Colin Maclaurin.

The department of Philosophy or Arts in the College had now reached its fullest seventeenth-century development. There were the four rotating Regents with their everlasting round of Aristotle, etc., necessary for graduation. There was the Regent of Humanity preparing entrants for the Bajan class, and perhaps occasionally lecturing to the whole College on classics. And there was now a Professor of Mathematics, with two lectures a week for volunteers. This was all. The Town Council had in 1620 (see above, p. 203) instituted a lectureship in Metaphysics, but they were at that time very fitful in such matters, and when the lecturer was, in 1627, turned out of the College by the Ministers (see p. 196, note) they never appointed any one to succeed him. It was a meagre apparatus of Arts teaching, but probably on a level with that of the other Universities of Scotland. The seventeenth century was the period of deepest depression for literature and science in Scotland. The College of Edinburgh, even in its Arts department, was secretly growing and gaining strength, and was soon about to burst its shell and emerge into that specialisation of teaching and research which is the prime characteristic of a modern University.

In the last quarter of the seventeenth century, a little before and after the conclusion of the first hundred years of the existence of the College, events occurred which gave it a new feature, gave it, in short, the beginnings of that which is now the great Medical School of the University of Edinburgh.

The origin of this new order of things was quite external to the College and its patrons; it rested with a small galaxy of accomplished, energetic, and some of them rather eccentric physicians, who, having been bred in foreign schools, were now congregated in Edinburgh. Chief and leader among them was Sir Robert Sibbald, and with him were associated Drs. Pitcairne, Andrew Balfour, Burnett, and Archibald Stevenson. Previous to this period Edinburgh had been remarkably infested with quacks.[1] And at

---

[1] The works of one of these have lived after him down to times within memory. Patrick Anderson in the seventeenth century advertised in Latin his "Angelic Pills," a sovereign remedy for all diseases, the secret of which he professed to have learned in Venice. His patent for these pills still exists; and there was, not long ago, an old "land"

this time medical practice in the city was greatly monopolised by the society of Surgeon-apothecaries. Sibbald and his friends set themselves to vindicate by degrees the position of Physicians and graduated Doctors of Medicine, and at the same time to advance the legitimate practice of Physic.

Sibbald states as his first principle : " I had learnt that the simplest method of physic was the best ; and those (*sic*) that the country afforded came nearest to our temper and agreed best with us." There may be something superstitious in this idea, but at all events it led Sibbald to investigate what *materia medica*, in the way of herbs, Scotland was capable of producing, and for this purpose to promote the establishment of a botanical garden. In this enterprise he was aided by his friend, Dr. Andrew Balfour, "a man of excellent wit, who had improved by his travels for fourteen years." The two, working together, got the use of a piece of ground belonging to Holyrood House, "of some forty feet every way." Such was the humble beginning of the Botanical Garden of Edinburgh. "We had," proceeds Sibbald, "by this time become acquainted with Mr. James Sutherland, a youth who, by his own industry, had attained great knowledge of the plants and of medals ; and he undertook the culture of it. By what we procured from Levistone and other gardens, and

in the High Street dedicated to the sale of "Anderson's pills," with a portrait of Anderson painted on the wall. About 1844 there was a litigation about the property in "Anderson's pills," as a question of succession under an entail. See Hill Burton's *Scot Abroad*, vol. ii. p. 117.

brought in from the country, we made a collection of eight or nine hundred plants there. We got several of the physicians in town to concur in the design, and to contribute so much a year for the charge of the culture and importation of foreign plants. Some of the Surgeon-apothecaries, who had then much power in the town, opposed us, dreading that it might usher in a College of Physicians; but by the care and dexterity of Dr. Balfour these were made friends to the design, and assisted us in obtaining of the Council of Edinburgh a lease to Mr. James Sutherland, for nineteen years, of the garden belonging to Trinity Hospital and adjacent to it.[1] And Dr. Balfour and I, with some others, were appointed by the Town Council visitors of the garden. After this, we applied ourselves with much care to embellish the fabric of the garden, and import plants from all places into this garden; and procured that several of the nobility concurred in contributing for some years. For the encouragement of Mr. Sutherland, some gifts likewise were obtained of money from the Exchequer, and the Lords of Session and Faculty of Advocates, for that use; and by Dr. Balfour's procurement considerable packets of seeds and plants were yearly sent hither from abroad, and the students of medicine got directions to send them from all places they travelled to, when they might be had; by which means the garden increased considerably every year."

[1] A low-lying site, east of what is now the North Bridge, now occupied by the North British Railway Company.

Such is the pleasing narrative which Sibbald gives of the steps so judiciously taken by himself and his colleague for introducing this important scientific improvement into Edinburgh. A few years later what had been done was associated with and incorporated into the College, for in 1676 the Town Council passed an order that, "considering the usefulness and necessity of encouragement of the art of Botany and planting of medicinal herbs, and that it were for the better flourishing of the College that the said profession be joined to the other professions, they appoint a yearly salary of £20 sterling, to be paid to Mr. James Sutherland, present Botanist, who professes the said art; and upon consideration aforesaid, they unite, annex, and adjoin the said Profession to the rest of the liberal sciences taught in the College, and recommend the Treasurer of the College to provide a convenient room in the College for keeping books and seeds relative to the said Profession." Nineteen years later, in 1695, the Town Council, after stating that "the Physic Garden is in great reputation both in England and foreign nations, by the great care and knowledge of Mr. James Sutherland," appointed him still more formally Professor of Botany in the College, with all emoluments, profits, and casualties, and with the "pension" of £20 sterling annually which had been formerly granted him.[1]

[1] The College of Surgeons of Edinburgh had got their patent from William and Mary in 1695. Sutherland, on this, immediately applied to have the instruction in Botany of their apprentices and pupils at a fee of one guinea each. This was granted, and Sutherland thus had a two-

In the meantime Sibbald and his friends had been working with energy and tact for the establishment of a College, "to secure," as he says, "our privileges belonging to us as doctors, and defend us against the encroachments of the Surgeons and Apothecaries, which were insupportable." This was by no means a new idea. As early as 1617 a proposal had been made for incorporating the Practitioners of Medicine in Scotland for the purpose of raising the character of Physicians and the standard of their acquirements. In 1621 James VI. issued a warrant to the Scottish Parliament for the establishment of a College of Physicians in Edinburgh; but, owing apparently to the religious dissensions of the time, the order was not attended to. In 1630 the matter was revived, and referred by Charles I. to his Privy Council, and again came to nothing. In 1656 Cromwell issued a patent instituting a College of Physicians of Scotland, and giving it extensive powers; but the death of the Protector occurred before the necessary preliminaries could be got through, so that the credit of procuring this national benefit was reserved for Sir Robert Sibbald and his allies. They adroitly enlisted the sympathies of Sir Charles Scarborough, who had accompanied the Duke of York as his

fold allegiance—to the College of Surgeons and to the "College or University" of Edinburgh. As time went on he seems to have grown remiss in his duties. In 1705 he was complained of as having neglected both the teaching of the Surgeon-apprentices, and also the yard (or garden) of the College of Edinburgh, of which he was keeper. The Town Council immediately cut down his salary, upon which he resigned.

physician to Edinburgh in 1680; they were supported by the Earl of Perth, who had previously been Sibbald's patron, and he persuaded several of the nobility to favour their design; finally Sibbald unearthed the warrant of James VI. above mentioned, and laid it before the Royal Duke, who, recognising his grandfather's signature, at once said that he "would see their business done." " So that it was resolved there should be a College of Physicians; but it took a long time of dispute before the Privy Council, in answering the objections of the Surgeons and of the town of Edinburgh against it. We soon did agree with the University and Bishops, and there were some conditions inserted in the patent in their favours;[1] and they became strong solicitors for us; so that, after long debates, the matter was concerted, and the draft of the patent agreed to by the Privy Council was sent up; and very soon after, by his Royal Highness' presentment, returned signed by the King." Sibbald himself turned the patent into Latin, and the great seal was appended to it on the 29th November 1681.

Thus was the College of Physicians of Edinburgh brought into existence, with the full concurrence of those who represented the interests of the Universities of Scotland. The conditions invested

[1] *i.e.* In favour of the Universities of Scotland. Sibbald says, "We did soon agree with the University and Bishops." That means with the University of Edinburgh, represented by its patrons, the Town Council; and with the Bishops (or Archbishops) of St. Andrews, Glasgow, and Aberdeen, as Chancellors of those Universities.

into the patent in favour of the Universities were as follows:—

1st. That the College of Physicians should have no power to erect a Medical School or confer degrees.

2d. That its patent should be without prejudice to the rights and privileges conceded to "the University or College" of St. Andrews, Glasgow, Aberdeen, and Edinburgh.

3d. That Graduates of the said Universities might freely practise Medicine in the other University towns. If they resided in Edinburgh they would be subject to the Bye-Laws of the College of Physicians; but all University Graduates might claim to be licentiated by the College, without examination and without fee.

All was harmonious. Already, in 1676, the Keeper of the Physic Garden had been incorporated among the Professors of the Town's College as teacher of Botany. And in 1685 the Town Council brought in three leading members of the College of Physicians to be Professors of Medicine in what, for the first time on record, they called "the University of this City." The Act of Council (24th March 1685) is as follows:—" The Council considering that the College of this City being from the original erection and foundation thereof, by His Majesty King James VI. of blessed memory, erected into a University, and endowed with the privilege of erecting professions (professorships) of all sorts, particularly of medicine, and that the Physicians have procured from his late Majesty, of ever blessed memory, King Charles II., a patent erecting them into a College of Physicians, and that there is therefore a necessity that there should be a Professor of Physic in the said College ; and understanding the great abilities and qualifications of Sir Robert Sibbald, etc., unanimously elect, nominate, and choose the said Sir Robert Sibbald to be Professor of Physic in the said University, and appoint convenient rooms in the College to be provided for him, wherein he is to teach the art of Medicine."

On the 9th September following, "the Council considering that by their Act of the date 24th March last, they had elected, nominated, and chosen Sir Robert Sibbald, Doctor of Medicine, to be Professor of Medicine in the University of this City, and had thereby appointed convenient rooms for him in the College for teaching the art of Medicine, and that he had compeared and accepted his office and made faith, and the Council considering that there is a necessity for more Professors of Medicine in the said University, and understanding the abilities and great qualifications of Doctor James Halket and Dr. Archibald Pitcairne, Doctors of Medicine, and their fitness to teach the art of Medicine in the said University, do therefore elect, nominate, and choose the said two doctors to be joined with Sir Robert Sibbald, His Majesty's Physician in ordinary, to be Professors of Medicine in the said University with the said Dr. Sibbald, and appoint convenient rooms in the College to be provided to them for teaching the said art of Medicine; but the Council declare the said Professors are to have no salaries from the good Town nor from the said University."

The foregoing Acts have been quoted on account of their phraseology, which is so remarkable as to demand explanation. Why did the Town Council suddenly alter the usage which had prevailed for more than a century, and style the " Town's College " a " University "? Not only did they do this, but they went out of their way to assert that the College had been established as a University from the first, thus reading into the existent charter of James VI. more than can be found there. It is true that "the University of Edinburgh" had been recognised by a Commission of the General Assembly (above, p. 209). And another circumstance may be remembered, namely, that the Lord Provost and Magistrates of that date evinced in other matters a peculiar desire to do honour to the College. But probably the real cause of the particular phraseology of the Acts was that it was an echo of the language used in a petition of the College of Physicians for the appointment of Sir Robert Sibbald as Professor. The Physicians may very likely in their petition have descanted upon the College of Edinburgh having been founded as a University, "with the privilege of erecting Professions of all sorts." And the Town Council, without verifying the reference, would embody into their Act the terms suggested to them. This explanation is confirmed by the fact that on some exceptional occasions in the eighteenth century the Town Council again spoke of "the University," but this was always on the occasion of creating new Professorships, and after the receipt of petitions on the subject. The Town Council no doubt adopted in their Acts the language used in the petitions; they were not on these occasions, nor in 1685, changing their views as to the character of the "Town's College."

But the above-quoted Acts of 1685 marked, not in their language but in their substance, a change of the greatest importance, and the inauguration of a new era. The Town Council, following the enlightened advice of the Physicians, had appointed, in general terms, three Professors of Medicine. They did not attempt to organise a school, nor did they propose any division of labour. They created, in fact, three joint Professors of the Theory and Practice of Physic, and left it to themselves what each should teach. They gave no salaries, only rooms and a title, and they assigned no duties. They were, in fact, establishing a Faculty of Medicine in the College, but they were as unconscious of what they were doing as Columbus was when he discovered the islands off the coast of North America.

It seems not to be recorded to what extent Sutherland as Botanist, and Sibbald, Halket, and Pitcairne as Professors of the Practice of Physic, availed themselves of their rooms in College, and gave lectures to Students. On the 14th February

1706, twenty-one years after his appointment as Professor, Sir Robert Sibbald published in the *Edinburgh Courant* the following characteristic advertisement :—

"*Quod Patriæ carissimæ, et in ea Philiatris, felix faustumque sit.*

"*Robertus Sibbaldus, M.D., eques auratus, Deo auspice historiam naturalem, et artem medicam, quam Dei gratia per annos quadraginta tres feliciter exercuit, docere in privatis collegiis incipiet, mensibus vernalibus hujus anni* 1706.

"*Monendos autem censet juvenes harum rerum curiosos, se non alios in album suum conscripturum quam qui callent*[1] *linguas Latinam et Græcam, omnem philosophiam et Mathescos fundamenta ; quod chirographis preceptorum testatum vult.*"

At the present day the form and the matter of this announcement seem equally remarkable. We should rub our eyes now if we were to meet in the columns of the *Courant* with an advertisement in classical Latin. The habit of writing and reading Latin familiarly has so completely passed away that few, except professional scholars, would be able to write as Sibbald did, or even to read off what he wrote, as easily as if it were English. The latter, at all events, any one intending to study medicine was expected to do at the beginning of the last century.

So far for the form : and now as to the matter.

---

[1] Strictly speaking, this should have been *calleant*. Otherwise the Latinity is excellent, as is also Sibbald's Latin version of the patent granted to the College of Physicians.

It would seem from the expressions used—"Sir Robert Sibbald, who has successfully practised Natural History and Medicine for forty-three years, will begin to teach in private courses of lectures (in privatis collegiis)"[1]—that this was a commencement, a first course of lectures, which Sibbald now, after being more than twenty years Professor, proposed to give. And the same impression is conveyed by the terms in which he lays down the qualifications for persons to be admitted to his lectures. The qualifications laid down by Sibbald for Students joining his class—the "Medical Preliminary," so to speak, which he prescribes—would astonish aspirants to Medicine of the present day. He says that he shall decline to enrol any Student who does not know Latin and Greek, all Philosophy, and the fundamental parts of Mathematics. This probably meant that none except Graduates in Arts would be admitted to the class. Sibbald was in a very different position from a modern Professor in the Faculty of Medicine. In his time there was no fixed Medical curriculum, no division of labour. He was willing

[1] The term "Colleges" was constantly employed in the last century to denote "courses of instruction." "Public Colleges" were regular and systematic prelections; "Private Colleges" implied more familiar intercourse with the Students, oral examinations, and the like. "Private Colleges" were sometimes added by Professors to their Public, or regular, courses of lectures. Thus Wodrow says of Craufurd, Professor of Ecclesiastical History (1731)—"He will give no private colleges but for money, so nobody comes to him." Bower is mistaken (vol. i. p. 376) in thinking that from the terms used it would appear that Sibbald "communicated his instructions privately in his own house, which was then in Carrubber's Close." Sibbald may very well have given his "private colleges" in the "convenient rooms" provided for him by the Town Council.

to pour out his mind (of course in Latin) on the topics that interested him—Natural History and the Practice of Physic; but he required as his audience young men who could follow his Latin and who had cultivated minds. *Nous avons changé tout cela;* the first Medical Professors in Edinburgh did each what seemed good in his own eyes. There was plenty of ability among them, but as yet no system. And in fact, the Professorships conferred upon them seem to have been treated by them as merely honorary titles.

We have now to notice the expansion of the College in a different direction, by an increase of its Theological department. This was due to the great Carstares, one of the most sagacious and patriotic statesmen that Scotland has ever produced. Long before he had any idea of becoming Principal of the College of Edinburgh we find Carstares working for the improvement of the Scottish Universities. He appears, like Henderson half a century earlier (above, p. 214), to have dreamt of a revival of learning in his country by means of the importation of Professors from abroad.

Early in 1691 he was at Utrecht, and Calamy, who was studying there at the time, records that "one of his principal aims was to pick up some that might be fit and qualified to make masters of in the several Colleges of Scotland, which had been before either too much neglected, or filled with improper persons."[1] And on his return to London shortly

---

[1] Calamy's *Historical Account of My Own Life*, vol. i. p. 172. See also Dr. Story's *William Carstares* (1874), p. 212.

afterwards, Carstares wrote to his brother-in-law, William Dunlop, who was Principal of the College of Glasgow :—" I have spoken to the King about allowing to the Universities some part of the Bishop's rents, and he seems to be much more inclined to do so than to give them to particular men. I shall not fail to push the matter as far as it will go, because it is service to the King and country. I could be content, too, if you fell upon some method to call a foreign Professor, such as Dr. Vries of Utrecht; if you get a call, I shall promote it." A little later he wrote to the same person :—" I think you may have an allowance for an extraordinary Professor of Divinity, and another of Philosophy, but I would have them from Holland, where they are very good, and I suppose it would please the King best."

The plan of Carstares for renovating the learning of Scotland from foreign sources was never carried out. But he succeeded in obtaining from William III. a grant to the Universities of £1200 sterling per annum out of the revenues of the Bishoprics, which had fallen to the Crown by the Act abolishing Episcopacy in Scotland. This gave an allotment of £300 per annum to each University, and it is needless to say that the University of Edinburgh ranked equally with the other three. By a sign-manual of 1693 each University was to receive an additional Professor of Divinity and ten Bursaries in Theology. In a special letter of donation to Edinburgh, 1694, it is stated that the four Professors are " to be called from foreign parts " by the

King and his successors (*dictis professoribus ab exteris per nos nostrisque successores vocandis et præsentandis*); this was evidently the suggestion of Carstares; part of his plan for renovating the Theology of Scotland. The Professor in Edinburgh was to have only £100 sterling per annum, and there were to be twenty Bursars in Theology, with £10 a year each.

This gift to the Universities was made a first charge on the proceeds of the "Bishops' Teinds;" no Professors, however, appear to have been appointed before the King's death in February 1702. But on the 10th November 1702 a Mr. John Cumming presented himself before the Town Council of Edinburgh, as having been appointed Regius[1] Professor of Ecclesiastical History in the College. It is not clear by whom Cumming's Commission was signed, probably this was done by Queen Anne as one of the early acts of her reign. The idea of having a foreign Professor of Divinity had been abandoned. And the new Chair had the province of Ecclesiastical History definitely assigned to it. This was perhaps the doing of Carstares, who soon acquired influence with Queen Anne.

Whether he had, or not, anything to do with the next move, we know not; but in 1707 Anne issued a sign-manual, in which she altered King William's

---

[1] This first appointment of a Regius Professor, as well as all subsequent appointments of the same kind, was received by the Town Council under a protest, which of course was a mere matter of form, that the admission of the Professor was not to prejudice the Town Council's rights.

disposition of the £300 a year granted to Edinburgh. This document stated that His late Majesty's pious intention in founding twenty Bursaries in Theology had been to provide qualified Ministers for the many vacancies in the Scottish Kirk after the Revolution Settlement;—but that this end was already fulfilled, "most of the Kirks being now being supplied with learned and pious Ministers; whereby, it now becomes of more use and benefit to our ancient kingdom to establish and settle a foundation for a Professor of the Public Law and the Law of Nature and Nations." To this Chair £150 a year was allotted as an endowment, and to provide that amount the Divinity Bursars were reduced to five in number.[1] Charles Areskine, "Professor of Philosophy in the College of Edinburgh" (*i.e.* one of the four Regents), was appointed the first Professor of Public Law. A certain amount of mystery hangs over the creation of the Chair; it was either, as some have suggested, a job, Areskine's influence at Court enabling him to obtain the diversion of Bursaries in order to create for his benefit a Professorship, which for a long time was of little or no use; or, on the other hand, it may have been a measure suggested or approved by Carstares for providing a scientific and philosophical basis for a future Faculty of Laws, in imitation,

---

[1] The Town Council protested against this alteration, but without avail. Dalzel (p. 294) denounces it as "a scandalous job, which ought not to have been consented to by Her Majesty's ministers, and which was resisted by the patrons, and the Principal, and Professors of the University." The patrons certainly resisted it, but there is no trace of Carstares, or any of the Professors, having done so.

perhaps, of the Dutch Universities. Whichever was the case,[1] the Chair of Public Law formed a new feature in the College of Edinburgh (though its possessor was for most of his time residing abroad, instead of lecturing to a class), and it was the last addition made to the establishment before the new start taken in 1708. The staff then had grown to be as follows: Principal, who was also nominally Professor of Theology; Professors of Divinity, Hebrew, and Church History; a Professor of Public Law; a Professor of Mathematics; four Regents of Philosophy; and a Regent of Humanity.

As the College grew in its teaching powers and in importance, questions as to its constitution and government under the vague terms of King James VI.'s charter naturally arose. The Town Council having, as we have seen, declared it, by an Act of 1685, to have been created as a University from the

[1] A curious fact relating to this matter may be here mentioned, namely, that there is in the University Library a book entitled *Hugonis Grotii De Jure Belli ac Pacis Librorum III. Compendium, Annotationibus et Commentariis Selectis illustratum. In usum studiosæ Juventutis Academiæ Edinensis.* Edinburgi, A.D. MDCCVII. It is by William Scott, one of the Regents at that time; it is dedicated to the Lord Provost and Town Council, and on the title page is written *Liber Bibliothecæ Edinensis ex dono Authoris, 4to Aprilis* 1707. In a Latin preface Scott tells us that the book had been printed for the use of a private class to whom he had previously dictated its contents as a preparation for wider studies, and he gives in full his opening address, delivered in his private class-room (*in auditorio privato*), on the study of Grotius. This shows that there was some little demand among the Students of the College for lectures on the Law of Nature and Nations. It is possible that Carstares may have suggested the delivery of these lectures as a first step towards the foundation of a Chair. But under the circumstances it is remarkable that the Chair, when founded, should have been given to Areskine and not to Scott.

first, the Bishop of Edinburgh, John Paterson, as if taking them at their word, in the next year put forward claims to be recognised as Chancellor of the University of Edinburgh. According to mediæval use the Bishop of a University town was almost invariably the Chancellor of the University; there had been no Bishop at Edinburgh when the College was founded, but now that there was a Bishop, and since the College had been declared to be a University, should not the Bishop be its Chancellor? James II. of England seems to have acquiesced in this view, and on the 19th March 1686 he granted to Bishop Paterson and his successors the office of Chancellor "of the College or University" of Edinburgh. Nothing, however, came of this, for on the 15th June 1686 the Scottish Parliament refused to ratify the appointment.[1]

Soon afterwards the King appears to have consented to rescind his decision in favour of the Bishops, and to constitute the Lord Provost of Edinburgh for all time coming Chancellor of the University. This concession was probably obtained by the influence of Sir Magnus Prince, Lord Provost for the time being and an Episcopalian. Certain curious circumstances are connected with this part of our history. Some light is contributed to it by a rare tract, entitled *A Short Account of Scotland, etc., Written by the Late Reverend Mr. Thomas Morer, Minister of St. Anne's within Aldersgate, when he was Chaplain to a Scotch Regiment* (London, 1715).

[1] Fountainhall's *Decisions*, vol. i. pp. 412, 418.

Morer was in Edinburgh in 1688, and paid a good deal of attention to the College. He says:—"The College was built about 1581, and passes for a University, but it is not really so. Yet a petition was made to King James VI." (this must be a misprint for James VII.) "to that purpose, who thereupon promised it should be done, but was not (*sic*), though the instruments are ready for the Royal allowance, and as the Principal told me, wants only peace and quietness to perfect the design."

This, then, was the statement made by the Episcopalian Principal Monro to the English chaplain who visited him: that James II. had orally given his consent to converting the College of Edinburgh into a University, and that a Deed drawn up for that purpose was waiting for the Royal sign-manual. Further on in his *Short Account* Morer says: "And so much for the College of Edinburgh, which, as an University, has the Lord Provost of the City for its Chancellor, and the Principal his Vice-Chancellor to govern it and despatch business." Instead of "has" in the foregoing sentence, Morer should have said "is intended to have," and then he would have been quite correct.

What was intended we know, because the University Library possesses the Deed[1] which King

---

[1] This document was mentioned in Dalzel's *History*, p. 224. It was submitted to the Commission of 1826-30, but, as never having been ratified, it was considered unimportant by them, and was not printed in their Report. The writer of these pages found the document amissing, and after much inquiry despaired of finding it. But it was at last discovered in an envelope labelled "College Library" among the papers

James II. was to have signed. It is a remarkable document in many ways. Assuming that it emanated from Sir Magnus Prince and the Town Council,[1] we see that they thought it expedient in getting the Lord Provost made Chancellor of the University, that it should be made clear that there was a University of which to be Chancellor. The natural way to do this would have been to say that King James VI.'s College, having prospered, etc., should now have all the privileges of a University, and be constituted as such. Instead of this, the draft signature falsifies history, adopts the phraseology of the Commission to Sir Robert Sibbald (above, p. 223), speaks of the College as having been originally "erected into a University," says that it was called "King James's University," and confirms, instead of creating, its rights as a University. It fixes the date of the foundation of the College in 1581, two years too soon; gives a highly-coloured representation of what had been done by the Town Council for the College; and speaks as if all sorts of valuable property belonged to the College. Its upshot is, however, to erect the College of Edinburgh into "a full and ample University," whereof the Lord Provost was to be Chancellor, and the Principal Vice-Chancellor. The change of dynasty prevented this from being carried out, and we have only to reflect what would have been the effect had it been carried out.

of the late Principal Lee, and was restored to the Library, after fifty-seven years' absence, by his son, the Rev. Professor Lee of the University of Glasgow.

[1] Appendix H. JAMES II'S DRAFT SIGNATURE OF CONFIRMATION.

Greater dignity would at that period have been conferred upon the College, and this Sir Magnus Prince no doubt honestly desired. But yet the powers of the Town Council were strictly reserved. All matters as to the regulation of degrees were to be carried out by the University "with consent and allowance of the said patrons." Thus, in view of subsequent struggles, the University would not have been in a much better position had this Deed obtained the Royal signature and passed under the Great Seal. In one respect, however, the members of the University would have profited; for the draft document exempted them, not only in regard of University property, but also of their private fortunes, from all rates and taxation whatsoever, which would be very agreeable at the present day.

But all this having fallen to the ground, the College was left on its old lines, and a question in course of time developed itself as to the rights of internal administration. After 1628, when the Town Council, by an elaborate code of regulations, settled the graduation system and the discipline of the College, the Principal and Regents were for a long time left to themselves to carry on the routine of administration. They of course deliberated among themselves as to arrangements and cases of discipline; they started a Minute Book, which came afterwards to be called the "Old College Record;" and from the middle of the seventeenth century onwards they began to consider and style themselves "the Faculty of Philosophy." This title was distinctly inserted into a paper of sixteen Articles for the improvement of College discipline, which they drew up in 1668 and submitted to the Town Council, who without comment confirmed the Articles. In extracts from the "Old College Record" from 1686 to 1699 we find repeated mention of "sittings of the Faculty" and "acts of the Faculty."

On the 15th December 1695 a new and peculiar function was performed by the College of Edinburgh. Hitherto it had only conferred degrees in Philosophy (or Arts) on Students who had gone through their course, but now all of a sudden we find it conferring an honorary degree in Civil Law on a certain Joseph Broun, who is said to have been an Englishman, and to have presented £15 to the Library in token of his gratitude. The history of this transaction is lost; the Town Council either sanctioned or, more probably, promoted the granting of this honorary degree, but it was no doubt voted by the "Faculty" and conferred by the hands of the Principal. To confer a degree in Civil Law, for the teaching of which there was as yet no provision, was a distinct enlargement of the degree-giving functions of the College, which by the Act of Parliament of 1621 had been defined to be a College of Arts and Theology.

After this it is no wonder that at the end of the century we find extracted from the College Record, without precise date assigned, an order for the punishment of dice-playing among the Students, which begins "*Senatus Academicus certior factus*," etc., showing that the Principals, Regents, and Professors had now got so far as to style themselves the Senate of a University. But they were soon to learn how devoid of legal claim to self-government as a University the College of Edinburgh was, how entirely any freedom of action which its officials enjoyed was a mere matter of sufferance.

Principal Rule appears to have died in 1701, so that there was a considerable interregnum between his death and the appointment of his successor, the great Carstares, in May 1703. The Regents and Professors were therefore without a head when on the 20th January 1703 they passed the following resolution :—

"*Sederunt* — Mr. Andrew Massie, Pr., Mr. William Law, Mr. James Gregory,[1] Mr. William Scott, Mr. Charles Areskine, Mr. Lawrence Dundas.

"The Faculty of Philosophy in the University of Edinburgh, taking to their consideration the reasons offered by Mr. Scott why his magistrand class should be privately graduated, and being fully satisfied with the same, do unanimously (according to their undoubted right contained in the charter of erection, and their constant and uninterrupted

---

[1] Gregory was Professor of Mathematics; Dundas, Regent of Humanity; the others were the four rotating Regents. The Professors of Divinity, Hebrew, Botany, and the Practice of Physic, not belonging to the Faculty of Philosophy, did not take part in this business; but according to the City Records, John Cumming, the newly-created Professor of Ecclesiastical History, appears to have signed the Act of the "Faculty of Philosophy," as if being reckoned as one of that Faculty.

custom in such cases) appoint the said class to be laureated privately upon the last Tuesday of April next, being the 27th day of the month."

This was clearly an ill-advised proceeding. It is difficult to understand what the Regents meant by their "undoubted right contained in the charter of erection." It looks like a piece of rash and ignorant bravado. The laureations, as we have seen above (p. 154), were public functions in which the Town Council, the Ministers, and even the College of Justice, had at one time taken considerable interest. That interest, after a century of their continuance, may have somewhat abated. Still it was a strong measure to say in any particular year that there should be no public graduation. There may have been good reasons for this in 1703, but the natural course would have been to lay these reasons before the Town Council and request sanction for the proposed arrangement. Instead of which, the Regents passed and recorded their own *fiat* in very ungracious terms. Their aggressive, not to say mutinous, language probably concealed some consciousness of the actual weakness of their position; and it was no less than a direct challenge to the Town Council to try conclusions with them, which that body did not hesitate to do.

The Lord Provost, Sir Hugh Cunningham, announced a visitation of the College, to be held on the 15th February 1703. On which day there were assembled in the Library the Lord Provost, Magistrates, and Council, bringing with them two

Assessors; namely, Sir James Stewart, Lord Advocate and a veteran in statesmanship, and Sir Gilbert Elliot, afterwards a Lord of Session and First Lord Minto; and eight Ministers of the City. The "Masters of the College" were called in, when there appeared the six persons above mentioned as forming the *sederunt* of "the Faculty," and in addition to them the Professors of Divinity, Hebrew, and Ecclesiastical History. It is observable that the Professors of Botany and Practice of Physic do not seem to have been reckoned among the " Masters."

The Lord Provost ordered the Laws given by the Council of Edinburgh, 1628, to be read, and especially the acts concerning Visitation, 1628 and 1663. He then said that he had seen "an unwarrantable Act of the Masters of the College, viz. the Professors of Philosophy, Humanity, Mathematics, and Church History, in which they asserted themselves a Faculty empowered by a charter of erection, etc.;" and "desired the pretended Act to be read."

The Lord Advocate (having previously conferred with the Regents and Professors) here mediated, and asked that the reading of the Act should be deferred, as the Masters were willing to pass from the Act, and to withdraw the protest they had previously made anent the electing of a Commissioner from the College to the General Assembly.[1] And his Lordship offered "to wait

[1] The practice had been for the College to elect their Member of Assembly in conjunction with the Town Council. Principal Rule,

upon any Committee of the Council, and make such overtures as might regulate such matters in time coming, to the honour of the Council, as patrons, and advantage of the Masters, with their due dependence upon the Council." The Masters were then interrogated individually if they agreed to the overture of the Lord Advocate, and they each severally gave their consent. The Meeting then terminated; the Lord Advocate agreeing to draw up a statement of the proceedings.

The patrons, to assert their authority, passed an order that Mr. Scott's class should be publicly graduated on the first Tuesday of May, but this order was not obeyed. On the 12th May Mr. Scott petitioned the Council, alleging that many of his class had dispersed into the country, and that "other insuperable difficulties falling in the way of a public graduation in this juncture, the same could not be performed, and craving therefore the Council to allow the said class to be graduated privately, *pro hac vice*." To this petition the Council assented. But the Regents had in the meantime very much taken the matter into their own hands; for as many as fourteen of the class had been already privately

however, always conformed with this practice under reservation that compliance with it should not be interpreted as a giving up by the College of its right to elect its own representative. In the interval between the death of Principal Rule and the appointment of Principal Carstares, the Regents being in their aggressive mood, one of them entered a protest against the Town Council's interfering in the election by the College of a Member of Assembly. And to this protest all the Regents and Professors, except one, subscribed their names. This was treated as an act of insubordination by the Town Council.

graduated, which the Town Council commented on, "expressly inhibiting" such conduct for the future.

This little conflict had been wholly unnecessary, for it is evident that private graduation would have been at once agreed to, if civilly asked for. And the result of the whole matter was to put back the growth of the independence of the College for some time to come. The Regents should never have raised a legal issue; but, as it was, the Lord Advocate, a man of great ability and experience, and very well disposed to the College, was called in to pronounce upon the legal aspect of the question, and he, after interposing so as to prevent any unseemly rupture between the parties, drew up a minute of the Act of Visitation, in which, after citing the charter of James VI., he laid it down that "conformably thereto, and ever since the erecting of the said College, the Magistrates and Council have had and exercised the only and full government of the said College." There was nothing more to be said on the subject; the "undoubted right" of the Regents "contained in the charter of erection," and their "constant and uninterrupted custom in such cases," vanished to the winds. Thus, at the beginning of the eighteenth century, the absolute powers of the Town Council over the College were declared by legal authority. And not only was this the case, but also what had occurred naturally stirred up a spirit of governing activity in the Town Council. On the 3d May 1703, when Carstares came to be installed as Principal, he was presented by the Lord Provost

with a fresh set of rules drawn up in Latin for his
guidance. Carstares was too old a statesman either
to quarrel with the patrons, or to suffer any deroga-
tion from the rights of his position. So with suavity
he addressed Sir Hugh Cunningham : " You may be
sure, my Lord, that I would have called for any rule
that may concern my post from the Keeper of the
Library, but I shall read the paper which your
Lordship hath given me; yet, my Lord, I cannot
but tell your Lordship and the other worthy magistrates of the city that are here present, that I look
upon myself as coming into this post upon no other
terms than what my predecessors did ; and that, as
to my part, all affairs relating to this College remain
entire." Gradually Carstares acquired a great deal
of influence with the Town Council; and, had he
been there a few months earlier to guide his Regents,
he would probably have restrained them from their
mistaken course of action.

The results of this continued to appear in exhibitions of authority on the part of the Town Council.
On the 12th May 1703 they passed an order that
all diplomas of graduation must have the Town's
Seal appended to them in a white iron box. The
Primar, with three or four of the Regents, were to
sign the diploma, and the Librarian was not to exact
above £4 (Scots) as a fee, while poor Students were
to have the diploma gratis. All certificates of
graduation were to make honourable mention of the
Town Council as patrons!

In October of the same year they issued a

WILLIAM CARSTARES,
Principal of the College of Edinburgh

vexatious order to the effect that as some of the Masters or Regents of the College had "never extracted or taken out their Acts of Admission," they were to have no more salary paid them until they should have done so.

And in 1704 they proceeded to a still more arbitrary act of authority in ordering the College Records to be seized[1] on the ground of certain alleged inaccuracies, which seem very trifling; the real blot in the eyes of the Town Council being, that " In the 19th page it is observed that the word *Faculty* is then first assumed, and without warrant,

[1] At first the order was that the book be "transsumed" with a view to its being corrected; Carstares, on behalf of himself and the Regents, craved, "with all submission," to have it recorded that it was not with their will that the book was delivered up. He was told that the book was only wanted for correction. But next year (1705) the Town Council "appointed the book belonging to the College of Edinburgh, entitled *Register of the University of Edinburgh*, to be put up in the charter-house; and ordained their clerk to write at the end of it, that the same was condemned as informal, and in many ways vitiated." It was kept by the Town Council thenceforward, but was produced, by the order of the Court of Session, at the great case of the Town Council *versus* the University in 1825-29. And now it was the fate of this luckless Record to perish in obscurity. It became part of the "process" in the lawsuit, and as such ought still to be in the Register House, where the other documents of the process lie, or else it should have been restored to the keeping of the Town Council. But we find it noted that the book was borrowed by Messrs. Cranstoun and Anderson, law agents for the Senatus, and never returned. And the writer of these pages on applying to Messrs. J. and F. Anderson, lineal successors to Messrs. Cranstoun and Anderson, and occupying the same premises, found it hopeless to inquire after a MS. volume received by their predecessors more than half a century before. Masses of documents had, in the meantime, been carted away and reduced to pulp by the papermaker. Such was the fate of this book; a few extracts, suited to the purposes of the defendants in the lawsuit, were printed, and these remain, but the "Old College Record" from 1645 to 1703 would surely have contained racy entries and perhaps valuable hints, and its loss must be deplored.

or any former practice, inserted in October 1686. And although the College had been now one hundred years standing before the said time, no record bears the word 'Faculty.'" This word "Faculty" was evidently as a red rag to the Town Council, and their anger at it made them forget that in 1668, eighteen years prior to the obnoxious entry, they had themselves endorsed a set of regulations, one of which bore that theses for graduation "must be revised and cognosced upon by the whole Faculty." They forgot also that "the Faculty" of the College of Edinburgh had been distinctly recognised in a letter under the Great Seal of William III. (1694), in which the words occur "as shall seem expedient to the said College or its Faculty" (dictæ academiæ vel facultati suæ expediens visum fuerit).[1] And still more did they forget their own declaration in 1685 (see above, p. 223), that the College of this City was "from the original erection and foundation thereof erected as a University." It was now made clear that the ordinary rights of a University were denied to be inherent in the College of Edinburgh, and at the same time that College was humiliated by being deprived of its Records.

Thus what may be called the first period of this history drew to its close under unpleasant circumstances the results of a rupture between the teachers of the College and their patrons the Town Council.

[1] This form of expression was doubtless used at the instance of Carstares, who had previously been in correspondence with Dr. Rule, and of course had learned from him to style the Principal and Regents of the College " the Faculty" as their proper official designation.

In itself this rupture was a sign of the growing strength of the College. The Regents and Professors doubtless thought themselves justified in claiming an independence equal to that enjoyed by the Senatus of any of the older Universities, on a level with which the College of Edinburgh had been repeatedly placed. But they were imprudent in stepping forward to assert their position without ascertaining, by legal advice, what it really was. They ignored the tremendous powers given to the Town Council by the charter of James VI. And hence they brought upon themselves the humiliation which has been related. The wisdom of Carstares soon restored happier relations, and there set in a halcyon period, which lasted, with hardly a cloud, for more than a century. After that the University, having grown exceedingly strong, again thought that it could throw off the government of the Town Council, but, as we shall see, with as bad success as the Regents met with in 1703.

Appendix F. Marischall College.

George Keith, fifth Earl Marischall, was educated at King's College Aberdeen, and was said at the age of eighteen to have been proficient in Greek, Latin, and Hebrew: he then went for further study to France, where he took the opportunity to perfect himself in the knowledge of arms and feats of athletic jugglery in vogue at the time. Proceeding to Geneva, he learned Rhetoric and Divinity from Theodore Beza. Keith then went the round of the Courts of Europe. After seven years' absence he returned to Scotland, and became "art and part" in the slaughter of his relative, William Keith, but got a remission under the Great Seal. He succeeded to the Earldom in 1581, and soon afterwards was mixed up in the Raid of Ruthven; but, sitting in an assize of Peers, he voted for the guilt of the Earl of Gowrie. He went to Denmark as ambassador to get the Princess Anne for James VI., and was joined there by the King. He bore all the expense of the embassy, amounting to 3156 merks. In 1583 he had been one of the Commissioners for the *Erectio nova* of King's College (see above, p. 90). This great, splendid, and highly-cultivated nobleman, who apparently united some of the violent spirit of the times with "the humour of a scholar," signed in 1593 a deed, which was styled *Nova Academiæ Abredonensis per Comitem Mariscallum, Auctoritate Regia, Erectio et Institutio.*

This document, which is the Charter of Foundation for Marischall College, is in many points curious and interesting. The preamble gives quite general reasons; there is no mention of what was probably the real object—to found a College on Reformation principles; it is only said that the want of public instruction (*publica disciplina*) is everywhere felt in the northern parts of Scotland. "We follow," says the Earl, "the example of Kings, Princes, Nobles, and Bishops, who have founded Colleges. We wish to institute at New Aberdeen a Gymnasium in the house formerly belonging to the Franciscans. Therefore we grant and mortify" (then follows a list of Church properties which had come into possession of the Earl). "These revenues for the edification of youth" were to be distributed among the following persons: a Gymnasiarch, three Regents, six pupils (Academiæ alumnos) a Steward, and a Cook.

In the course of teaching prescribed, we see that the *Regia Erectio* of the College of Glasgow (above, pp. 84-87) is copied, and often its exact terms are reproduced. Thus, the Gymnasiarch must be learned in Hebrew and Syriac; the Regents are each to be confined to special subjects, "so that the youths ascending by degrees may find at each stage a teacher worthy of their zeal and ability." In these and many other details we see the ideas of Andrew Melville.

But the *Regia Erectio* was drawn up for a College which was within a previously-existing University, and this was not the case at New Aberdeen. Lord Marischall's charter, however, ignores this difference of circumstances, and delegates, for instance, various functions to the Chancellor, while making no provision for the appointment of such an officer. Perhaps it was intended that the office of Chancellor should be retained in Earl Marischall's family—but this is never specified.

Throughout the deed the word *Academia* is used in a twofold sense, sometimes meaning the "College," sometimes the "University." Thus, when it is said that none of the Bursars may sleep "*extra Academiam,*" the four walls of the College are implied; when it is enjoined that the Rector be elected "per omnes *Academiæ Suppositos*" divided into four nations, we have terms only applicable to a University. Evidently Lord Marischall's *Academia* was to be at once a College and a University. Degree-giving powers were assumed for it. The Gymnasiarch or Principal was to graduate such Students who deserved it at the end of a four years' course. The idea plainly was that the Bursars on the foundation would form a nucleus, but that these would be supplemented by a large number of outside Students, who, divided into nations, would elect their several *Procuratores*, by whom the Rector would be elected. The Rector was to exercise all the functions—"*quæ Rectores Academiæ Glasguensis, Edinburgensis, vel cujusris alterius*"—are understood to have the power or duty of exercising. We observe here that the Rector of the College of Edinburgh is placed on the same footing with the Rector of the University of Glasgow, which is the more remarkable, as in 1593, when this deed was drawn, the office of Rector at Edinburgh had not been separated from the Principalship, but had been given as a mere courtesy title to Rollock. There was in the charter no recognition of the University of Old Aberdeen. In one matter only, namely, in the examination and admission of the Masters of Marischall College, the Principal of King's College was to be called in to assist.

An Act of Parliament of 1593, after stating in preamble that George Earl Marischall "has both founded and erected a College within the burgh of New Aberdeen," ratified the foundation, and gave the College "all freedoms, franchises, liberties, free privileges and jurisdiction, that to a free College within this realm by law and practice is known to appertain." But the important proviso was added that "the Masters, members, students, bursars, and whole inhabitants of the said College shall be subject to the jurisdiction of the Provost, Bailies, and Council of the said burgh of Aberdeen, in all things to be done and committed by them *outside the walls of the said College*, and within the territories or freedom of the said burgh." Thus the Legislature regarded Marischall College as bounded by its walls, and not as a University in the mediæval sense. But by ratifying the charter they ratified the power of granting degrees which had been assumed in the charter. And the Act of 1621, by placing the College of Edinburgh on the same footing as Marischall College, confirmed the legality of its degrees.

APPENDIX G. HISTORY OF THE UNIVERSITY MACE.

THERE used to be a tradition that in 1683 Bishop Kennedy's tomb at St. Andrews was opened in search of treasures which had been hidden there during the Reformation troubles, and that, besides other things, five silver Maces were discovered, whereof two were kept in St. Andrews and the other three distributed to the Universities of Glasgow, Aberdeen, and Edinburgh. As a matter of fact there are now three Maces at St. Andrews, and these may very likely have been found in Kennedy's tomb. But there is no probability in the story that the other Universities were presented with Maces issuing from that receptacle. It is certain that the College of Edinburgh possessed a Mace of its own in 1640, which was carried before Henderson, as Rector, though how it was obtained is not recorded. This Mace had a history: it was borrowed by the Town Council "for use of the public" in 1651; and was restored to the College Librarians in 1655; and in 1660 it was "lent to the Macer of the Committee of Parliament, till they get one of their own." "On the night betwixt the 29th and 30th October 1787" (as reported by Professor Dalzel, then Librarian) "the door of the Library was broken open by thieves, and the mace stolen from the press where it was usually deposited." The Magistrates immediately, but without effect, offered "a reward of ten guineas for the discovery of the delinquents."

On the 2d October 1789, as stated in the *Caledonian Mercury*, "William Creech, Esqre. (the College Bailie) in name of the

Lord Provost, Magistrates, and Council, presented to the Senatus Academicus of the University of Edinburgh, assembled in the Library, an elegant new silver Mace, decorated with the Royal Ensigns of King James VI., the Founder of the College, and with the Arms of the City and University beautifully enchased, and having the following inscription engraved on one of the compartments under the Crown:

> Nova Hac
> Clava Argentea
> Academiam Suam Donavit
> Senatus Edinburgensis
> Consule Tho. Elder
> Prætore Academico
> Gul. Creech
> A.D. 1789."

There was a very special and extraordinary reason for this act of liberality, namely, that public opinion in Edinburgh had come to attribute the theft committed in the College to one of the Town Council themselves. This was the notorious Deacon Brodie, a man of highly respectable exterior and popular manners, who seems to have associated himself with the lowest ruffians in a series of burglaries, while others he committed single-handed. His habits of cock-fighting and gambling probably required larger funds than his trade, that of a cabinetmaker, would supply; while his skill in that trade would be serviceable to him in his additional vocation of burglar. He was tried and condemned to death on the 29th August 1788 for robbing the Excise Office; and after his execution people began "to put two and two together," and to lay the affair of the College Mace at the Deacon's door. The hypothesis seems probable; for Deacon Brodie's official position, as one of the patrons of the College, would make him well informed as to the place of custody of the Mace, while his proclivities would induce him to abstract it. At all events it is said that the Town Council were so "black affronted"[1] at the disgrace brought upon them by an unworthy member of their body that they hastened to get the matter hushed up by having a new Mace made and presented to the College.

[1] See Lieut.-Col. A. Fergusson's biography of *The Hon. Henry Erskine* (1882), p. 309.

Mutual compliments were then interchanged between the Town Council and the Professors; and Principal Robertson, in name of the Senatus, "respectfully received and gratefully acknowledged" the gift. And the new Mace (which is the one still used by the University) came, in fact, just in time to be carried in procession at the laying of the foundation-stone of the new University Buildings in November 1789.

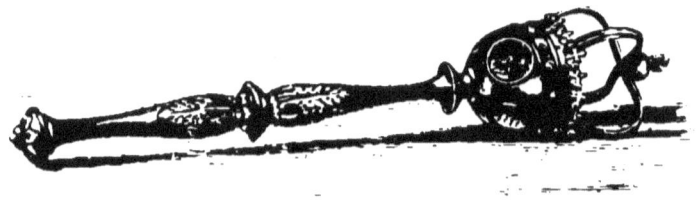

In the above-quoted description of the Mace the "Arms of the University" are mentioned. These Arms seem to have been devised for the express purpose of being engraved on the Mace. And the University acquired at the same time not only its Mace, but also armorial bearings and a Common Seal. On the 3d October 1789 "Mr. Dalzel reported that whereas the University were not in possession of a Common Seal for affixing or suspending to their Diplomas or public Deeds, but were under the necessity at every graduation of applying for one of the City seals, which was inconvenient and unsuitable to the dignity of the University, he, with the approbation of several of his Colleagues, had desired Mr. James Cummyng, of the Lyon Office, to make out a device, which had been done accordingly; and that Mr. Robert Boswell, the Lyon King of Arms's Deputy had consented at the desire of Mr. Fraser Tytler to issue a patent from the said office (without demanding the usual fees) authorising the College to use the said Device as their Arms in all time to come, *viz. Argent on a Saltire Azure between a Thistle in chief Proper and a Castle on a Rock in base Sable a Book expanded Or;* as the same are represented on one of the compartments of the new Mace. Which having met with the approbation of the Senatus Academicus, they ordered the said Arms to be engraved on a Seal, to be used for the future as the Seal of the University."

APPENDIX H. DOCUMENT LABELLED SIGNATURE OF CONFIRMA-
TION IN FAVOURS OF THE UNIVERSITY OF EDINBURGH, 1688.
(PRESERVED IN THE UNIVERSITY LIBRARY.)

OUR SOVERAIGN LORD taking into his Royall consideration the many large and ample priveledges and Immunities granted by his Matie's Royall Grandfather King James the Sixth of blessed memorie and since ratified and confirmed by his Matie's Royal ffather and Brother to and in favours of the university of Edinburgh, His Matie also out of his ffatherly care and Royall zeall for the promotting and encouraging pietie and learning being no less desirous that the s^d university should have all due encouragements and protections from his Matie and his Matie's Royall Successors, THEREFORE His Matie with advice and consent of his Matie's Right trustie Cousin and Councellour James Earl of Perth etc. Lord High Chancellour of the Kingdome of Scotland John Marquess of Athol etc. Lord privie seal his Matie's well beloved and trustie cousins and councellors William Duke of Hamilton etc. George Duke of Gordon etc. his Matie's well beloved cousins and councellours John Earle of Tweeddale etc. John Earle of Belcarres etc. George Viscount of Tarbot etc. Lord Register His Matie's commissioners for the Thesaurie comptrollers and Thesaurie for new augmentations and also with advice and consent of the Remnant Lords and others Commissioners of his Matie's exchequer within the s^d Kingdome ORDAINS an charter to be made and past under his Matie's great Seall of the s^d Kingdom of Scotland ratifieing and approving and for his Matie and his Matie's Royall successors perpetually confirming likeas his matie with advice and consent fors^d by these pnts Ratifies and approves and for his Matie's Royall Successors perpetually confirms all and sundry Erections Donations Mortifications Charters Infeftments former confirmations and all other rights and securities whatsomever granted by his Matie's Royall Grandfather King James the sixth His Matie's Royall ffather King Charles the first and his Matie's Royall Brother King Charles the second of blessed memorie or by any other persons to and in favours of the s^d university of Edinburgh and to the Principall professors Regents Masters scollars students Bursars Janitors and all other officers and members of the samen of all and hail the fabrick and buildings belonging to the s^d university with the yard and pertinents thereof and of all and sundry the lands rents tenements possessions annual rents Teinds and other goods belonging to them and all priveledges Immunities liberties and exemptions enjoyed or that might been enjoyed by them of whatsomever tenor qualitie contents and nature the samen be of in haill heads clauses and circumstances of the s^ds Charters erections and Donations dispensing hereby with the generality of this present ratification and declairing the samen to be valid effectuall and sufficient to the s^d university and to the s^d principall professors other masters and members of the samen as if everie particular Charter either of Erection Donation and Mortification were herein Insert and specially set down whereanent and with all and sundry other objections which may be made or alleadged against the validitie of the s^ds rights or this present confirmation his Matie for himself and for his Matie's Royall successors hath dispensed and by thir dispenses forever. AND FURTHER his Matie considering the many good and thankful services done to his Matie and his Royall progenitors by the Provost Bailies Councill and communitie of the burgh of Edinburgh patrons of the s^d university and the great sums of money Doted and Mortified by them to the use thereof at the erection of the samen in Anno on thousand five hundred and eightie on years and of the great charges and expenses since bestowed by them in erecting the buildings thereof being now beutified with a goodly fabrick and furnished with a famous library and good store of mathematical instruments and other furniture befitting an university and of the great care taken by them in managing the mortifications bestowed upon the s^d university overseeing the same and placeing therein from time to time since the foundation thereof professors under whom it has and does flourish with great success and his matie out of his sincere and ffatherly care and Royall zeall for propagating learning so necessarie and profitable both to church and State being willing to further testifie his Royall kindness favour and signall good will to the s^d universitie being named by his Matie's Royall Grandfather KING JAMES UNIVERSITIE with advice and consent fors^d hath not onlie taken and revived but hereby takes and revives the s^d University of Edinburgh and haill schools and faculties thereof and the

Principall professors and other Members of the samen with all and Sundry their priveledges Immunities exemptions Lands revenues tenements and other goods gear als well moveable as reall spirituall as temporall either within the s^d city of Edinburgh as in any other place within the s^d Kingdome unto his Matie's and his Royall Successors' firm grace Royall care protection and patrocine now and in all time coming. But also in fortification of all the former erections Donations Mortifications charters Infeftments and other rights of the s^d Colledge erected and (? an) universitie and but prejudice to any thereof in any sort his Matie of his Royall authority princely power certain knowledge and proper motive hath of new constitute created erected and Incorporated and by the tenor hereof for his Matie and his Royall Successors with advice and consent above written of new makes constitutes creates erects and Incorporates the s^d university of Edinburgh in an full and ample universitie to be called now as of befor and in all time coming KING JAMES'S UNIVERSITIE of new giving granting disponing and for his Matie and his Royall Successors with advice and consent fors^d perpetually confirming to the s^d university Principall professors Regents Masters Members whatsomever thereof all and haill the Lands Rents tenements possessions annual rents teinds and other goods belonging to them and all and whatsomever priveledges Immunities Liberties and exemptions they formerly possesst or might have possest and enjoyed and that in the most full and ample manner are may or can be possest and enjoyed by any other university within or without the s^d ancient Kingdome admitting the generality hereof to be als valid as if the s^{ds} lands teinds priveledges exemptions and others fors^d were particularly enumerate Insert and Ingrossed hereintill with the not doing whereof and with all that may be objected against this present new gift and erection his matie for himself and his Royall Successors with advice and consent fors^d hath dispensed and be thir presents dispenses for ever. AND HEREBY DECLAREING that the Provost Bailies and town councill of Ed^r have been are and shall be the sole and undoubted Patrons of the s^d universitie and have the alone right and power of nominating and presenting to all places and professions either for the time vacant or that may afterwards fall to vake belonging to the s^d universitie and hereby nominating appointing and ordaining

Likeas his Matie of his royall good will and pleasure with consent fors^d by the tenor hereof nominats appoints and ordains the R^t Honourable Sir Magnus prince present Provost and his Successors provosts of Ed^r (excluding all others) to be now and in all time coming chancellours of the s^d university with full power and priveledge to the s^d universitie (But prejudice of the general priveledges above written) of having and enjoying the profession of Philologie als well in the Hebrew Greek Latin Orientall ffrench and other Languages as in all its other parts the professions of historie Mathematiques Philosophy Medicine Law and Theologie in all their parts and all other faculties and professions of all arts and sciences whatsomever whither (*sic*) already established or to be established in the s^d universitie and that are or may be teached in any other universitie within or without the s^d ancient Kingdome and to preserve and maintain such of the s^d professions as are already established. And for further promotion and advancement of learning with consent and allowance of their s^d patrons to revive or erect such of the s^{ds} professions or such part of the same as are in desuetude or not yet established in the s^d universitie. And with consent fors^d to form themselves from time to time into such faculties and societies as their number frequencie Revenues and Rents will allow and maintain. And to conferre the Degrees of Batchelours Licentiats Doctors and all other degrees suitable in the s^{ds} respective arts and sciences according to the usuall and accustomed ceremonies which degrees are to be conferred by the Principall as Vice-chancellour of the Universitie ex officio with the advice and concurrence of the respective faculties which the receivers of the s^d degree shall be of and with power to the fors^d Chancellour of the s^d universitie with the Bailies and Council of Ed^r to visit the s^d universitie and take the administration of the rents and revenues thereof and to take care of the schools chambers dwelling houses and other ffabricks belonging thereto. AND LASTLY with the speciall priveledge that the s^d universitie Principall professors Regents Masters and Members thereof whatsomever their Lands rents possessions and goods reall or moveable belonging either to their offices or their private fortunes shall be free and exempted from all stents taxations cesses Impositions customs exactions and collections Imposed or to be imposed upon the subjects of the s^d Kingdome and of all watchings wardings leveings hosts and other burdens or services whatsomever als well not named as named bygone present as in all time coming. Hereby discharging all and sundry his Matie's subjects Tacksmen Collectors Waiters and all other whom it effeirs from troubling or molesting the s^d universitie of Ed^r Principall Masters and Members thereof their lands rents possessions or goods whatsomever either reall or personall belonging to the communitie of the s^d universitie or to themselves in particular for the s^{ds} taxations cesses and others fors^d bygone and in all time coming and of their offices in that part and that they do nothing contrarie to the fors^d priveledges Immunities and exemptions hereby granted unto them under all highest pain. And his Matie faithfullie promisses in verbo principis to cause the fors^d Charter to be ratified in his matie's next parliament by his Matie with consent of the estates thereof and ordains the samen Charter with this declaration of his Matie's will to be contained therein to be a sufficient warrant for that effect and that the fors^d charter be further extended in the best and most ample forme with all clauses needfull and that precepts be orderly directed thereupon in form as effeirs. Given at

CHAPTER V.

THE DEVELOPMENT OF THE FOUR FACULTIES IN THE UNIVERSITY OF EDINBURGH, 1708-1858.

"From precedent to precedent broadening down."

I. THE period of time traversed in the last chapter was, as regards the national history, an "hour of crowded life," full of vicissitudes and death-struggles for religious and civil liberty, and culminating in the Revolution Settlement and the Union with England. But to the historian of the University of Edinburgh, as such, all those stirring crises are indifferent; for his purpose they are *nihil ad rem*, because none of them really affected the condition or progress of the University. All that can be said about them is that times of religious conflict are always unfavourable to learning and science, and that the period of the Covenanters was no exception to this rule. For the rest, political changes affected the *personnel* of the College of Edinburgh from time to time during the seventeenth century, but never its institutions. Owing to Cromwell coming into power Colville was for some time kept out of the Principalship,[1]

---
[1] As will be related in Vol. II.

Robertus Leightonus S.S. Th.
professor Primarius et
Academiæ Edenburgenæ Præfectus.

and Leighton was put in. It was a great blessing to the College for the time to have Leighton as its Principal, but he cannot be said to have changed the College in any way. Again, when William III. and the Presbyterians got the ascendency, a Royal Commission removed the Episcopalian Principal Monro and Professor Strachan from their appointments, but no organic changes ensued. The Town Council appear always to have followed the Government in religious as well as political principles. The attendance of Students was said never to have been affected by the troubles of the times. As a rule the Students were Covenanters, and they rioted and " burnt the Pope " when the Duke of York was at Holyrood, but nothing serious came of it.

The first great organic change, which in fact turned the College of Edinburgh into a University, was made immediately after the Union with England. And in the ensuing period of peace and prosperity there came the successive steps of the extraordinary process of development which we have now to relate. It has been seen before how the *Book of Discipline*, and Andrew Melville, and all the most enlightened Reformers, aimed at the introduction of professorial teaching into the Universities of Scotland, and yet how all the Universities down to the eighteenth century clung to the practice of " Regenting." Now at last, in Edinburgh, the change was to be made. Carstares was now Principal, and we cannot doubt that he would see and seize every opportunity which occurred for raising the University teaching of his country, though, like a Baron Stockmar, he did not appear in what was being done. In 1707 a remarkable thing occurred; for William Scott, one of the Regents, "obtained a patent from the Crown for the profession of Greek, by the which he was constitute her Majesty's sole Professor of Greek in the University of Edinburgh."[1] It is difficult not to suppose that Carstares had a hand in this. We have before seen (p. 233, note) that this same William Scott had commenced teaching Public Law in the College with a view to obtaining a chair of the subject to be founded by Queen Anne, but that Areskine, by his family influence, had stepped in and secured the Chair. Perhaps now, as a *solatium*, Carstares, who was high in favour with the Queen, obtained him this patent to be Professor of Greek.

The move was not only a proper one in itself, but it was consistent with the views of the Parliamentary "Commission for visitation of Universities, Colleges, and Schools," who in 1699 made an order for the specialising of Greek in the Universities. They laid it down that the teacher of the first class was to be "fixed and not ambulatory;" throughout the whole year he was to teach "only the Greek Grammar and proper Greek authors, without teaching so much as any *structura syllogismi*, or anything

[1] We get this information from a curious paper written by Colin Drummond in 1731, and afterwards discovered and printed in the *Scots Magazine* for 1829. Drummond succeeded to the Chair of Greek in 1730, and the object of his paper was to protest against other Professors infringing on his monopoly of the subject.

belonging to the course of Philosophy." And "for the better encouragement of said fixed teacher of Greek, no scholar bred at school in Scotland and not foreign bred" was to be admitted to learn Philosophy "unless he had learned Greek, at least for the ordinary year, under the said fixed Greek master." This order of the Commission, however, seems to have been disregarded, just as was another and less judicious order, which they often repeated, for the production of a stereotyped course of Philosophy for common use in the Universities.

Scott's patent as Professor of Greek in the University of Edinburgh would have put him nearly in the position desired by the Commissioners of 1699. But his admission as such was opposed by the Town Council, as having the sole power of appointing Professors, and also by the other three Regents, who thought themselves entitled to teach Greek as well as Philosophy. Out of this, perhaps by the manipulation of Carstares, arose conferences in which the Town Council, the Ministers, and the members of the College, took part, and which resulted in the Town Council's Act of 1708. By this Act Scott retained the Professorship of Greek, while other changes were introduced, which may have merely seemed a satisfactory compromise to the parties concerned, but which in reality constituted vital improvements in the teaching system of the College.

In their Act of 16th June 1708 the Town Council said that "taking to their consideration what may be the proper methods for advancing of learning in their own College of Edinburgh, they have agreed upon the following articles as a rule of teaching in the said College: *Primo* that all the parts of philosophy be taught in two years, as they are by the most famous Universities abroad; *Secundo* that, as a consequence of this article, there be but two philosophy classes in the College, to be taught by two of the four present Regents; *Tertio* that in the first of these classes the students be taught Logic and Metaphysic and in the last a compend of Ethics and Natural Philosophy." Three other articles were added in which the Town Council constituted a Professor of Pneumatics and Moral Philosophy, to be apparently the apex of the whole teaching establishment. He was to have a voluntary class in his own special subject, and to be allowed a larger salary than the rest because he would get no fees. They also constituted "a fixed Professor of Greek," whose class was to be below the two classes in Philosophy, but was not necessarily to be passed through by a Student wishing to join the Philosophy course at once. They offered the appointments thus created to the existing Regents, to be chosen by them in order of seniority; and the result was that Laurence Dundas became Professor of Humanity; William Scott, Professor of Greek; Colin Drummond, Professor of Logic and Metaphysics; Robert Stewart, Professor of Natural Philosophy; and William Law, Professor of Moral Philosophy.

In this arrangement the handiwork of Carstares is traceable : he probably took advantage of the conferences to indoctrinate the Town Council and the Ministers with his views, and to get them to begin moulding the College after "the most famous Universities abroad," that is to say, after Utrecht and Leyden. This tinge was effectually given during the Principalship of Carstares, and a few years later we shall have evidence that the teaching of the University of Edinburgh, in almost all its departments, had become distinctively Dutch. But the important thing in 1708 was that the Arts Faculty was henceforth to consist, not of rotating Regents, but of specialised Professors. It is true that some vestiges of the old system lingered a while, for the senior Professor of Philosophy was to teach "a compend of Ethics and Natural Philosophy," but Stewart soon dropped the Ethics and Aristotelianism in general, and became a Natural Philosopher of the school of Newton. It was a mighty change, and the example of it was followed by the other Universities of Scotland : by Glasgow in 1727, by St. Andrews in 1747, by Aberdeen in 1754.

The curriculum for Arts laid down was as follows :

(1.) The class of the Professor of Humanity (now restricted to Latin) remained at the bottom, but it was no longer infra-Academical ; it constituted the first year of the Arts course, and from 1710 onwards the Students belonging to it were matriculated, which the Pupils of the Regent of Humanity never had been.

(2.) Next came the class of the Professor of Greek. This was called the "Bajan class," from old associations, though it was now properly the class for second year Students. But persons coming from other Universities, or who, on examination, showed the requisite proficiency, might pass over both the Humanity and Greek classes. A similar practice had long previously been allowed under the Regenting system. Those who on entrance were placed in the second, third, or fourth year class, were called *Supervenientes*, and they were often very numerous.

(3.) Then came the class of the Professor of Logic, which, as being next above the Bajans, was now called the "Semi" class. It was the third year's course for an ordinary Student, and the first of the two years to be devoted to Philosophy.

(4.) Finally there was the Natural Philosophy, or "Magistrand" class, which conducted the Student to his degree.

In addition to the four Professors, to whom the above different stages of the Arts curriculum were entrusted, there were also the Professors of Mathematics and of Moral Philosophy giving lectures, attendance upon which was voluntary. In fact, there seems to have been some feeling of reaction at this time against the Procrustean uniformity of the old system, and a good deal of *Lehr-und-Lern Freiheit* was introduced. One remarkable result of this was, that teaching and learning soon grew to be thought of more importance than graduation.

Of old, when it was each Regent's part to conduct all his pupils through the various stages and get them laureated, there was a sort of pressure put upon every Student to graduate. There were great fluctuations in the number of those graduating, owing to special circumstances from time to time, but, on the whole, graduation was the rule. In 1704 as many as sixty-five took the Master of Arts degree, and in 1705 the extraordinary number of one hundred and four. But after 1708 it was not the interest or concern of any Professor in the Arts Faculty (except the Professor of Natural Philosophy, who got fees for laureating his class) to promote graduation. The old ceremonial of public laureation in the presence of the leading personages of Edinburgh (see above, p. 154) was abandoned, and the degree rapidly fell into disregard. This became most decisively apparent in the middle of the eighteenth century; in 1749 there were only three graduates, and after that date down to the very end of the century only one or at most two persons were admitted in each year to the Master of Arts degree, with the exception of the year 1778, when there was a batch of honorary degrees in Arts. We shall relate presently various efforts made, down to 1858, to reform and revive the Arts degree system, but it will be convenient beforehand to take a glimpse at the teaching given in the Arts Faculty of Edinburgh under the new system; which we are enabled to do owing to the programmes of the classes in the University having been published by the Professors themselves in the *Scots Magazine* for 1741. In that year we find the Professor of Humanity advertising two "colleges" or courses of lectures—the one his "usual college," from the 1st October to the end of July; the other his "private college," from the 1st November to the 1st June. In the former or general class, which seems to have lasted ten months on end, a great deal of work was got through; but it was of a kind belonging rather to a school than to a University. The old entrance examination in Latin, instituted by Rollock, had been abandoned, and the Professor apparently took nothing for granted. He proceeded to ground his class in Latin; he began with Cæsar, and then went on to more difficult authors. He spent "a part of each morning in going over the material part of Ruddiman's *Grammar*, and then Vossius's *Compend of Rhetoric;* after which his students composed orations in Latin, and delivered them before him and the whole class. He likewise read Drummond's *Compend of Ancient and Modern Geography.*" In the private class grammar was no longer taught, but parts of Terence, Cicero, Horace, Tacitus, Suetonius, and Pliny the younger, were read.

Of Greek there were at this time two Professors: Colin Drummond, who had held the Chair of Greek for eleven years, had now retired from the performance of its ordinary functions; and under the honorary title of "Professor of Greek and Philosophy" he gave "lectures for the benefit of students in Physic and Anatomy on Hippocrates' *Aphorisms* and Rufus Ephesius, *De appellationibus corporis humani.*" He had thus become a useful appendage to the Faculty of Medicine. His junior colleague, Robert Law, who was now the real teacher of Greek in the University, did work properly belonging to one of the lower classes in a grammar school. He taught "Greek Grammar; the *New Testament;* a *Delectus* containing some fables of Æsop, some of Lucian's dialogues, two orations of Isocrates, and the *Table* of Cebes; three or four books of Homer's *Iliad;* and Upton's *Collection.*" "In another college for the more advanced" he read and explained critically two books of Homer, some Demosthenes, and two plays of Euripides.

This record of the classical department in the University of Edinburgh in 1741 reflects a state of things which was general at the time in Scotland, which lasted on into the present century, and of which many vestiges still remain. It shows us industrious Professors doing the work of schoolmasters. And the causes of this were two; free entrance to the University, and the deficiency of the grammar schools. Not only had the scheme of the *Book of Discipline* for the creation of higher schools and for a four years' curriculum of Greek for schoolboys (see above, p. 65) never been carried out, but the existing Burgh Schools had actually been depressed by absurd regulations[1] giving to the

---

[1] For instance, in 1672, the following Act was passed by the Privy Council:—"Forasmuch as it is necessary for the advancement of learning that all due encouragement be given to the Professors and

Universities a monopoly of teaching Greek. And these regulations the Universities had with short-sighted selfishness clung to and upheld. It is true that the schoolmasters by degrees came to evade these laws; Colin Drummond, in his paper of 1731 above quoted, indicates that half the Students in the "Semi" class (going straight to Philosophy, and skipping over the Latin and Greek classes) came with a smattering of Greek from the country schools, and Jupiter Carlyle, in his *Autobiography*, said that having "learnt Greek pretty well at school," he omitted this subject altogether from his University curriculum (1735). Still the grammar schools were poor, and there was no idea throughout Scotland in the last century of the greatness of Hellenic culture. The Universities could not overtake the deficiencies of the schools, or turn out a great classical scholar to be afterwards Professor, and so the level of classical learning was kept down throughout the

---

Masters of Universities and Colleges, and that the practice of some persons in taking upon them without warrant or allowance of any in authority to draw together numbers of scholars and to teach them those languages and parts of Philosophy which are proper to be taught in Universities, is contrary to the Laws of this Kingdom, and tends accordingly to the prejudice of Universities and Colleges by rendering some of the Professors therein altogether useless: Therefore, we the Lords of the Privy Council do hereby prohibit and discharge all persons whatsoever, who are not publicly authorised or allowed, conform to the Act of Parliament, to gather together any number of scholars and to teach them Philosophy or the Greek language, and grant warrant to direct letters at the instance of the Professors and Masters of Universities or Colleges of this Kingdom against all such persons as contravene this Act, charging them to desist and cease from so doing in time coming, with certification if they fail to give obedience, other letters shall be directed to charge them thereto *simpliciter* under the form of rebellion."

country, and this was especially the case with regard to Greek.[1] The remedy would have been to revert to the old plan of seeking as Professors, scholars who had been educated abroad; this and the reorganising of the relations between the Universities and the schools would have improved the education of Scotland.

The eighteenth century is admitted to have been a very dead and stagnant time in the English Universities, and especially at Oxford. The cause of this was that in Oxford the Colleges had swamped the University, and each College privately taught its own Students through the instrumentality of clerical Fellows only waiting for livings. Of this system general perfunctoriness and lassitude, not to mention "port wine and prejudice," were the natural results. Graduation went on, but it had been reduced to a nonentity: the University was ready to confer a degree upon any one whom any College might recommend.[2] However, all this time the University

---

[1] Scotland during the sixteenth and seventeenth centuries had a great reputation for its Latin Scholarship. Puffendorff says in his *Introductio ad Historiam Europæam* (1680), p. 201 : "*Est quoque Scotorum gens ingeniorum præstantissimorum ferax et maxime Latinæ linguæ cognitione illustrium.*" And Morhofius *De pura dictione Latina* (1725), p. 41, says : "*In Scota gente plures fuere qui linguæ Latinæ studiosiores fuere quam in Anglis.*" (Both authors are quoted by M'Crie.) But it was one of the points of similarity between the Scotch and the French, that neither of the two nations ever took very kindly to Greek. Whether this was due to external causes, or was connected in some way with other national characteristics, it would be hard to say. But it seems a fact that while German and English scholars have inclined to Hellenism, French and Scottish scholars have till lately confined themselves to Latinity.

[2] The following is Lord Eldon's account of his examination by one of the members of his own College for a degree in Arts :—"I was

of Oxford, though merged into a congeries of Colleges, had its *genius loci*, its beautiful buildings and gardens, and a classical atmosphere, fed from a number of highly-endowed grammar schools, which devoted their whole teaching to Latin and Greek. In all these respects it presented a great contrast to the small, poverty-stricken, ill-housed University of Edinburgh, which stood, "like a lodge in a garden of cucumbers," in a country well-nigh destitute of secondary schools. But, on the other hand, the University of Edinburgh had a great advantage in that it had renounced the collegiate and tutorial method of teaching, and had adopted the plan of teaching by Professors. In this new system lay all the possibilities of specialised learning and science. A Professor appointed to pursue for life a particular subject, and, with the whole University teaching of that subject placed in his hands, was in a very different position in point of authority, responsibility, and incentives to exertion from either a Regent or a College tutor. A man of any ability, placed in a Professorial Chair, would be sure to make something of it. It is true that in the departments of Latin and Greek this advantage was neutralised, because the Professors, owing to the low state of proficiency in their Pupils, were not free to start above the level of school teaching, and had to act the part of tutors

examined in Hebrew and History. 'What is the Hebrew for the place of a skull?' I replied, '*Golgotha*.' 'Who founded University College.' I replied that 'King Alfred founded it.' 'Very well, sir,' said the examiner, 'you are competent for your degree.'" And accordingly, on the 20th February 1770, it was conferred upon him.

COLIN MACLAURIN, MATH. PROF. EDIN.

From an Original Painting in the collection of the Earl of Buchan

instead of that of professors. But in the other departments of the Arts Faculty this depressing influence was not felt, and in them it was shown that the University of Edinburgh had caught, more quickly and effectually than the English Universities, both the Baconian impulse and the Newtonian impulse.

We see this from the rich programme of Mr. Colin M'Laurin, F.R.S., Professor of Mathematics, published in the *Scots Magazine* in 1741. He gave "every year three Colleges, and sometimes a fourth, upon such of the abstruse parts of the Science as were not explained in the former three." The first course contained: Demonstrations of the ground of Vulgar and Decimal Arithmetic; Six books of Euclid; Plane Trigonometry and use of tables of Logarithms, Sines, etc.; Surveying, Fortification, and other practical parts; the elements of Algebra; and a lecture on Geography once a fortnight.

The second course consisted of: Algebra; the Theory and Mensuration of Solids; Spherical Trigonometry, the doctrine of the Sphere, Dialling, and other practical parts; Conic Sections, with the theory of Gunnery; the elements of Astronomy and Optics.

"He begins the third College" (says the *Scots Magazine*) "with Perspective; then treats more fully of the Astronomy and Optics. Afterwards he prelects on Sir Isaac Newton's *Principia*, and explains the direct and inverse method of Fluxions. At a separate hour he begins a College of Experimental Philosophy, about the middle of December, which continues thrice every week till the beginning of April ; and at proper hours of the night describes the constellations, and shows the planets by telescopes of various kinds." All this busy teaching of important and interesting subjects was comprised in the time between the 1st November and the 1st May, so that the Professor left himself six months in the year for his own researches.

In the old Regenting times in Edinburgh "Natural Philosophy" had meant the *Physical Lectures* of Aristotle and the *Sphere* of Sacrobosco. In 1741 things were different; the following is a list of the text-books and subjects which Mr. Robert Stewart, Professor of Natural Philosophy, undertook to teach:—Dr. John Keill's *Introductio ad veram Physicam;* Mechanics from several other authors; "Hydrostatics and Pneumatics from a manuscript of the Professor's own writing;" Dr. David Gregory's *Optics;* Sir Isaac Newton's *Of Colours;* the several parts of the Eye, with their uses, and the Phenomena of Vision ; the different kinds of Microscopes and Telescopes ; Dr. David Gregory's *Astronomy;* some propositions of Newton's *Principia;* Astronomical Observations, both ancient and modern ; exhibitions of experiments in Mechanics, Hydrostatics, Pneumatics, and Optics. All which was clear of Mediævalism and the Ptolemaic system, and was essentially modern and progressive.

In the phraseology of those days, what we call the "Professor of Logic and Metaphysics" was styled the "Professor of Rational and Instrumental[1] Philosophy." The course given by this Professor (Mr. John Stevenson) in 1741 lasted nearly eight months, and comprised the following text-books and subjects:—*Heineccii Elementa Philosophiæ rationalis;* an abridgment of Locke's *Essay on the Human Understanding;* "Metaphysics, in lectures upon De Vries' *Ontologia;*" the grounds of criticism in lectures upon Longinus *On Sublimity*, and the *Poetic* of Aristotle. And he gave a separate "college" on the History of Philosophy, with *Heineccii Historia Philosophica* as a text-book. The Students had to defend and impugn Theses, as an exercise in the art of reasoning. This course of teaching seems to have been based partly on Dutch systems of Philosophy, partly upon Locke. Though Rhetoric was not specified in the title of Stevenson's Chair, it belonged to it; and the most valuable part of his teaching consisted in his lectures on the grounds of criticism, of which a further account will be given.

Last in the Arts Faculty came the Professor of Moral Philosophy, or as he then called himself, the "Professor of Pneumatical and Ethical Philosophy." We have had previously two mentions of "Pneumatics" as a branch of Mechanics,—the doctrine of the air; but now we have the term used, as in the language of the Schoolmen, to denote the doctrine

---

[1] "Instrumental," of course, referred to the term *Organum*, given to the logical treatises of Aristotle,—Logic being regarded as the instrument of thought and science.

of spiritual substances, such as God, the Angels, and the souls of men. The first branch, then, of the teaching of this Professor (Dr. John Pringle) was a metaphysical, and perhaps mystical, system of Natural Theology, for which he mentions no textbooks. His second branch was Moral and Political Philosophy, deduced chiefly from Cicero, Marcus Antoninus, Puffendorff, and Lord Bacon, and "illustrated with an account of the rise and fall of the ancient governments of Greece and Rome, and a view of that form of government which took its rise from the irruptions of the Northern nations." The course lasted for six months, and the Students had to write and deliver discourses upon points of " Pneumatical " or Moral Philosophy. It is striking that all through these programmes there is no mention of Aristotle. The reaction against the old system of Regenting had been complete. The Arts Faculty of the University of Edinburgh (with the exception of its classical department) had been remodelled after the example of Leyden and Utrecht. And in supplement to the Dutch influence, it borrowed inspirations from Bacon, Newton, and Locke. Its teaching during the latter half of the eighteenth century was decidedly fresher than that of Oxford.

We have not only the programmes of these old Professors in the Arts Faculty for our information, but it so happens that we possess a lively commentary on their personal performances in the shape of the reminiscences of Dr. Alexander Carlyle, who was a Student in Arts and Divinity at the University from November 1735 to April 1743, and who records without reserve his impression of the various Professors. He approved of Ker (Professor of Latin) as "very much master of his subject." M'Laurin he found "the clearest and most agreeable lecturer in Mathematics" that he had ever heard. Stewart, Professor of Natural Philosophy, was "worn out with age and had never excelled." Colin Drummond, who was still Professor of Greek in 1735-36, was "an old sickly man who could seldom attend, and used substitutes," so that Carlyle, who "had learnt Greek pretty well at school," omitted this subject. From Stevenson's class in Logic and Rhetoric Carlyle thought that he got more benefit than from any of the other classes; and this he thought due to the judiciousness of the Professor, and also to "the effect which criticism and rational Logic have upon the opening mind." He did not think much of Pringle's course in Moral Philosophy, except for the elegant Latin address which he gave once a week. Carlyle's remarks point to one disadvantage under which the University, down to 1858, continued to suffer; namely, the want of a system of pensions which would have enabled superannuated Professors to retire from duties for which they were no longer competent.

The Arts Faculty of the University had been constituted by the creation of five Professorships in 1708; but their number was increased in 1760 by the addition of a Chair of Rhetoric and *Belles Lettres*.

This came to pass in the same way in which several other Chairs in other Faculties were established; namely, that when some new subject had been successfully taught in the City the Town Council recognised it and dubbed the teacher of it "Professor," without giving him any salary, and leaving him to make the best of his position. In 1748 Lord Kames had induced Adam Smith to give a set of lectures in Edinburgh on Taste and Composition. These lectures gained the Chair of Logic at Glasgow for Adam Smith in 1751. A successor to him, as lecturer in Edinburgh, appeared in the person of Mr. Watson, afterwards the historian of Philip II. In 1758 he was promoted to the Chair of Logic at St. Andrews. And on the 11th December 1759 Dr. Hugh Blair, Minister of St. Giles, with the consent of the Senatus and Town Council, began to read lectures on Rhetoric and *Belles Lettres* within the walls of the College. Next year the patrons appointed him Professor, but without salary. His courses, however, were so well attended, and excited so much interest, that an application was made to the Crown to endow and assume the patronage of the Chair. This was done, and in 1762 George III. granted a commission to Dr. Hugh Blair as Regius Professor of Rhetoric, with a salary of £70 per annum out of Bishops' Teinds, a convenient remnant of the old Episcopal Church of Scotland, which was used for the endowment of several Professorships. The introduction of this new Chair made a change in the teaching of the Arts Faculty, for since 1708 Rhetoric had been attached to the Chair of Logic, but after 1760 it became the province of a separate Professor, and thus came to embrace a systematic course of lectures upon English literature. And the Arts curriculum thus made up remained unaltered, except so far as regards the proclivities and the calibre of the successive Professors, until very recent times.

But when we speak of a curriculum it must be remembered that as soon as graduation fell into disregard no such thing as a curriculum could really continue to exist. The main subjects of Arts teaching were there, but each Student attended such classes as he or his friends might think advisable. The Senatus Academicus, however, from time to time, made valiant, though abortive, attempts to revive an interest in graduation. In November 1738, "It being represented by the Principal (Wishart *secundus*) that some Students of Philosophy, who had been conversing with him and some of the Professors, were willing to print and defend Theses publicly in order to their receiving the degree of M.A., *viz.*, Hugh Blair,[1] William Mackenzie, John Wotherspoon, William Cleghorn, and Nathaniel Mitchell,—this University meeting unanimously agreed and allowed the same, as being a probable mean of retrieving the honours of that Degree; and for the encouragement of any who shall be at the charges of this public trial (*i.e.* printing their Theses)

---

[1] Afterwards Professor of Rhetoric. Wotherspoon became famous as a writer and preacher at Paisley and in America.

the Masters are resolved that they shall be eased of the Promoter's fees and other College dues." And on the 23d February 1739 the five candidates mentioned in the above Minute having printed Theses and publicly defended the same—each of the four candidates impugning the fifth—"in a public and frequent meeting" in the Common Hall, were all graduated by the Principal.

It will be observed that this qualification for a degree was an entirely novel one. In lieu of passing an examination each candidate was to print and defend a Thesis. This idea seems to have been borrowed from the Faculty of Medicine, for the old custom in the Arts Faculty had been that the Regent should promulgate a Thesis which each of his pupils was bound to defend. But now each candidate for a degree in Arts was invited to draw up his own Thesis and defend it. However, this exercise seems to have been a voluntary one in 1738, obtained by private arrangement with some clever Students. The Senatus at the same time drew up a new set of rules for graduation in Arts, in which they improved on the system introduced by the Town Council in 1708. They enacted that "none shall be admitted to the degree of Master of Arts unless they have studied three years in Philosophy, either here or in some other University, during which time they shall be obliged to have attended on the Mathematics and Moral Philosophy as well as the Semi and Magistrand class (see above, p. 264); and unless they undergo a public examination upon their Greek and all parts of Philosophy, to be conducted in the Common Hall by at least two Masters of the Faculty of Arts and in the presence of two or three more of the Professors." By this rule attendance on the classes of Mathematics and Moral Philosophy was to be made compulsory. The conditions thus laid down for a degree were good enough; but how if no one cared to obtain the degree?

In order to secure some candidates the Senatus tried to make Arts graduation compulsory for those who were going to enter the Ministry. They resolved " that the Professor of Divinity be enjoined that he shall receive no new Students of Divinity, nor consider them as scholars under his care, who cannot produce a certificate for having got the degree in Arts; and that such as are already listed students in Divinity shall have the degree gratis; and that the Rev. Professor of Divinity should advise such students to take the degree for a good example in this matter." This was a good intention, and had the rule issued from the General Assembly of the Church of Scotland it would doubtless have been efficacious. Coming merely from the Senatus it appears to have had no permanent effect.[1] Indeed

[1] Some of the Divinity Students of the time seem to have availed themselves of the offer of Senatus to give them degrees, *ex gratia*, without examination. Among these was probably John Home, the author of *Douglas*, who graduated in 1742. Certainly "Jupiter" Carlyle, who graduated in 1743, must have got his degree in this way. He had enrolled himself as a Divinity Student in 1738-39, and therefore was among the number of those to whom the degree was offered. See his *Autobiography*, p. 52. He never speaks of having been examined in the University.

it may be doubted whether the Senatus Academicus could legally impose conditions on persons wishing to prepare for the Ministry. Unless the General Assembly ratified those conditions they would certainly have no validity. It would probably have been better for the Church of Scotland if all entering the Ministry during the eighteenth century had been obliged to graduate in Arts; but perhaps the General Assembly thought that to enact this would be making the Universities too important. They probably remembered the words of warning addressed to their predecessors by John Knox on his death-bed: "Above all things preserve the Kirk from the bondage of the Universities. Persuade them to rule themselves peaceably, and order the schools in Christ; but never subject the pulpit to their judgment, neither yet exempt them from your jurisdiction."[1]

Arts graduation, then, being unpatronised by the Church, rapidly fell to zero. But in 1778 there appears to have been a repetition of what occurred in 1738, for the Professors found four of the Students willing to prepare and defend Theses.[2] The Senatus marked the occasion by conferring honorary M.A. degrees on three of their own body who had not

[1] Letter of John Knox to the General Assembly at Perth, on 5th August 1572—the last he wrote. See Laing's *Knox*, vi. p. 619.
[2] These were William Greenfield (afterwards Professor of Rhetoric), John Erskine, Alexander Mitchell, and Joseph Ewart. The subjects of their Theses are recorded:—1. *De methodis Exhaustionum atque Rationum primarum et ultimarum.* 2. *De Sermonis natura et indole.* 3. *De Inductione.* 4. *De Causis Eloquentiæ.* Each of these is styled "*Dissertatio Inauguralis.*"

previously graduated: Dalzel, Professor of Greek; Dugald Stewart, then Professor of Mathematics; and Bruce, Professor of Logic. They also drew up afresh elaborate regulations for a private and also a public examination of candidates for degrees. In the latter a Thesis or Dissertation on some point of literature or science was to be recited by the Student, with *annexa* or propositions attached to it, on which he was to be questioned. All which became absolutely a dead letter.

From this time onwards, as all desire for the M.A. degree seemed to have expired, attendance on the Arts classes became purely voluntary, except so far as the General Assembly should choose to interfere by regulating the education of aspirants to the Ministry. The General Assembly have never to the present day made graduation in Arts necessary for ordination; but they did require attendance on the Arts classes. In 1776 it was enacted that "none be admitted to trials in order to be licensed but such as have produced to the Professor of Divinity, at the time of being enrolled" (as Divinity Students) "either a diploma of Master of Arts or a certificate bearing that they have gone through a full course of philosophy at the College," the classes of "which the student must attend in such order as is prescribed" in his own University. The Church then left something to be decided by the Universities. And accordingly the question arose, and gave matter for much inter-University discussion, as to what should be "the Course of Philosophy" prescribed to persons wishing to become Divinity Students. The University of Glasgow in 1803 tried to get it laid down that the course was and always had been one of three sessions. But the other Universities carried against them the resolution that no one should be admitted to the M.A. degree who had not attended in separate sessions—(1) Greek; (2) Logic; (3) Moral Philosophy; (4) Natural Philosophy; and that this course should be required from Students previous to their enrolment in the Divinity Hall. It seems curious that the Universities of Scotland should have agreed upon a course which made Natural Philosophy compulsory without making any provision for the study of Mathematics, so necessary as a basis for Natural Philosophy. But in 1809-10 the Senatus of the University of Edinburgh, after much consideration and the report of a Committee, resolved to make attendance on the Mathematical class necessary for future Students of Divinity. And so matters rested with the Arts Faculty, the authority of the Church over a section of the Students being a certain assistance towards filling their classes. In 1812 the Senatus appointed a Committee to draw up new statutes for degrees in Arts, "the former ones having so conspicuously failed." But no result came of this, and graduation in Arts had to wait for the Royal Commission of 1826 and the Executive Commission of 1858 for its revival.

II. The Arts Faculty of the University of Edinburgh, in contradistinction to the Regents or Tutors of the College, was completely founded, as we have seen, in 1708. The commencement of a Faculty of Laws had been made a year previously by the creation of a Regius Professorship of Public Law in 1707 (above, p. 232), and the establishment of that Faculty was completed during the first quarter of the eighteenth century. It may appear surprising that the Metropolis of Scotland, and the seat of the highest Law Courts, should have been left so long without any school for Legal Science, so that those wishing to qualify themselves as lawyers had still to go to Utrecht, Leyden, Groningen, or Halle, as in former times Scotchmen had betaken themselves for the same purpose to Paris and Orleans. Long previously, in the sixteenth century, there had been two attempts made, both without effect, to establish the teaching of Law in Edinburgh. The first was Bishop Reid's bequest (1558) for the creation of a College of Arts and Law, which came to nothing. The second was the wise and liberal movement of the College of Justice (1590) for the creation of a Professorship of Laws, which, by causes now inscrutable, perhaps by the prejudiced opposition of James VI. (above, p. 188), was frustrated. By the end of the seventeenth century the want of home teaching in the Civil Law and Scots Law was sufficiently felt to induce some of the Advocates to meet the demand by giving private lectures on these subjects. In 1698 an Act of the Scottish Parliament appointed Alexander Cunningham " Professor of the Civil Law in Scotland." But this was a very curious transaction, the particulars of which shall be recounted in an Appendix.¹ Suffice it here to say that Cunningham never taught Civil Law, and was not intended to do so; his Professorship was a mere honorary title, and he had no connection whatever with the University. It is said that John Spottiswoode (great-grandson of Archbishop Spottiswoode; born 1667; educated at the College of Edinburgh; and afterwards a Law Student at Leyden; admitted Advocate 1696; and Keeper of the Advocates' Library from 1703 till 1728) "had the honour of being the first who opened schools, in his own house indeed, for teaching professedly the Roman and the Scottish Laws, which he continued to teach at Edinburgh, though not in the University, for six-and-twenty years."²

Spottiswoode's example was followed by others; one of these was James Craig, who had been for some years lecturing upon Civil Law, when, in 1710, the Town Council determined to take him up into the University. They elected and appointed him Professor of Civil Law, and assigned him a classroom. "But in regard there is no foundation of salary to the said Professorship," the Council declared that "he is not to expect any salary as Professor aforesaid. And the said Mr. James Craig compearing accepted his office in the terms above mentioned, and gave his oath *de fideli administratione.*"

The Chair of Civil Law was thus started by the Town Council, as the first Chairs of Medicine had

---

¹ See Appendix I. ALEXANDER CUNNINGHAM.
² Chalmers' *Life of Thomas Ruddiman* (1795), p. 35.

been, without any salary attached. It seems, however, to have been a working Chair from the commencement.[1] Craig held it from 1710 till 1732, and it was only during the first seven years of that time that he remained without a salary. In 1716 an Act of Parliament (3d George I. *cap.* 5) "for continuing the Duty of two pennies Scots, or one sixth of a penny sterling, on every pint of ale and beer that shall be vended and sold within the City of Edinburgh, for the benefit of the said City," specified among the objects to which the Duty was to be applied, the "settling a salary upon the Professor of Law in the University of Edinburgh, and his successors in office, not exceeding £100 per annum," to commence from the 11th November 1717. And the Act of 1722 (9th George I. *cap.* 14), for further renewing this Duty, renewed also the assignment of £100 for the salary of the "Professor of Civil Law," as he was now more accurately designated. In addition it provided for the payment of £100 yearly to a "Professor of Universal Civil History and Greek and Roman Antiquities, in the said University;" and of £100 yearly to a "Professor of Scots Law." And the same Act prescribed the mode in which future vacancies in these three Chairs of Civil Law, Scots Law, and Universal History were to be filled up, namely, the Faculty of Advocates were in each case to nominate and present to the

---

[1] Craig had two courses, one of *Institutes*, another of *Pandects;* for the latter he used as a text-book Van Eck's *Principia*, his own interleaved copy of which is in the library at Riccarton.

Town Council a leet of two persons, from whom the Council were to be bound to choose one and admit him to the vacant Professorship.

The Chair of Universal History, which in 1722 was placed on a permanent footing by Act of Parliament, had been established with a temporary endowment of £50 a year by the Town Council in 1719. The Order which they passed on the subject is not without interest. They say: "Considering the great advantages that arise to the nation from the encouragement of learning by the establishment of such professions (professorships) in our College, as enable youth to study with equal advantages at home as they do abroad, and considering the advantages that arise to this City in particular from the reputation that the Professors of the liberal Arts and Sciences have justly acquired to themselves in the said College; and that a profession of Universal History is extremely necessary to complete the same, this profession being very much esteemed and the most attended of any one profession at all the Universities abroad, and yet nowhere set up in any of our Colleges in Scotland," etc.—"they agree that a Professor of Universal History be established in the College of this City." And they then proceeded to nominate and elect Mr. Charles Mackie to the Professorship thus created.

The terms of this resolution, with its comparison of the Universities of Scotland, into none of which had the teaching of History been introduced, with "the Universities abroad," where History is "very much esteemed," and the classes in it "the most attended"—seem to reflect the mind of Carstares. It is true that he had died more than three years previously to this act of the Town Council. But the influence which he had exercised lived after him. And the fact that Charles Mackie, the first Professor of History, was the nephew of Carstares, suggests the belief that the arrangement made in 1719 was only the carrying out of measures which Carstares had quietly urged upon the Town Council. In all probability Carstares was greatly instrumental in founding both the Arts Faculty and the Faculty of Laws, and we may conjecture that he wished to bring in the study of Universal History as one of "the liberal Arts and Sciences." This last object has been frustrated owing to a certain legal complexion having been given to the Chair of History from the commencement. Mackie, being an Advocate, devoted part of his course to lecturing upon the law procedure of the Ancients, and got himself styled in the Act of 1722 "Professor of Universal Civil History and *Greek and Roman Antiquities.*" At the same time the patronage of the Chair was virtually placed in the hands of the Faculty of Advocates, which meant that the chair should always be filled by an Edinburgh Advocate. The Chair of History has never taken its proper place as a new and important school in the Faculty of Arts. It has always tended to serve as an appendage to the Faculty of Laws. And it will be seen hereafter that this tendency was confirmed by the Commission of 1858, which assigned to it Constitutional Law and History as its distinctive province.

There was yet another Chair in the Faculty of Laws, which at the request of the Town Council had been provided with a salary of £100 a year by the Act of 1722. This was the Chair of Scots Law, which the Town Council founded on the 28th November 1722 much in the same way as they had founded the Chair of Civil Law, that is to say, by taking up into the University an individual who had been already lecturing on the subject outside. Alexander Bayne, Advocate, "represented how much it would be for the interest of the Nation and of this City to have a Professor of the Law of Scotland placed in the University of this City, not only for teaching the Scots Law, but also for qualifying of Writers for His Majesty's Signet." Whereon the Council, "being fully apprised of the fitness and qualifications of Mr. Alexander Bayne of Rives, Advocate, to discharge such a province, elect him to be Professor of the Law of Scotland in the University[1] of this City."

During the remainder of the eighteenth century the Laws Faculty consisted of three Professors (of Public, Civil, and Municipal Laws), and besides them there was the Professor of History, part of whose teaching was for the benefit of future lawyers. If we look at the programmes of 1741, as preserved in the *Scots Magazine*, we observe that the then incumbents of those chairs (who had each in early life

[1] They here echo the terms used in Bayne's petition.

studied Jurisprudence at Leyden[1]) leant very much to Dutch authorities. Thus George Abercromby, "Professor of the Law of Nature and Nations" (as he called himself), lectured upon Grotius' *De jure belli et pacis;* and Thomas Dundas, Professor of Civil Law, took Van Muyden's *Compend* as his text-book in lecturing upon the *Institutes* of Justinian, and Voet's *Compend* in lecturing on the *Pandects.* John Erskine, "Professor of the Scots or Municipal Law," not being able to draw from a foreign source, took as his text-book Sir George Mackenzie's *Institutions.* Charles Mackie, who simply styles himself "Professor of History," taking as his text-book *Tursellini Epitome Historiarum,* seems to have given a full and valuable course upon Universal History, "adducing the authority of the best historians;" "referring to remarkable passages in the *Grand Corps Diplomatique,* Rymer's *Fœdera,* and other vouchers;" and "taking occasion to detect many vulgar errors in History." He also gave "a separate college on the Roman Antiquities," especially in reference to the Law Procedure of the Romans. Mackie was the only one among the Professors of 1741 who notified that all his lectures would be delivered in Latin, though some of the others[2] followed this practice,

---

[1] See the *Album Studiosorum Academiæ Lugduno Batavæ,* 1575-1875, in which their several names appear.

[2] Dr. Somerville, who attended the University 1756-59 complained of Dr. Stevenson's Logic lectures being delivered in Latin and difficult to follow. He also mentions that the lectures in Church History "were composed in Latin ; but after the first the Professor began every prelection by recapitulating the preceding one in English."—*My own Life and Times,* p. 20.

which soon fell into disuse. He decidedly belonged to both Faculties, Arts and Laws, but, as has been already observed, his Chair afterwards got a narrower and more exclusively legal province. There was no graduation in Laws, except what was honorary, in the eighteenth century, but there was regular teaching in Civil and Municipal Law; the teaching of Public Law was from the first intermittent, and, as we shall see hereafter, the Chair ultimately was treated as a sinecure, and from 1831 it was left vacant until 1862, when it was revived by the Commission appointed under the Act of 1858.

At the close of the last century two proposals were made for adding Chairs to the Faculty of Laws, and it may at first sight seem strange that both these proposals met with opposition from the Senatus Academicus. But such was then and has often been the operation of the University system in Scotland, where, each Chair being slenderly endowed in the matter of fixed stipend, each Professor is chiefly dependent on the fees of his Students, and jealously guards against any encroachment upon the monopoly which he enjoys of teaching his subject. This feeling, as we shall see in numerous instances, gives rise to an extreme conservatism, which resists even the most desirable changes.

On the 12th December 1796, it having been reported to the Senatus Academicus of the University of Edinburgh that the Society of Writers to the Signet had created among themselves a Lectureship on Conveyancing, and contemplated applying to the Crown to erect that Lectureship into a Professorship in the University, the Senatus "unanimously disapproved of the proposal, as neither conducive to the improvement of the course of Law Studies, nor consistent with due regard to the rights and interests of the established Professor of Scots Law."

In June 1798 Dr. Duncan, Professor of the Institutes of Medicine, memorialised the Town Council, stating that he had been in the habit of giving one lecture per week on Medical Jurisprudence, and recommending them to found a Professorship of the subject. This move, which in itself was a very proper one, was made by Dr. Duncan in the interest of his son, who afterwards became a distinguished Professor. But when the Senatus were invited to give their opinion on the proposal, they at once condemned it on the ground that "the multiplying of Professorships, especially on new subjects of education, does not promise to advance the prosperity or dignity of the University;" and that the most essential parts of Medical Jurisprudence might be taught by existing Professors.

The Senatus by this course of action were able to delay, but not ultimately to prevent, the additions to the University staff which had been proposed. The Town Council and the Crown Officers took a more enlightened view of the question; and on the 1st May 1807 a Commission came down from George III. creating "a Professorship of Medical Jurisprudence and Medical Police," "as taught in every University of reputation on the Continent of Europe," with an endowment of £100 a year out of Bishops' Rents; and appointing Dr. Andrew Duncan, junior, to be the first Professor. On condition, however, that he was not to interfere with any of the courses of lectures now delivered in the said University. Principal Baird, not satisfied with this proviso, read a paper reserving to the Senatus or any Professor the right of protesting in future against the establishment of a Regius Professorship of Medical Jurisprudence. This, of course, was *brutum fulmen*, and a Chair valuable to Students both of Law and of Medicine was added to the University.

The second proposed Chair was longer delayed, and it was not till 1825 that the Society of Writers to the Signet, having petitioned the Town Council to turn their Lectureship on Conveyancing into a Professorship, and having undertaken to provide a perpetual salary of at least one hundred guineas, the Town Council acceded to these terms. Setting aside the objections of the Senatus, they gave a Commission, as Professor, to Macvey Napier, who had acted as Lecturer on Conveyancing since 1816. It was arranged that in future the patrons of the Chair were to be two delegates from the Town Council, two from the Writers to the Signet, and the Deputy Keeper of the Signet.

III. The history of the Medical School of the University of Edinburgh cannot be separated from the history of extra-Academical Medicine as practised and taught in the City. In fact, the course of events was this: a Medical School having been begun to be formed outside the University, some of the members of that School were, first in an honorary way and afterwards more substantively, incorporated into the University as Professors. And so the Medical Faculty of the University had its quasi-fortuitous beginning, from which it grew to be an independent and famous School of Medicine. But one of its greatest advantages has been, that it has continued to be surrounded by extramural rivals, who have kept its Professors up to the mark, and sometimes eclipsed them, and who have always been in training to fill up the ranks of the University whenever vacancies occurred.

It has been observed that though the practice of dissection was legalised in Edinburgh as early as 1505,[1] no progress in Anatomical or Medical Science for nearly two centuries after that period was made in Scotland, owing to the poverty and distracted state of the country; while in Italy, Belgium, Holland, and France, Anatomists of great note were flourishing, and in England Harvey had discovered the circulation of the blood.

But, as we have seen above (pp. 217-226), towards the close of the seventeenth century certain accom-

---

[1] The Charter of the Surgeons and Barbers of Edinburgh, dated 1505, granted them the privilege of having "once in the year a condemned man after he be dead to make anatomy of." See *Historical Sketch of the Edinburgh Anatomical School*, by John Struthers, M.D., Professor of Anatomy in the University of Aberdeen, p. 18, from which the above remark is quoted.

plished physicians, who had been educated abroad, resolved to give a new start to Medicine in Edinburgh. Hence came the establishment of the Physic Garden, and of the College of Physicians; and then the Town Council took in the Keeper of the Physic Garden to be Professor of Botany in their College, and three chief members of the College of Physicians to be Professors of Medicine. These last appointments were almost entirely honorary; class-rooms were provided for the so-called Professors, but teaching was left optional, and certainly none of them taught systematically. This, however, was the tentative outset—a sort of false dawn—of the University Medical School.

The first impulse having come from the newly-created College of Physicians, the second came from the College of Surgeons, who, having got a fresh royal charter in 1694, and also a grant from the Town Council of unowned dead bodies, opened an Anatomical theatre in 1697. But at first they had no special Anatomist; whenever a body was to be dissected they divided it into ten parts, which were dissected and lectured upon during ten[1] successive days by different members of their own body appointed for the purpose. In 1705, however, they adopted a new system by appointing one of their number, Mr. Robert Elliot, to the sole and per-

[1] The Town Council had laid down curious rules for the treatment of subjects. "All the gross intestines" were to be buried within forty-eight hours, and the rest of the body within ten days. And the dissection was to be during the winter season only, from one equinox to the other.

manent charge of teaching Anatomy.[1] Elliot, on his appointment, petitioned the Town Council for some pecuniary encouragement for the task which he had undertaken, stating that he "was of intention to make a public profession and teaching of anatomy for instruction of youth, to serve her Majesty's lieges both at home and abroad, in her armies and fleets, which he hoped, by the blessing of God, would be a mean of saving much money to the nation, expended in teaching anatomy in foreign places, besides the preventing of many dangers and inconveniences to which youth were exposed in their travels to other countries." All which being approved by the Council, they granted the petitioner an allowance of £15 sterling per annum, "as an encouragement to go on in the said profession," but "with the express provision and condition that the petitioner take exact notice and inspection of the order and condition of the rarities of the College; and that an exact inventory be made of the same and given in to the Council." In these informal terms Elliot became incorporated into the Town's College as Professor of Anatomy,[2] with a salary of

[1] It appears that this change was decided on in consequence of a rival teacher of anatomy, not being a member of the College of Surgeons, appearing in the town, and offering to give public demonstrations gratis, if allowed the use of the theatre and dead bodies. See Gairdner's *History of the College of Surgeons*, p. 32.

[2] The terms of the Council's minute (29th August 1705) would seem to imply that Elliot was only appointed Keeper of the Museum in the College. In subsequent minutes, however, he was referred to as "Professor of Anatomy," but without specification as to whether he was a Professor in the College. At last, in 1720, his successors, Drummond and M'Gill, are spoken of in the City Records as "conjoint Professors of Anatomy in this City and College."

£15, all his teaching being done in the theatre of the Surgeons.

The Surgeons themselves appear never to have designated Elliot as "Professor." He was their "public dissector of anatomy." The Town Council, by the charter of James VI., had the sole right of creating Professorships within the City; they made Elliot a Professor, and in 1708 they appointed Adam Drummond, Surgeon Apothecary, to be conjoint Professor with him; and subsequently to this appointment Drummond was admitted by the College of Surgeons to the use of their theatre. On the death of Elliot, in 1716, John M'Gill, Deacon of the Surgeons[1] (answering to the President of the College of Surgeons at the present day), was conjoined with Drummond, and they were styled by the Town Council in 1720 "conjunct Professors of Anatomy in this City and College." Thus, as in the case of Medicine and of Law, so in the case of Anatomy, successful practice or teaching had grown up outside the College, and then the practitioners or teachers were dignified by the Town Council with the title of Professors, and were given a more or less close connection with the College or University.

In the meantime, in a similar way, the impulse coming from without, a Professorship of Chemistry had been created in the University of Edinburgh. This occurred in December 1713; it has been

---

[1] The Deacon of the Surgeons was at this time, and indeed till 1833, a member, *ex officio*, of the Town Council.

observed that in the course of the same year a Chair of Chemistry had been established at Cambridge, and possibly this circumstance may have been present to the mind of Dr. James Craufurd, who had been Boerhaave's pupil at Leyden, and who appears to have made proposals to the patrons of the College that he should be authorised to teach Chemistry in Edinburgh. These advances were graciously received by the Town Council, who, using the same preamble as they had employed in creating the first Medical Professorships in 1685 (that the College of this City had from its origin been erected into a University, etc.), and adding that it was expedient to provide for Scotsmen the means of learning Physic and Chemistry at home, proceeded to "elect, nominate, and choose Dr. James Craufurd to be Professor of Physic and Chemistry in the said University, and appoint convenient rooms to be appropriated to him." They added, as they had done when they consented to make James Craig Professor of Civil Law, that Dr. Craufurd was "not to expect any salary as Professor." These terms were accepted; and in this permissive way the Chair, afterwards made illustrious by the name of Black, came into existence. Craufurd does not appear to have given regular annual courses of Chemistry. It is recorded of him that he gave such courses "sometimes."[1] Perhaps he did not find adequate encouragement from the attendance of Students; and it must be remembered that he was

[1] Bower's *History*, ii. 126 and 170.

Professor of "Physic" also, and may have lectured in that capacity. The specialisation of subjects in the Medical Faculty was as yet only incipient. But the idea of procuring a complete organisation for medical education in Edinburgh had been already conceived by John Monro, a distinguished Army Surgeon of King William's army, who, after much foreign travel and experience, had settled in Edinburgh at the beginning of the century, and was President of the Surgeons in 1712-13. It is said that "about the year 1720 he communicated to the Physicians and Surgeons a plan which he had long formed in his own mind, of having the different branches of Physic and Surgery regularly taught at Edinburgh, which was highly approved by them."[1] But he had already done more than form the plan in his mind; he had taken the first and most important step towards its realisation, by dedicating his only son to the project, and training him from early boyhood to take the lead in its fulfilment. Nobly did Alexander Monro, *Primus*, carry out the ideas and aspirations of his father. And that father is described as long afterwards passing his old age at a country-seat in Berwickshire, happy in the renown of his affectionate son, and in the success of his favourite plan, "the founding of a Seminary of Medical Education in his native country."

The merely *amateur* and perfunctory character of the Professorships of Medicine which had been created by the Town Council in 1685 is clearly

[1] *Life of Alexander Monro*, p. 12.

DR. ALEXANDER MONRO, PRIMUS.

FROM A PORTRAIT BY ALLAN RAMSAY.

proved by the fact that John Monro, some thirty-five years later, thought of establishing *de novo* a Seminary of Medical Education. But this had to be done, and it was done by Alexander Monro, who became in reality the founder of the Medical School, not only of the University, but of the City of Edinburgh. Alexander Monro was born in 1697; and, showing an early enthusiasm for the study of Medicine, was admitted by his father's influence to assist at the post-mortem examinations made by the Surgeons; he learned a little Anatomy from the demonstrations of Drummond and M'Gill, attended some of the occasional courses in Chemistry given by Craufurd, and got some instruction in plants from George Preston, then Keeper of the Physic Garden, and Professor of Botany in connection with the College. Young as he was, he had acquired practical experience in Medicine and Surgery by acting as his father's apprentice.

But all this was insufficient, and at the age of twenty he was sent off to study for two years in London, Paris, and Leyden. In London he studied Anatomy under Cheselden, and the Anatomical preparations which he made there and sent down to Edinburgh were considered so striking that Drummond, the "conjoint Professor of Anatomy in this City and College," declared himself ready to resign his office to the young man, when he should return home—which generous offer, Bower thinks, was suggested to Drummond by his kinsman, George Drummond, then an influential Town Councillor, and afterwards the greatest of the Lord Provosts of Edinburgh. Monro, proceeding to Paris, attended classes in the hospitals, and the Anatomical teaching of M. Bouquet. "At Leyden he became the favourite and admiring pupil of the great Boerhaave."[1] Returning to Edinburgh in the autumn of 1719 he was examined by the College of Surgeons; and then Drummond and M'Gill actually resigned their conjoint Chair in his favour, though he was only twenty-two years of age; and the College of Surgeons having formally recommended him to the Town Council, he was appointed by that body in January 1720 to be "Professor of Anatomy in this City and College," on a salary of £15 sterling per annum.

After eight months spent in preparation, Monro opened his class in the theatre in Surgeons' Hall,[2] in the presence of the Lord Provost and other dignitaries, to a class of fifty-seven Students, who were thenceforth regularly taught from October to May.[3] This class became steadily consolidated: for the first decade of years its average number was 67; for the second decade, 109; for the third, 147. It appears from the City Records that as early as

[1] Struthers, *Historical Sketch*, p. 21.
[2] Built in 1697 on the site of what had been part of the Blackfriars' ground. In this century it was the scene of Robert Knox's teaching. In 1832 the Surgeons removed from it to Nicolson Street, and it then became part of the Old Royal Infirmary, and was used as a fever ward.
[3] Monro's courses were not limited to Anatomy; they included instruction in Surgery and Surgical Treatment, and even some general lectures on Physiology.

during the second session Monro's class had been joined by Students "from all the several parts of Scotland, as also from England and Ireland." Encouraged by this success, Monro applied to the Town Council in 1722 for a permanent status in the University. He naturally wished, and felt it due to himself, that he should hold a position equivalent to that enjoyed by Professors in other Universities, a position of security and independence. But what he asked was contrary to the traditions and instincts of the Town Council, who, partly from the love of authority, but partly also, no doubt, from the mistaken idea[1] that it would be unsafe to grant life-tenure of office to the University teachers, had repeatedly laid down the rule that Regentships and Professorships were tenable only during the pleasure of the patrons; and so lately as August 1719 had reaffirmed this principle in a general Act upon the subject. But now, as if overborne by the brilliancy and success of the young Monro, and probably acting under the advice of George Drummond, they departed from their former rulings, and "for his

[1] Municipal corporations are naturally prone to this idea; they have no great respect for men of learning or science, and they think that such persons should be treated like the *employés* in a mercantile establishment. They forget that anything like insecurity of tenure attached to Professorships, which are seldom well-paid offices, would greatly deter able men from seeking them. The Merchant Company of Edinburgh, who in 1869 liberally founded a Chair of Commercial and Political Economy in the University of Edinburgh, marred their gift to some extent by insisting that each appointment of a Professor to fill the Chair should be only for a period of seven years, though with power of re-election. This practically renders the Professor liable to be dismissed at the end of seven years, if his views, politically or otherwise, shall have displeased the electors.

better encouragement, of new again nominated" Monro "sole Professor of Anatomy within this City and College, and that *ad vitam aut culpam*, notwithstanding any Act of the Council formerly made to the contrary." Thus a most important precedent was laid down, which was never afterwards departed from, altering the whole policy of the Town Council towards the University, and giving Professors a position of independence and respectability which they had never before enjoyed.

The next step in the epoch-making career of Monro was the removal of his Anatomical teaching from the Surgeons' Hall to a theatre within the College buildings. In April 1725, shortly before the close of his annual session, furious indignation was roused in the minds of the lower orders in Edinburgh by the spreading of a report that graves in the Greyfriars Churchyard had been violated by some of his Students, and corpses exhumed for dissection. A formidable mob surrounded Surgeons' Hall threatening its demolition.[1] And nothing but very spirited and energetic measures on the part of the Magistrates could have prevented the wrecking of the Hall, and the destruction of the Anatomical preparations which Monro had during several years laboriously accumulated. There may very likely have been some foundation for the rumour which had excited the public mind. The number of "unowned bodies" in Edinburgh, the population of which was then only 25,000, would be but small, and

[1] Bower, ii. 182.

quite insufficient to supply subjects to a school which was beginning to be enthusiastic in dissection. Even after Elliot had commenced teaching, the want of subjects was felt, and an undoubted case of body-snatching in the Greyfriars Churchyard occurred in 1711, which called forth a strong denunciation from the College of Surgeons. The advent of Monro of course increased the zeal of Anatomical Students: and the Students of all denominations in Edinburgh at that day were a bold and turbulent set. There was an increasing alarm as to what might be done; in 1721 the College of Surgeons ordered a clause to be put into the indentures of apprentices against violation of the churchyards; in 1722 a second case of body-snatching was stated to have taken place, and the clause was made more stringent; in March 1725, just before the tumult above mentioned, the Professor of Anatomy was ordered to report to the College of Surgeons on all bodies received by him, and to obtain permission for their use.[1]

Such was the state of feeling when the Greyfriars Churchyard was again violated, and the mob rushed to Surgeons' Hall to stop the teaching of Anatomy. The tumult was appeased by the Magistrates, who offered "a reward of £20 sterling to those who would discover the persons that were accessory to stealing dead bodies;" and shortly afterwards the session of the Anatomy class came to a close. But it is no wonder that when Monro had again to commence lecturing he should desire to do

[1] Struthers, p. 22.

so in safer quarters. Within the walls of the College, the towered gateway of which was guarded by a Janitor, his theatre and his specimens would not be exposed to that immediate attack by storm with which he had been threatened in Surgeons' Hall. He therefore petitioned the Town Council to allow him a theatre, as Professor of Anatomy, in the University of Edinburgh. And they, entirely meeting his views, "appropriated a fit place in the said University to be adapted to the said theatre for public dissections, and teaching the students under his inspection." And thus the Chair of Anatomy was removed from the premises and the partial control of the College of Surgeons; it ceased indefinitely to belong to "this City and College;" it was localised within the University, and became the Chair which has been subsequently filled by several great Anatomists, worthy followers of Alexander Monro, *Primus*.

There is one contemporary name which can never be dissociated from the achievements of the first Monro, and the establishment of the Medical Faculty of the University, and that is the name of George Drummond,[1] the greatest Ædile that has ever governed the City of Edinburgh, and the wisest and best disposed of all the long list of Town Councillors and Provosts, who during 275 years acted as patrons of the College or University. The Medical Faculty was the creation of the eighteenth century, and it has been the boast and glory of the

[1] See Appendix J. GEORGE DRUMMOND.

University of Edinburgh ever since. Bower says of George Drummond that "from the year 1715 to the time of his death, in 1766, nothing was done in regard to the College without his advice and discretion;" and this period is synchronous with that of the establishment of the Medical Faculty. It seems not too much to say that, but for Drummond, the Medical School of the University might have had a far less auspicious start, and it is even possible that the leading Medical School of Scotland might have been located at Glasgow instead of in the Metropolis. Drummond was greatly instrumental in placing the young Monro in a Professor's Chair, and he afterwards invariably supported and assisted him. And in several other cases, during his fifty years of influence, he recognised genius and fostered it.

There was one especial measure fundamentally necessary to the realisation of John Monro's idea of a Medical Seminary in Edinburgh which was carried out by the conjoint labours of Alexander Monro and George Drummond: and that was the establishment of the Royal Infirmary of Edinburgh. Without a large public hospital of the kind a practical School of Medicine could never have existed, and, on the other hand, such a hospital would be, as it has been, an inestimable boon to the sick and wounded poor. The reasons in favour of such an institution were set forth by Monro in a pamphlet, which was circulated in 1721, but at the time little public encouragement was given to the scheme. In 1725, however, when Drummond became Lord Provost for the first time, he provided a basis for a subscription list by getting some of the funds of a "Scottish Fishery Company," which was then being dissolved, allocated for the establishment of an Infirmary. The College of Physicians took the matter up, and subscriptions for some years continued to flow in. At last, in 1738, the foundation-stone of that building, which was till recently the "Royal Infirmary of Edinburgh," was laid, and a great public enthusiasm on the subject was manifested. Drummond and Monro were appointed "the Building Committee," and they paid the workmen with their own hands. All classes contributed: landowners gave stone; merchants gave timber; farmers lent their carts for carriage of materials; even the masons and other labourers gave one day's work out of the month *gratis*, as it was a building for the benefit of the poor.

In the meantime the Town Council had been taking measures, doubtless under suggestion from the Monros and other leading members of the Physicians and Surgeons, to supplement the teaching of Anatomy and Surgery now provided, and establish the systematic teaching of Medicine. They passed an Act in August 1724 wherein, "considering the great benefit and advantage that would accrue to this City and Kingdom, by having all the parts of Medicine taught in this place; and likewise considering that hitherto the Institutes and Practice of Medicine, though the principal parts thereof, have not been professed or taught in the said College;— therefore they hereby institute and establish the foresaid Profession of the Institutes and Practice of Medicine in their said College, and do elect, nominate, and choose Mr. William Porterfield, Doctor of Medicine in Edinburgh," to be Professor. They granted him all "powers, privileges, and immunities" enjoyed by any other Professor, but at the same time no salary ; and, mindful how the Professorships of Medicine which they had created in 1685 had borne no fruit in the shape of teaching, they inserted the clause that "Dr. Porterfield by his acceptation, binds and obliges himself to give colleges (*i.e.* courses of lectures) regularly, in order to the instructing of students in the said science of medicine."

Even this stringent contract does not appear to have had the desired effect ; there is no evidence that Porterfield ever lectured. The City Records are, as so often happens with them, silent about particulars which one would have expected them to narrate. In about a year and a half after Porterfield's formal appointment, two other Professors were with equal formality appointed to fill his Chair, without any word to indicate how that Chair had become vacant, whether by resignation, or supersession, or how. The facts, however, which Bower has elicited, suggest a conjectural explanation of the matter. Porterfield appears to have been a man of considerable private fortune, of great ability and accomplishments, but with a speculative[1] rather than

---

[1] See Bower's *History*, ii. 200-203. Porterfield brought out in 1713 a mathematical demonstration of the strength of the bones to resist transverse fracture. And in 1759 a *Treatise on the Eye*, in which

a practical turn of mind; more suited to deal with Natural Philosophy in application to Medicine than with the Practice of Physic. And withal, he is said to have been a man of peculiar temper and much self-will. Under all these circumstances it is not difficult to suppose that Porterfield, though he had been warmly recommended by the College of Physicians as one who was "otherwise well qualified, and also disengaged from the necessary business of all other public professions," and though he accepted the compliment implied in his appointment to be Professor of the Institutes and Practice of Medicine, yet, when he came to face the duties of the Chair, found that they would be irksome to him. Being above the necessity of lecturing for fees,—if he found other able Physicians in Edinburgh anxious to do so, he may very likely have stepped aside in their favour, and have signified to the Town Council his resignation of the appointment which they had conferred upon him; though it seems extraordinary that this resignation should not have been recorded.

However this may be, we find four members of the College of Physicians, Drs. John Rutherford, Andrew Sinclair, Andrew Plummer, and John Innes, pressing forward into the breach. What these gentlemen first did was, in November 1724, shortly after the date of Porterfield's appointment, to apply for the keeping and use of the College garden, with

metaphysical and mathematical ideas were combined with anatomical and physiological observations, and which contained no reference to the diseases of the eye.

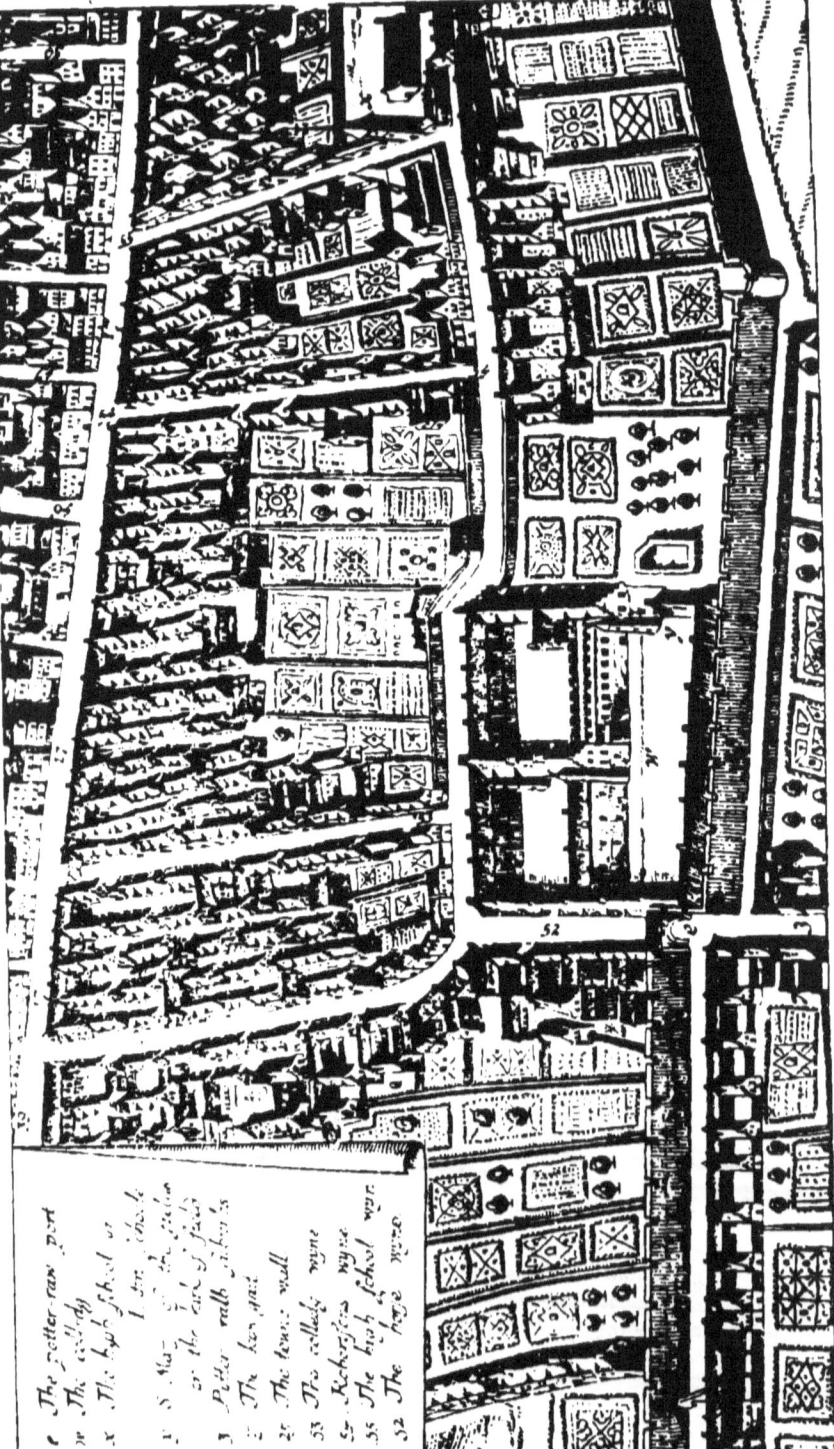

From Gordon of Rothiemay's BIRD'S EYE VIEW, 1646.

the view of rearing pharmaceutical plants therein. They proposed to set up, at their own cost, a chemical laboratory in conjunction with the garden, their object being to supply the apothecaries' shops with drugs. And they undertook to keep and leave the garden in good order if they should be allowed a ten years' lease of it. The College garden was a large space of ground which had belonged to the old Kirk-of-Field, and which ran along the east side of the College, where the causeway and houses of Nicolson Street and South Bridge Street now are, and extending away to join the grounds of the Blackfriars. It is clearly shown in the plan of Edinburgh drawn by Gordon of Rothiemay in 1617 (see opposite). There was also a strip of garden along the south face of the old College buildings, where South College Street now is. The "yard" (or garden) of the College had been hitherto, at least nominally, under the keeping of the Professors of Botany; but the first Professor, Sutherland, had ultimately neglected the College yard. And the four petitioners, in 1724, speak of it as having been "formerly let to Mr. George Preston" (the third Professor of Botany), and as having "for some years lain in disorder." Perhaps the Professor of Botany found the keeping of the Physic Garden of the City sufficient to occupy his whole time, and did not care to provide a second edition of the same in connection with the College. It is indicative of the enterprising spirit of the Physicians in Edinburgh of those days that four of them should have formed themselves into a little company for the production of vegetable drugs from this neglected College yard. The Town Council approved of the proposal, and granted the request of the applicants. An ulterior result of the movement seems to have been to bring the four Physicians into prominence, and into a sort of relationship to the College, which very soon became closer.

In February 1726 Rutherford, Sinclair, Plummer, and Innes presented another petition to the Town Council, "craving the Council to institute the Profession (of Medicine) in the College of Edinburgh, and appoint the petitioners to teach and profess the same." And in their preamble they stated that they had already, "under the Council's protection, undertaken the professing and teaching of Medicine in this City, and, by the encouragement which the Council had been pleased to grant them, had carried it on with some success." Thus Porterfield had mysteriously vanished from the scene; whether he had simply stepped back, on second thoughts, into philosophical retirement, or whether differences had arisen between him and the patrons, we cannot tell; but at all events the coast was clear, and the Town Council were asked to institute Professorships of Medicine, just as if none had hitherto existed. Apparently the petitioners had been supplying Porterfield's place as a lecturer by giving lectures on Medicine in the Town; or, if Porterfield lectured, then they had been playing the part of extra-mural rivals, with the sanction of the Town Council.

That body, in reply, took the same tone as the petitioners had done; they utterly ignored the Commission which they had given to Porterfield only eighteen months before, and enunciated afresh that "it would be of great advantage to this College, City, and Country, that Medicine in all its branches be professed here, by such a number of Professors of that science as may by themselves promote students to their degrees, with as great solemnity as is done in any other College or University at home or abroad." These were important words, and the Act in which they are contained, passed under the Provostship of George Drummond, constituted the charter of the Medical Faculty of the University of Edinburgh. Hitherto there had been isolated measures, and the title of "Professor" had been conferred in an honorary way upon individuals. But now for the first time the Town Council showed that they understood what is necessary to make a University Medical School—namely, a sufficient staff of Professors to instruct Students in all the main branches of Medical Science, and then conduct them to graduation with all the guarantees that the degree of any other University could give. And such a staff the Town Council were now resolved to create.

It is true that prior to 1726 the degree of Doctor of Medicine had not infrequently[1] been

[1] The first Medical degree conferred by the University was in 1705; the second in 1710. Altogether twenty-one degrees were conferred on the recommendation of the College of Physicians prior to 1726, of which, however, two were admissions *ad eundem*, granted to

conferred by "the University of Edinburgh"; but this had been invariably done at the instance and by the recommendation of the Royal College of Physicians. Thus we find a minute of that body, dated 1710, which narrates that "the President and three Fellows of the Royal College of Physicians having been appointed by the said College[1] to take trial of the learning and qualification of Mr. Jonathan Harly, in order to his obtaining the degree of Doctor of Medicine, having discoursed with the said Mr. Harly, and prepared several questions, both in the theory and practice of Medicine, do find him a man of good learning, and sufficiently qualified for obtaining the degree aforesaid; and therefore we recommend him to the Reverend and Honourable the Principal, Professors, and Masters of the University of Edinburgh, that they will be pleased to confer the degree of Doctor of Medicine on the said Mr. Jonathan Harly." One peculiarity here was that the recommendation for a degree was made, not to the Town Council as patrons, not to the Lord Provost as Rector or Chancellor of the University, but directly to the Principal and Professors as the degree-giving body, and the fountain of Academical honour. And in this understanding

Doctors of other Universities. It is noted in the Graduation Book that no Thesis was produced by any of the twenty-one persons thus graduated.

[1] That is to say, the Royal College of Physicians. These words, however, were endeavoured to be wrested, in an action of the Senatus Academicus against the Town Council, so late as 1850, to mean "that these Examiners were selected by the Principal and Professors of the College" of Edinburgh.

the Town Council appear to have tacitly acquiesced. It is therefore the more surprising that on other occasions they should have refused to recognise that the Town's College contained within itself a "Faculty" or Senatus Academicus.

But in 1726 they were bent on strengthening their College and raising it to the dignity of "any College or University whatsoever." And especially they resolved to give it the means of educating and examining for itself candidates for its degrees in Medicine. They proceeded, accordingly, to "unanimously constitute, nominate, and appoint, Drs. Andrew Sinclair and John Rutherford, to be Professors of the Theory and Practice of Medicine; and Drs. Andrew Plummer and John Innes, to be Professors of Medicine and Chemistry[1] in the College of Edinburgh; with full power to all of them to profess and teach Medicine in all its branches—to examine candidates, and to do every other thing requisite and necessary to the graduation of doctors of medicine." They conferred these appointments *ad vitam aut culpam;* but they were to be unaccompanied by any salary out of the City's revenues.

This Act of 1726 not only established the Medical Faculty of the University by creating four Professorships in Medicine, in addition to the Chair of Anatomy already existing, but it also for the first time recognised on the part of the Town Council

[1] Craufurd, who in 1713 had been appointed "Professor of Chemistry in the University of Edinburgh," must now have either deceased, or else have voluntarily discontinued his occasional courses of lectures (see above, p. 297).

the right of the Principal and Professors to "deliberate and vote on the affairs of general concern to the College." Of course the practice of so deliberating and voting had long existed, but it had never been recognised, and on one occasion, at least, the right had been formally denied (see above, pp. 240-246). But now the Council, being in a more reasonable frame of mind, recognised the practice, and proceeded to regulate it by ordaining that of the four new Professors "two only[1] shall at one time have the privilege of voting with the other Professors in College affairs." They were to enjoy this privilege in alternate years; first, one Professor of the Theory and Practice of Medicine, and one Professor of Medicine and Chemistry were to be privileged for a year to deliberate and vote, and then for the next year they were to be disfranchised, and the other pair were to come in. The term "Senatus Academicus" is never used in the Act, but the existence of such a body is clearly implied by its provisions. And, as if acting on the encouragement which they had received, the Principal and Professors met in the subsequent October as a *Senatus Academicus*, and having recognised the five Medical Professors as a Medical Faculty, entered them as such in their minutes.

The Town Council had not exactly defined the provinces of the four Professors whom they appointed; it appears, however, that while Dr.

[1] The reason for limiting the new Medical votes in the College Councils is not known. Perhaps the Arts Professors may have made a representation on the subject. The restriction was removed by an Act of the Town Council on the 26th February 1729.

Plummer lectured on Chemistry, or rather Chemical Pharmacy, Dr. Innes ignored the term "Chemistry" in his commission, and simply taught the Practice of Physic conjointly with Dr. Rutherford, who lectured on Boerhaave's *Aphorismi de Cognoscendis et Curandis Morbis.* Dr. Sinclair, who had chosen the Institutes of Theory of Medicine as his province, took the *Institutiones Medicæ* of the same author for his text-book. There was no longer any *dilettante*-ism about the Medical Professorships in the College; systematic courses were henceforth delivered, though for a time there was a want of originality about them, as they were entirely a reproduction of the system of Boerhaave.[1]

On the same day (9th February 1726) on which the Town Council added four new Professors to the staff of the College they also proceeded to appoint a Professor of Midwifery, not, however, for the College, but for the City. It was hardly contemplated in those days that Medical Students should go through a course of obstetrics, the whole practice and profession of which was then left to females. But one Mr. Joseph Gibson, a Surgeon of Edinburgh, had outstepped his era, and had for some time practised this important art in the town of Leith, and, supported by the recommendations of members of the Colleges of Physicians and Surgeons, he now applied to the Town Council to create him a Pro-

[1] The notices in the *Scots Magazine* of the courses of lectures in the University of Edinburgh for 1741 do not contain any particulars as to the teaching of the Medical Professors beyond what is above given.

fessor, which they did, nominating him "Professor of Midwifery in this City and privileges," with power to him "to profess and teach the said art, in as large an extent as it is taught in any city or place where this profession is already instituted." And with this appointment they joined a system of rules for the regulation of the practice of Midwifery in Edinburgh. Here again we have an instance of a branch of study elevated into a Professorship owing to suggestions from without. As Bower says: "This institution, like every other connected with the history of Medicine in Edinburgh, originated with the colleges of Physicians and Surgeons." At first, as in other cases, the Professorship of Midwifery was general and unattached, but subsequently it was incorporated into the University. On the death of Gibson in 1739 he was succeeded by Mr. Robert Smith, who received a commission appointing him "Professor of Midwifery in this City's College," "with the same privileges and immunities which the other Professors in the said College do enjoy, or that are known to appertain to a Professor of Midwifery in any other well regulated city or place."[1]

The next great step in the progress of the Medi-

---

[1] The researches of Professor A. R. Simpson (see his Introductory Lecture on the *History of the Chair of Midwifery*, etc., Edinburgh, 1883, pp. 9, 10), lead to the conclusion that Joseph Gibson was the first person who ever received the title of "Professor of Midwifery." Professor Simpson says that none of the title-pages of the obstetric treatises prior to 1726 indicate that the authors had that title. And he refers to Killian's *Geburtslehre*, p. 23, for the fact that the University of Strasburg was the first on the Continent to have a Professorship of Midwifery, dating from 1728, *i.e.* two years after Gibson had received

cal School of the University was made in 1746, when George Drummond, after an interval of twenty years, returned to office as Lord Provost, in the autumn succeeding the battle of Culloden. The Royal Infirmary, his creation, had then been opened, and one of the first acts of his administration was to institute clinical lectures in the Infirmary. The Managers, by his advice, permitted all Students of Medicine, upon paying a small gratuity, to attend the hospital. Dr. Rutherford, as Professor of the Practice of Physic, commenced delivering clinical lectures in the winter session of 1746-47, and was immediately attended by a large number of Students. Rutherford's clinical courses were continued over twenty years, and he thus solidly inaugurated that practical instruction in Medicine for which the University of Edinburgh has been distinguished.

We have seen that in 1726 the Senatus Academicus recognised five Professors as constituting the Medical Faculty, namely, those of Anatomy, Institutes of Medicine, Practice of Physic, and two joint Professors of Medicine and Chemistry. The next expansion in the Faculty took place in the province of Botany. The Town Council, so long back as 1676, had given the title of "Professor of Botany in the Town's College" to Mr. Sutherland, Keeper of the Physic Garden. But this was an outside and quasi-honorary Professorship, and no systematic

his appointment in Edinburgh. The Town Council then, in speaking of "other cities and places where this profession is instituted," were unconscious that they were doing something original, and were not following, but founding, a precedent.

teaching in Botany seems to have been given, either by Sutherland or by his two successors in the appointment, Charles and George Preston. At last Dr. Charles Alston appeared on the scene; he had devoted his life to the study of Botany, and had especially imbued himself at Leyden with the ideas of Boerhaave on this science. On returning to Edinburgh about the year 1720, aged thirty-seven, he seems to have got the sinecure office of King's Botanist in connection with the gardens of Holyrood, and to have begun giving some lectures. Eighteen years later, in the year 1738, George Preston died, and the Town Council, "considering that were a Professor of Medicine and Botany elected and installed in the City's College, it would in a great measure contribute to the advancement of learning, etc.; they therefore appoint Dr. Charles Alston, etc." And this vigorous man, commencing when he was fifty-five years old, delivered two courses of lectures annually for the next twenty-two years—one on Botany and one on Materia Medica. And so the teaching of these two subjects got regularly established in the University.

What had been thus begun was diligently carried forward by Dr. John Hope, who in 1761 was appointed by the Town Council "Professor of Botany and Materia Medica." Like his predecessor, he gave an annual course in each of these subjects, and he laboured indefatigably in introducing the Linnæan system into Scotland. But subdivision and specialisation of science was required in order to give the Medical School of the University its complete organisation. In 1768 Dr. Hope received a commission from the King as Regius Professor of Botany, and he then appears to have recommended to the patrons that the province of Materia Medica should be separated from his Chair and entrusted to other hands. Accordingly Dr. Francis Home, who was well qualified by study and experience at home and abroad for this charge, was appointed to a separate Professorship of Materia Medica, which he worthily inaugurated during a period of thirty years.

In 1770 the Medical School of the University received a fresh augmentation directly from the hands of the Crown, for in January of that year we find recorded a petition of Dr. Robert Ramsay, setting forth that he had been appointed by the King, on the 13th March 1767, Regius Professor of Natural History, and Keeper of the Museum in the University, with a salary of £70 per annum; and praying to be admitted Professor, under the usual reservation of the town's rights, and to be appointed by the Town Council Keeper of the Museum, with a commission from them, which petition the Council graciously acceded to, on condition that Dr. Ramsay conform to their regulations, and deliver to the clerk a full list or inventory of the curiosities belonging to the University.

Unfortunately, the paucity of those curiosities and, in fact, the want of a proper Museum[1] of

[1] See Appendix K. THE NATURAL HISTORY MUSEUM OF THE UNIVERSITY.

Natural History, put great difficulties in the way of Dr. Ramsay, who appears, either from this or some other cause, to have seldom attempted lecturing. The Chair of Natural History, like so many others in the University of Edinburgh, made a lame start. But on the death of Ramsay Dr. John Walker, a Scotch clergyman of great ability, who had acquired considerable note as a naturalist, received from the Crown the newly-instituted Professorship, and he, with great zeal and energy, both enlarged the Natural History collections in the University, and gave regular courses of lectures, which were attended by a good number of the Students, and also by many *amateur* pupils of riper age.

During the fifty years between 1720 and 1770 there were instituted in the University of Edinburgh eight Chairs belonging to the Faculty of Medicine (Anatomy, Institutes of Medicine, Practice of Physic, Chemistry, Midwifery, Botany, Materia Medica, and Natural History), and a system of clinical teaching in Medicine, had been organised. This foundation of a great Medical school was mainly due to the impulse which came from the Edinburgh Colleges of Physicians and Surgeons, seconded by the good-will and sagacity of George Drummond. But some credit must also be given to the Government of that day. Dr. Somerville[1] says: "I know it to be a fact that Provost Drummond, the most meritorious benefactor of the community over which he

[1] *My Own Life and Times*, 1741-1814, by Thomas Somerville, D.D., Minister of Jedburgh, p. 380.

presided, did not find himself at liberty to promise any preferment at the disposal of the Town Council of Edinburgh without the previous consent of Lord Milton, the delegate and political agent of Archibald Duke of Argyll. It was fortunate for the public that in the enlightened scheme for filling the Chairs in the University with the ablest candidates, the Duke of Argyll concurred with Lord Provost Drummond." Nothing, indeed, could be more fortunate or more creditable to the patrons than the selection made by them of Professors to fill the various Chairs; but the personal qualifications of those Professors must be reserved for subsequent consideration.

The Faculty of Medicine might soon have been still farther increased, had it not been for the resistance of the Senatus Academicus. But in fact almost every subsequent addition to the Faculty, beyond the original eight Chairs, met with determined opposition from existing Professors, owing to that conservatism to which allusion has been already made (above, p. 290); and thus improvements in the University system had to be forced upon the University from without. In 1777 the College of Surgeons, being desirous to have Surgery taught in the University by a separate Professor, memorialised the Crown on the subject. But they were defeated by the influence of Alexander Monro, *secundus*, who selfishly demanded to keep the teaching of Surgery, as well as of Anatomy, on the ground that both his father and himself had taught both subjects (above, p. 300, note). He was supported by Principal

Robertson and by the other Medical Professors, and the Town Council granted him a new Commission, "expressly bearing him to be Professor of Medicine and particularly of Anatomy and Surgery;" they, however, reserved power to themselves or their successors in office "to separate the offices of Professor of Anatomy and Surgery at any time after the decease of the said Dr. Alexander Monro." Dr. A. Hamilton (Chairman of the Surgeons and afterwards Professor of Midwifery) protested against this, because "as the surgeon must be formed by witnessing practice on the living body, the Professor of Anatomy could not give the rudiments of the art of Surgery."[1] But in vain; for more than fifty years deference continued to be paid to the interests of the Monro family, and the separate teaching of Systematic Surgery was prevented in the University.

The introduction of Clinical Surgery was, however, unopposed; this occurred in 1802, when Mr. James Russell, Surgeon, petitioned the Town Council to the effect that, "The high reputation which the University of Edinburgh enjoys as a school of Medicine, whither Students resort even from the continents of Europe and of America, is greatly due to the clinical instruction in Medicine here given; *that* it is expedient to add to this clinical instruction in Surgery also; *that* Mr. Russell

---

[1] See Dr. Gairdner's paper *On the History of the Medical Profession in Edinburgh* in the *Edinburgh Medical Journal* for 1862, p. 700.

himself undertook in 1786 to give some clinical lectures in practical Surgery, and that in seventeen years he has given twenty-four courses of such lectures and has received high testimony in their favour; he therefore prays the Town Council to erect his Lectureship into a Professorship in the University, under the title of 'the Clinical and Pathological Professor of Surgery.'" This petition having been referred to the Senatus Academicus, they, after conference with the Managers of the Royal Infirmary, reported in favour of it,—on condition that the rights of the Professor of Anatomy and Surgery be not interfered with, and that the " Professor of Clinical Surgery " do not give courses of Systematic Surgery.

The Town Council accordingly took steps for obtaining from the Crown some endowment for the Chair which was to be established, and, with the assistance of the Dundases, they were successful in this attempt. In June 1803 there came down a Commission from George III. creating a Chair of Clinical Surgery in the University of Edinburgh with an endowment of £50 per annum out of the "Bishops' Rents," and appointing Mr. James Russell as the first Professor;—with clauses, however, protecting the rights of the Professor of Anatomy and Surgery, as had been suggested by the Senatus.

The want of a separate Chair of Systematic Surgery began to be more and more felt, especially owing to the comparative incompetence of Alexander Monro, *tertius*, who (as "conjoint Professor to his aged father") was monopolising the subjects of Anatomy and Surgery. In 1804 the College of Surgeons published an advertisement in which they said that they "have appointed Mr. John Thomson, 'Professor of Surgery to the College' and have directed him to deliver annually during the Winter Session, a course of lectures on the Principles and Practice of Surgery." They added that these lectures would be "a valuable addition to the system of Medical Education in the University." The Senatus Academicus were at once up in arms against this announcement. They wanted to take legal proceedings, on the ground that the rights of the Town Council were being infringed, but they were advised by their Faculty of Laws not to do so, as "the restraining clause in the Royal charter of 1582 does not appear to have been acted upon to the effect of restraint and exclusion, and therefore probably would not be enforced by a Court of Law." For instance, they pointed out that a "Professorship of Conveyancing" had been instituted by the Writers to the Signet (above, p. 290) not many years ago, and never interfered with.

The Senatus refrained on this occasion from going to law, but they were still busying themselves about a memorial for getting Mr. John Thomson stopped from holding the Professorship of Surgery which the College of Surgeons had conferred upon him, when all of a sudden, on the 7th November 1806, they were informed that a Commission from George III. had come down erecting a "Professorship of Military Surgery in our University of Edinburgh," to be endowed with an annual salary of £100 from Bishops' Rents, and appointing Mr. John Thomson to be first Professor. The Town Council apparently considered themselves bound by the terms of their commission (above, p. 322) to Alexander Monro, *secundus*, who was still alive. They therefore had gone to work by a side wind to get the teaching of Surgery in the University supplemented. The new Royal Commission was received by the Senatus under protest from the Monros that it encroached upon their rights, and that it had been obtained "in consequence of surprise and misconception and want of due information on the part of His Majesty's Ministers."

In 1816 the Town Council proposed the creation of a Chair of "Comparative Anatomy and Veterinary Surgery." The Senatus opposed this and petitioned against it, though one of their body, who was always enlightened and liberal—Dr. Duncan senior—refused to join in their petition, protesting "that such a Chair would be no prejudice to any existing Professorship, and would be highly advantageous and creditable to the University."

In 1829 the Royal Commission, which was then sitting, having informed the Senatus that they meant to recommend the establishment of a separate Chair of Surgery, Dr. Monro, *tertius*, protested against this on the grounds that "Surgery" was included in his Commission; *that* he had prepared a course of lectures on the subject; and *that* his pupils had always continued numerous in spite of the rivalry of other schools. He perhaps would not have admitted that this last circumstance was due to the fame of the Medical School of the University and not to his own merits. But it was well known that many Students, after paying him his fees and nominally enrolling in his class (with a view to graduation) had gone outside the University for instruction in Surgery, and had thus been obliged to pay for the same subject twice over. Monro added the very curious reason that it would be hard on him to restrict him to Anatomy, as he could only teach it imperfectly, owing to the deficiency of bodies for dissection. He said that there were only one hundred unclaimed bodies *per annum* in Edinburgh, and that fifty during the winter months was an inadequate supply for all the teachers of Anatomy.

But the protests of Dr. Monro received their *quietus* in September 1831, when the matter was cut short by a resolution of the Government to establish, in accordance with representations from the Town Council, not only a Chair of Surgery, but also one of Pathology. The announcement of this intention caused great excitement in the Senatus, who expressed their sentiments on the subjects in a letter to the Town Council. Their dislike to the proposed Crown appointments led them even to say that the patronage of the University had better be left in the hands of the Town Council, who were "always impartial and amenable to public opinion." This language, used for the purpose of the moment, was very different from that which the Senatus had employed a few years previously, nor did they afterwards adhere to the same view, as will be shown in a subsequent chapter.

On the 11th October 1831 Commissions from William IV. were presented, nominating Dr. John Thomson and John William Turner, Esq., to be respectively Professors of Pathology and Surgery in the University of Edinburgh. There were certain peculiarities in these appointments. They gave no stipend to either of the Professors from Bishops' Teinds or otherwise; on the other hand, the Commissions gave each Professor *power "to examine candidates* and do everything that may be required and necessary to the graduation of Doctors of Medicine." This clause might be construed as making the classes of Pathology and Surgery necessary for Medical graduation, and it was thus an interference on the part of the Crown with the regulations of the University. And as such it was protested against, of course without effect, both by the Town Council and the Senatus. The latter body sent up a long representation to Lord Melbourne to the effect that a Chair of Pathology was unnecessary and inexpedient, as the Chair of the Practice of Physic covered this subject; and as to a Chair of Surgery, that they would agree to separate teaching of Surgery, provided that so long as Monro gave a distinct course of lectures upon it, this should be considered equivalent to the course of the new Professor. To this representation Lord Melbourne, then Home Secretary, vouchsafed only a brief reply —that the thing was done and there was an end of it, and that if the Senatus felt themselves aggrieved they might go to law. Thus two most important Chairs were introduced against the wishes of the Senatus Academicus, and the foundation of these Chairs in 1831 completed the Professorial staff of the Faculty of Medicine, a Chair of Clinical Surgery having been added in 1803 to the eight previously existing Chairs of the Faculty; a Chair of Military Surgery in 1806; and a Chair of Medical Jurisprudence, belonging to the Faculties both of Laws and of Medicine, in 1807 (above, p. 291). The number of the Medical Professorships was thus raised to thirteen, and there was now almost a superfluity of the teaching of Surgery. But on the death of Sir George Ballingall, Professor of Military Surgery, 1856, Syme, the Professor of Clinical Surgery, wrote to Lord Panmure, then Secretary of State for War, recommending that the Chair of Military Surgery should be removed from Edinburgh to the neighbourhood of some great Military and Naval Hospital. The Crimean War had doubtless called attention to the subject, and the Government approving of Professor Syme's suggestion suppressed the Chair of Military Surgery in the University of Edinburgh, thus reducing the Medical Faculty to its present complement of twelve Professors.

We have related above (p. 265) the decline of Arts graduation in the University of Edinburgh during the last century. With the Medical classes

PROFESSOR JAMES SYME.

FROM A PHOTOGRAPH

during the same period the case was exactly opposite. From the date of the establishment of the Medical Faculty in 1726 to the end of the century, the custom of graduation in Medicine took root, and the number of these receiving the degree of Doctor of Medicine steadily increased. At first, from 1726 to 1748, under half-a-dozen names on an average each year are recorded in the *List of Graduates in Medicine*. From the middle of the century, just when the graduations in Arts were dwindling to nothing, Medical graduations rose to an average of over a dozen per annum. And, on a rough computation, after 1770 over twenty of these degrees were taken annually; after 1780 over thirty; and at the end of last century over fifty. During the early part of the present century the number soon rose to a hundred; in 1824 as many as one hundred and forty took the M.D. degree; and in 1827 the high-water of Medical graduation (prior to the Universities Act of 1858) was reached, there being one hundred and sixty Medical Graduates, whereof fifty were Scotch, forty-six English, thirty-six Irish, and the rest from the West Indies, Canada, and other colonies, with a few from foreign countries. Of course the Medical degree had a solid professional value, which increased in proportion as the Medical School of the University advanced in public estimation.

While these degrees were being increasingly sought after by Students, the Medical Faculty and the Senatus Academicus were watchful over the conditions under which they should be conferred.

In 1767 *Statuta Solennia* were enacted within the University for the ordering of Medical degrees. For the Arts Faculty regulations in the English language would, at that date, have been considered good enough. But the Medical Faculty had always about them an air of old-fashioned dignity; and it was quite in keeping with their wigs and gold-headed canes that they should put forth statutes couched in not unclassical Latin. The *Statuta Solennia* of 1767 were afterwards, from time to time, slightly modified;—in 1777, in 1783, in 1811, in 1813, in 1814, in 1818, in 1823, and in 1825; but, on the whole, it may be said that the system laid down in 1767, and the form of examination for Medical degrees then prescribed, remained the same in their essential particulars down to 1833, when new *Statuta* were promulgated, which introduced essential changes into the system, especially as regards the mode of examining candidates for degrees.

The chief features of the scheme of the *Statuta Solennia* of 1767 were as follows:—

1st. No one was to be admitted as a candidate for a degree in Medicine who had not thoroughly completed a course of study in all the branches of Medical teaching in this or some other University. Ten years afterwards (in 1777) this rule was defined to mean: "The candidate shall have attended classes in Anatomy and Surgery, Chemistry, Botany, Materia Medica and Pharmacy, the Theory and Practice of Medicine, and the lectures in Clinical Medicine given in the Royal Infirmary." No change in this list of subjects was made till 1825, when Midwifery was added as a necessary subject, and the candidate was required to have gone through a three months' course in any two of the following:— Practical Anatomy, Natural History, Medical Jurisprudence, Clinical Surgery, and Military Surgery. In 1783 the course of Medical study necessary for graduation was fixed at three years, of which at least one year was to have been passed at the University of Edinburgh. In 1825 the course was raised to four years, with exceptions in favour of Masters of Arts, Surgeons to the Army, Navy, or East India Company, and Hospital Assistants.

2d. The candidate, having applied to the Dean of the Medical Faculty three months before the Graduation day, was to be privately examined, at the house of one of the Professors, as to his literary attainments in general, and as to his proficiency in the different branches of Medicine.

This Examination comprised what is now called the "Preliminary Examination in Arts." It decided whether a candidate knew enough Latin to be allowed to graduate. It also enabled the Faculty to judge, no doubt with sufficient accuracy, whether a candidate had not better be sent back to his Medical studies for another year. Many were so sent back, but as the whole transaction was private no disgrace attended failure at this trial. In 1811, however, such private investigations appear to have been discontinued.

3d. The next step for a candidate, who had passed the first ordeal, was to submit a Medical Thesis to one of the Professors, who was to read and correct it, and, if he approved it, to sign it accordingly.

4th. The candidate was next to be examined more minutely by two Professors, in the presence of the Faculty, on the different branches of Medicine.

5th. Then two of the Aphorisms of Hippocrates were to be given him for explanation and illustration. He was to make his comments in writing, and defend them before the Faculty.

6th. Next he was to have two cases (*morborum historiæ*) given him, with questions attached. He was to return answers in writing, and defend them before the Faculty.

7th. Then, if all had previously gone well, he was to have his Thesis printed by the University printer, and present copies to each member of the Faculty of Medicine. And on the Graduation day he would defend his Thesis, and then receive the Doctor's degree.

8th. All the above-mentioned exercises, both oral and written, were to be in the Latin language.

This system, substantially unchanged, continued in vogue till 1834, when for the first time Theses written in English were accepted.[1] An Emeritus Professor, still living, describes his own examination

---

[1] The Senatus Academicus having resolved in October 1833 that for the future the language of Medical Theses should be optional, on the next Graduation day (1st August 1834), out of one hundred and ten graduates only nineteen presented Latin Theses, the rest English ones. In 1835 there were two Latin Theses; one was by a Spaniard, the other by an Irishman named Epaphroditus Young. In 1837 two; in 1838 one; in 1840 the last of the Latin Theses was given in by a student from Jamaica.

in 1831; how he attended, in evening dress, at the house of one of the Professors, and, taking his place at a table round which all the Medical Professors were assembled, was asked questions by each of them successively in Latin, to which he replied in the same language. Such an examination must have been extremely incomplete. That which is now divided into three stages — the First and Second Professional and the Third or Clinical Examinations—was then all got through in a single sitting by means of a few oral questions, without either examination papers or practical examinations. And both examiners and examinee were doubtless hampered by having to interchange ideas in what was to both of them a dead language.[1] But the Medical Examinations of the University were greatly improved by the *Statuta* of 1833, which substituted English for Latin as the language for both oral and written tests, and in lieu of the private house system introduced Examinations held within the University and divided into two stages; the first scientific (in Anatomy, Chemistry, Botany, Institutes of Medicine, and Zoology), the second professional (in Materia Medica, Pathology, Practice of Medicine, Surgery, Midwifery, and Medical Jurisprudence). Each stage consisted of both written and oral examinations. The system only required a little improvement by the Commission of 1858 to become perfectly efficient and thorough.

[1] A graphic account by the late Sir R. Christison of his own examination under this system will be given subsequently.

IV. When we consider the enlightened views of the Reformers as to what a School of Theology should be, the zeal of the people of Edinburgh in the seventeenth century for the endowment of a Chair of Divinity in their College, and the desire of Henderson, and afterwards of Carstares, to have learned teachers of Theology brought to Scotland from abroad; above all, when we consider that the General Assembly had special supervision of the "Divinity Halls" in the Universities, we cannot but be struck by observing that the period during which the Faculties of Arts, Laws, and Medicine were developed in the University of Edinburgh brought no corresponding development to the Faculty of Divinity. A Chair of Ecclesiastical History had been added in 1702 (above, p. 231); after this matters remained *in statu quo* for nearly one hundred and fifty years, and the condition of the Divinity School of the University in the middle of the last century, as depicted by contemporary records, seems deplorable. In the University programmes published in the *Scots Magazine* for 1741 the "Professors of Divinity" were stated to be (1) "The Rev. Dr. William Wishart, Principal of the College and First Professor of Divinity." The latter title, however, was honorary; the Principal did not lecture; "his chief business being to have the over-sight of the College; to take an account of the proficiency of the students in Philosophy and the Languages; to preside in University meetings; and to confer all degrees." (2) "The Rev. Mr. John Gowdie, Professor of Divinity," who lectured "on *Ben. Picteti Theologia Christiana* and on some parts of the sacred text." (3) "The Rev. Mr. Patrick Cuming, Professor of Church History," who gave lectures "on *Jo. Alphonsi Turretini Compendium Historiæ Ecclesiasticæ.*" The Professor of Hebrew in 1741 did not advertise himself among the Professors of Divinity, but among the "Professors of Arts and Sciences." He taught Leusden's *Hebrew Grammar*, and "analysed the Old Testament in Hebrew."

Even if we reckon the Professor of Hebrew as belonging to the Faculty of Divinity, that gives us a Faculty of only three Chairs, as the Principal was only nominally a Professor. But attendance on two out of three of those classes was left optional to the Divinity Students. Thus Dr. Somerville, referring to the Hebrew class in 1759, when a very able man, Dr. Robertson, was Professor, says:[1] "When I was a student of divinity Hebrew was little cultivated, or altogether omitted, by the greater number of the theological students." And of the Church History class he says: "Dr. Cuming, as required by the terms of his appointment, delivered a lecture once a week during four months of the Session, on Church History. Attendance at this class not being an indispensable qualification for probationary trials, few of the Divinity Students attended." Thus the only Theological teaching which was required in those days by the General Assembly, as a preparation for the Ministry, was that given in the Divinity Class of

[1] *My Own Life and Times*, p. 18.

Professor Gowdie. Of its quality we may form a conception from the lively and irreverent reminiscences of "Jupiter" Carlyle. "The Professor," says he, "though said to be learned, was dull and tedious in his lectures, insomuch that at the end of seven years he had only lectured half through Pictet's *Compend of Theology.* There was one advantage attending the lectures of a dull professor—*viz.* that he could form no school, and the students were left entirely to themselves and naturally formed opinions far more liberal than those they got from the Professor. This was the answer I gave to Patrick Lord Elibank, one of the most ingenious and learned noblemen of his time, when he asked me one day, many years afterwards, what could be the reason that young clergymen of that period so far surpassed their predecessors of his early days in useful accomplishments and liberality of mind—viz. *that the Professor of Theology was dull and Dutch and prolix.* His Lordship said he perfectly understood me, and that this entirely accounted for the change." Carlyle adds: "In the following winter (November 1741) I attended the Divinity Hall at Edinburgh again for three or four months, and delivered a discourse *De Fide Salvifica,* a very improper subject for so young a student, which attracted no attention from any one but the Professor, who was pleased with it, as it resembled his own Dutch Latin."

If torpid Professors of Divinity were a condition favourable to the production of clergymen of that type which "Jupiter" admired and represented—namely "Moderates," who were at the same time men of the world, and presentable in society—that condition was not permanent in the University of Edinburgh. Many earnest and some distinguished men held Chairs in the Faculty of Divinity down to 1858. But any one can see that the system of education for the clergy in Scotland during last century was loose, and that the standard was low. To have left matters so was discreditable to the General Assembly; it is difficult to conceive why they should never have returned to the educational ideas of the Reformers, or why the "Moderates" should not have perceived that learning in Theology is not necessarily connected with fanaticism. Graduation in Divinity should certainly have been introduced, but it was not, though honorary and complimentary titles of Doctor of Divinity were conferred from time to time, more or less deservedly, on various clergymen and divines. The first batch of these were three Nonconformist clergymen from England; Edmund Calamy, Daniel Williams, and Joshua Oldfield, who were made Doctors of Divinity by Carstares in 1709. Altogether one hundred and thirty-two degrees of this kind were conferred by the University of Edinburgh during the eighteenth century.

Very late in its history the Faculty of Divinity received an addition. This was in 1847, when a Commission from Queen Victoria erected a Chair of Biblical Criticism and Biblical Antiquities, "subject to the Laws and Regulations of the Church of Scotland," and appointed Dr. Robert Lee thereto. No endowment was attached to the Chair, but the Professor was to be provided for by being made a Dean of the Chapel-Royal. During previous negotiations the General Assembly had acquiesced in the founding of this Chair, on condition that no additional burden was to be thrown by it on the Divinity Students, that is to say, that there would be no fees, and that attendance on the Class would be voluntary.[1]

We have now traced the complete formation of the four Faculties of Arts, Laws, Medicine, and Divinity, from the beginning of the eighteenth century down to 1858. But during that period there were added to the University some other Chairs also, which, since the University has no Faculty of Science, were placed in the Faculty of Arts as the recognised asylum for nondescript Chairs. These were (A) Practical Astronomy (founded 1785); (B) Agriculture (1790); (C) Music (1839); (D) Technology (1855).

(A) On the 25th September 1785 George III.

[1] On the presentation of this Commission the then Principal, Dr. John Lee, delivered a quasi-protest against it: *First*, on the ground that the Chair was unnecessary, its subjects being embraced in the teaching of the Professors of Hebrew and Church History. And, with great knowledge of the past, he descanted on "the lights thrown" on Biblical Criticism by various bygone Professors. But he said that the new Professor would be well received. *Secondly*, he objected to a Chair founded without an endowment, pointing out that the Deanery fund was being constantly diminished by the augmentations of stipend for Parochial Ministers, so that the support for the Professorship (even if all future Professors of this subject were to be Deans) was precarious. This, however, was learned conservatism, and the Chair of Biblical Criticism has been, of course, a great gain to the University.

signed a Commission creating a Chair of Practical Astronomy, in the following terms :—" Whereas We considering the great advantages which Navigation and the useful Arts derive from the cultivation of Practical Astronomy and that it is of great importance in the education of youth, and especially of those who are destined for the naval line, that they be instructed in the principles and practice of Astronomical science, and that the institution of a Professorship for these purposes in our University of Edinburgh will be a great improvement in the education there :—Therefore We have agreed with advice and consent of the Lord Chief Baron, and the other Barons of Exchequer in that part of the United Kingdom to erect and endow a Profession in our said University of Edinburgh under the name of the 'Profession of Practical Astronomy.'" Then follows the appointment of Robert Blair, M.D., the first Professor, and a salary of £120[1] from Bishops' rents is assigned to the Chair. This Professorship was probably instituted at the suggestion of the Town Council, its first object being, perhaps, to provide for the instruction of mates and skippers in the merchant service shipping from the port of Leith. But to perform this or any other function the Chair of Practical Astronomy absolutely failed. It was a *coup manqué* from the first, and its history has

---

[1] Professor Leslie, in his evidence before the Universities Commission of 1826, says of this salary : "It was intended to be the largest in the College, and I well know that the Professor expressed no small degree of disappointment on being told that the salary attached to the Chair of Law of Nature and Nations was much greater."

been a curious one. The Government while providing a liberal endowment (according to the ideas of those times) for the Professorship, declined to undertake the expense of furnishing the Professor with the necessary appliances for teaching. Dr. Blair presented his Commission to the Senatus early in 1786, but having no observatory or instruments at his disposal he was unable to open a class. Professor Wallace says of him in his evidence before the Commission of 1826 : " I have no doubt he would have executed most faithfully the duties of his office. At the time of his appointment he was a zealous student and cultivator of Astronomy and Optics ; but he could not carry his views into execution, because Government declined to erect an Observatory for the use of the University."

Blair had been forty years " Professor of Practical Astronomy " when the Royal Commission commenced their sittings in Edinburgh ; and on their calling for a list of the Professors in the University they received one from which Blair's name was left out. When they inquired the reason of this, they were told : " He has never attended any of our meetings ; he has not been in the University but once or twice for many years." Thus Blair not only did not teach, but he held himself aloof from the Senatus,[1]

---

[1] The University Records show that Dr. Robert Blair, from the first, after his induction into the Senatus in February 1786, absented himself from all their meetings. Even on the great occasion of laying the foundation-stone of the New Buildings, when almost all the other Professors were present, his name does not appear as having been with them.

and took no part in their deliberations. The Senatus in return left him out of their lists. And it is curious that Bower, who brings down his *History* of the University to 1829, makes no mention of the foundation of the Chair of Practical Astronomy, nor of the first Professor of that subject.

Dr. Robert Blair was not called upon to give evidence before the Commission; he was then very old, and probably infirm, and he died while the Commissioners were still sitting in 1828. They then reported: "Without an Observatory furnished with proper instruments, the class could not be usefully taught. The Professorship now being vacant, we humbly recommend that no nomination should be made for that class until a suitable Observatory, attached to the University, can be provided." In accordance with this advice the Chair of Practical Astronomy was kept vacant for four years, and during that time negotiations were carried on between the Government and the "Astronomical Institution," a private society in Edinburgh, who had built an observatory[1] on the Calton Hill, which, however, was not connected with the University. And on the 1st October 1834 there came down a Commission of William IV. to Thomas Henderson, as Professor of Practical Astronomy, saying: "Whereas an agreement has been concluded betwixt the Lords Commissioners of our Treasury and the members of the Astronomical Institution of Edinburgh, whereby the latter have given the use of the Observatory at Edin-

[1] See Appendix L. EDINBURGH OBSERVATORY.

burgh erected by them and the Instruments therein contained to the Professor of Practical Astronomy in the said University to be appointed by us;—therefore," etc., Henderson is appointed Professor "with all the rights and privileges belonging to any other Professor," but with no requirement to teach, or other mention of Professorial duties. And in the same Commission he is appointed Astronomer-Royal for Scotland, and required to "make Observations for the extension and improvement of Astronomy, Geography, and Navigation." He is to report these observations twice a year. "And the said Thomas Henderson shall have an established salary of £300 yearly." This salary was assigned to the conjoined offices of Professor of Practical Astronomy and Astronomer-Royal for Scotland. But by the terms of the Commission onerous and important duties were exacted from the Astronomer-Royal, while on the Professor no specified duties were imposed.

Under these circumstances it is not surprising that Henderson became for ten years a zealous and devoted Observer, and indeed is said to have killed himself by hard work; but on the other hand he so far followed the example of the sinecurist Blair as to give no lectures in the University. It has frequently happened that astronomers, absorbed in pursuing their nightly observations and daily calculations, have evinced a repugnance to teaching, as being an interruption to what they consider their more serious work. On the death of Henderson in 1846 the present Professor, Charles Piazzi Smyth, was appointed under a Commission from Queen Victoria in terms precisely similar to Henderson's Commission. For a few sessions he tried the experiment of giving a six months' course of lectures at the University, and had an attendance of some twelve Students. But he found the labour of preparing and delivering lectures by day, when he had to observe by night, too intolerable, and at the same time that small fruit seemed likely to result from the class, who were, for the most part, of an *amateur* character. He therefore relinquished the attempt, and " limited himself," as he states in the *University Calendar*, " to *receiving* any matriculated applicants for Practical Astronomy, ascertaining in a friendly manner something of their calibre and objects, and then advising or assisting such gentlemen afterwards in their studies, at various periods through the Session." The Professor described to a Parliamentary Commission, appointed in 1876 to inquire into the state of the Royal Observatory at Edinburgh, his experiences of "the calibre and objects" of those who applied to him. He said: " One or two in the course of several years may be good students, in whose progress I should feel an interest; but the majority are elderly gentlemen, who expect that if they take a ticket in the University they will acquire a right to send their families, their children and servants, up to the Observatory to be shown the stars through the telescopes there!" No doubt the Astronomer-Royal is right in keeping the *profanum vulgus* out of his " Uranienburg," and it would perhaps be unreasonable to expect him to give courses of lectures in the University. But after all, the Observatory, as well as the Professor of Practical Astronomy, belongs to the University. And it is probably the most desirable course that a few Students, with whose qualifications and objects the Professor is satisfied, should be received like apprentices to do practical work within the Observatory. This, however, would necessitate the enlargement, in fact the rebuilding, and the better equipment of the Observatory, as recommended by the above-mentioned Parliamentary Commission. Such a consummation may be realised in the future. In the meantime it must be said that the Chair of Practical Astronomy, which has now been in existence nearly a hundred years, has contributed next to nothing to the educational resources of the University.

(B) The Chair of Agriculture was the first Chair in the University of Edinburgh founded by a private benefactor, all the previous Professorships having been instituted either by the Town Council or by the Crown. In the middle of the eighteenth century Lord Kames had stimulated Dr. Cullen to give some lectures on the Science of Agriculture; and in 1788 Dr. Walker, then Professor of Natural History, gave a much fuller course on the same subject. Bower thinks that this "suggested to Sir William Pulteney[1] the idea" of presenting a Chair

[1] Sir William Johnstone Pulteney is mentioned in Dr. Carlyle's *Autobiography* as "Mr. Johnstone." He was sixth son of Sir James Johnstone of Westerhall, county Dumfries, and was born in 1729. In 1760 he married the heiress of Daniel Pulteney (cousin of the Earl of

of Agriculture to his old *Alma Mater*, the University of Edinburgh. On the 7th July 1790 the "College Bailie" and another of the Magistrates came to the Senatus introducing " Dr. Andrew Coventry of Shanwell," and presenting a Commission from " William Pulteney Esq. of Solway Bank," appointing him to be Professor of Agriculture in the University. The Commission narrated that Mr. Pulteney had placed £1250 in the hands of the Town Council, who had given him a bond for it,

Bath), who brought to him the princely fortune of the Pulteney family. Mr. Johnstone then took his wife's name, and called himself Johnstone-Pulteney. In 1794 he succeeded his elder brother, Sir James Johnstone, who had died without issue, in the family baronetcy. He was thus "Mr. Johnstone Pulteney" when he founded the Chair. He died "one of the richest subjects in Britain," in 1805. Dr. Somerville says of him : " Sir William Pulteney's character has been misunderstood and undervalued by those to whom he was only known superficially, and who formed their opinion from the temper and habits he discovered in reference to his personal accommodation and household economy. His apparent expenditure was considered as shamefully penurious compared with the amplitude of his fortune, and his carefulness in personal and domestic expenses was so paltry and sordid as to become proverbial. But with all this narrowness, his beneficence—often voluntary and unsolicited—surpassed the example of most of his contemporaries who had acquired the greatest celebrity for the munificence and extent of their generosity. I was informed by Mr. Alison of the Excise Office, one of Sir William's confidential agents in works of charity, that after he became opulent he had always a large sum afloat in benevolent speculations. He ever showed an anxious attention to find out genius and talents languishing in circumstances of obscurity and neglect, that he might find the means of bringing them into notice. And he enjoyed the satisfaction of receiving the most pleasing testimonies of the personal gratitude of many of his protegees, afterwards celebrated for public services which were the fruits of the talents fostered and matured under his beneficent patronage. Sir William Pulteney sat in the House of Commons for several successive Parliaments, and acquired high reputation on account of his knowledge and attention to business. He never attached himself to any party, nor solicited or accepted any ministerial office."—Somerville's *Life and Times*, pp. 260-262.

at four per cent interest, obliging themselves and successors to pay an annual salary of £50 to the Professor.[1] Pulteney was to have the patronage of the Chair during his lifetime; afterwards it was to be vested in three public bodies—the Judges of the Court of Session, the Town Council, and the Senatus. The Professor was to be bound to deliver "a set of Instructions or Lectures on the subject of Agriculture, respecting the nature of soils and manures; the modes of cultivation; the succession of crops; the construction of implements of husbandry; the best and most successful known practices; the manner of instituting experiments to ascertain the effect of any proposed practice in any soil or climate; and the best manner of introducing or training skilful labourers and country artificers, where these may be wanting."

The presentation of this Commission produced even more than the usual number of protests. *First*, the College Bailie, *pro forma*, protested against the rights of the Town Council being prejudiced by a private individual having founded a Chair. *Secondly*, the Professor of Natural History protested that the new Chair was not to hinder him from teaching

[1] There is a letter extant from Pulteney to Professor Adam Ferguson, dated 21st March 1789, which shows that he had declined to accede to a suggestion that he should make the endowment of the Chair more ample. He says: "I am not of Principal Robertson's opinion that it would be right to make the salary higher, because our object is to make it an object to the Professor to exert himself very much and by no means to make this a sinecure. If the Town could contrive to give him a habitation of any sort, however small, in the College, it would be a great point and would connect him more with the University."

"any branch of Natural Science." *Thirdly*, the Professor of Botany protested against this last protest,—that the Professor of Natural History could not claim the right of teaching Botany. And *fourthly*, Dr. Andrew Coventry, the new Professor, protested against any one but himself giving "a separate course of Georgical lectures." After all this fencing, the Chair was inaugurated, and caused no manner of discord or difficulty in the University. It was perhaps the first Chair of Agriculture that had been introduced into any University.

Dr. Andrew Coventry, after holding the Chair for thirty-six years, gave evidence before the Commission of 1826. And he came very well out of the ordeal: he had delivered thirty-two courses, some of them consisting of more than one hundred and forty lectures each. His classes had ranged in number of Students from seventy-eight as a maximum to thirty as a minimum; and this, in regard to a subject not available for either graduation or ordination, must be considered a success. His lectures had been attended by the sons of practical farmers, Writers who had the management of estates, Divinity Students, and others. From the Divinity Students he never exacted a fee. He had other avocations, and was frequently called to London as a witness before Parliamentary Committees, and for this reason he had "of late years" taken to lecture only in alternate winters, persuading persons who wished to attend him during any session when he was to be absent to put off doing so, and attend the classes of Chemistry and Botany in the meantime. After this statement of matters it seems rather surprising that the Royal Commission of 1826-30 should have recommended that the Chair of Agriculture should be abolished, "unless a class could be provided for it, and taught regularly." But that Commission, as will be shown subsequently, though very able and zealous, were sometimes too sudden and drastic in their recommendations, as indeed Commissions who have only to report, without the responsibility of carrying measures into effect, are apt to be.

(C) The Chair of Music was also a private foundation, and its institution was connected with circumstances most important in the history of the University. "General John Reid," says Bower (iii. 368), "of Woodstock Street, Oxford Street, London, was a native of Perthshire, and educated at the University of Edinburgh. He entered the army very early in life, and continued in it upwards of sixty years. He was a General in His Majesty's army, and Colonel of the 88th Regiment of foot, and had seen a good deal of service both in Europe and America, where he possessed extensive estates, which were forfeited during the unfortunate contest with the colonies." General Reid[1] had one daughter, who was married to a Dr. Stark Robertson. But it would seem that this marriage had not been pleasing to the General, for in 1803 he made a Will, leaving the liferent of his property to his

[1] See Appendix M. GENERAL REID.

GENERAL REID.
FROM AN OLD PORTRAIT.

daughter, but expressly ordering that the interest of his estate was to be paid into her hands alone, and not to be subject to the debts, control, or disposition of her husband. On her death the property was to go to her children, if she had any, in specified proportions, but on the express condition that each one of them benefiting by the estate was to take the name of Reid. Failing issue to his daughter, Reid devised—" it being my wish and desire that the said John Stark Robertson shall not inherit or possess any part of my property"—that (with the exception of a few legacies) the bulk of the estate should be applied, in the first place, in "establishing and endowing a Professorship of Music in the College and University of Edinburgh, where I had my education and passed the pleasantest part of my youth ;" and, in the next place, " in making additions to the Library of the said University, or otherwise in promoting the interest and advantage of the University, in such way as the Principal and Professors thereof for the time being shall in their discretion think most right and proper." He directs his trustees in that case to apportion a fund for "the endowment and maintenance in all time coming in the said University of a Professor of the Theory of Music, an art and science in which the Scots stand unrivalled by all the neighbouring nations in pastoral melody and sweet combination of sounds." The salary of such Professor "not being less than £300 of good and lawful money of Great Britain." And the residue of his estate is to be made over to the

Principal and Professors of the said University for the purposes aforesaid. He concludes by saying: "And as I am the last representative of an old family in Perthshire, which on my death will be extinct in the male line, I therefore leave two portraits of me, one when a Lieutenant in the Earl of Loudoun's regiment, raised in 1745; and the other when a Major-General in the army, to the Principal and Professors of the said University of Edinburgh, to be disposed of in such a manner as the Principal shall direct; and to that University I wish prosperity to the end of time."

The Will containing these quaint and pleasing terms was signed in 1803. Three years later, when there was apparently no prospect of a family to Mrs. Stark Robertson, Reid added a codicil to it, giving more specific instructions as to a particular duty to be performed by his Professor of Music, as follows: " After the decease of my daughter Susanna Robertson, she dying without issue, I have left all my property in the Funds, or in Great Britain, to the College of Edinburgh, where I had my education, as will be found more particularly expressed in my Will; and as I leave all my music-books (particularly those of my own composition) to the Professor of Music in that College, it is my wish that in every year after his appointment, he will cause a Concert of Music to be performed on the 13th of February, being my birthday, in which shall be introduced one Solo for the German Flute, Hautboy, or Clarionet; also one March and Minuet, with accompaniments by a select Band, in order to show the taste of Music about the middle of last century, when they were by me composed, and with a view also to keep my memory in remembrance; the expense attending the Concert to be defrayed from the general fund left by me to the College, and not from the salary to be paid to the Professor of Music, from which there is not to be any diminution."

The good General died in 1807; and his Solicitors, in forwarding a copy of the Will and Codicil to the Senatus, seemed to consider it almost certain that the residuary legacy would come to the Principal and Professors of the University, to whom it had been devised. They enclosed an estimate of what it would amount to—namely, £52,114.

Such was the Reid Bequest, which was not only a compliment to the University, but also gave the Senatus Academicus very great strength and encouragement, by assuring to them the ultimate possession of an independent fund to be at their own disposal, for "promoting the interest or advantage of the University." Mrs. Stark Robertson, however,

> " Like to a stepdame or a dowager
> Long withering out a young man's revenue,"

kept them very long out of their reversion. In 1819 the Senatus, representing to some of the Edinburgh banks that Mrs. Robertson was sixty years old and childless, obtained from them a loan of £3000, on the security of the bequest, for the purchase of a collection in Natural History for the

University Museum. But Mrs. Robertson lived nineteen years more after that, and it was not till 1838 that news came of her death in Paris, at the age of seventy-nine. The trustees, Mr. George Kinloch, Mr. E. Marjoribanks, and Sir Edward Antrobus, at once decided that they could not take the responsibility of parting with the estate without an order of Chancery. They therefore paid the money into Chancery, and invited the Senatus to an amicable suit. In 1839, under an order of the Court of Chancery, General Reid's Trustees proceeded to appoint Mr. John Thomson as first Professor of the Theory of Music,[1] whom they had chosen from a list of several candidates, being satisfied of his professional attainments and private character. The appointment was quite in accordance with the wishes of the Senatus, Mr. Thomson being the son-in-law of Dr. John Lee, who next year became Principal; after it was made, the trustees had no other duty left but to hand over to the Senatus the residuary estate, under General Reid's Will, which was then declared to amount to £73,000, or thereabouts. The history of the Reid Fund, and its disposal by the Senatus, and the law-suits it gave rise to, will fall to be treated of elsewhere; we are only here concerned with the institution of the Chair of Music. The Town Council, following the suggestions of the Senatus, laid down that the first and all subsequent Professors of the Theory of Music should be bound

[1] This title was given by order of the Town Council, who passed an Act establishing the Chair.

to give courses of public lectures comprehending "the phenomena and philosophy of Sound in so far as connected with musical intonation; the laws of Harmonies, with their application to the Theory of Music; the explanation not only of the ordinary rules of Thorough Bass, but also a clear exposition of methodical composition in double, triple, and quadruple Counterpoint; and the practical application of all the principles and doctrines appertaining to the Science. Further, that joined with these discussions the Professor shall exhibit the History of the Science, with a critical analysis of the works of all the classical masters, ancient as well as modern, and such improvements as the progress of the Science may from time to time suggest." Such was the comprehensive programme of teaching laid down for the Professors of the Theory of Music, but it may be doubted whether it has ever been completely realised. There were many difficulties in the way: the first Professor died after a short tenure of office, and some of his successors had an equally short incumbency; the demand for lectures of the kind prescribed would be limited by the number of Students intending to take to Music as a profession; and the class-room provided for this department was so incommodious that in 1846 the Professor reported that it was not in a condition to allow him to deliver lectures, as the cold and damp were felt by the Students, and were injurious to his instruments. It was not till 1858 that the foundation-stone of the present Music class-room was laid.

Further details relating to this Chair will be given in connection with the biographies of the different Professors, and with the history of the Reid Fund. It may be sufficient here to mention that the Reid Concert, after being at first held in a small way, and giving rise to many heartburnings as to the distribution of tickets, has for a long series of years been conducted on a splendid scale, and has not only celebrated with the greatest honour the birthday of General Reid, but has come to be the nucleus of a Musical Festival for Edinburgh, and has thus done much to develop musical taste in the city. At the same time the Chair has been used not only for the instruction of the few Students wishing to become professional musicians, but also for the training of large choruses of all classes of the Students; and this has exercised a very humanising influence. Besides all this the Chair of the Theory of Music probably still possesses unrealised potentialities of usefulness, which remain among the "un-called up capital" of the University of Edinburgh.

(D) The Chair of Technology arose out of a movement made by the Senatus in 1852 to transfer the rich Natural History collections which had been amassed by Professor Jameson, and which were acknowledged to be "second only to those of the British Museum," to the nation. These collections had outgrown the Museum completed for them in 1820 on the west side of the University Buildings; and it was proposed that the Government should take them over and place them in a National

Museum, which should still be an addition to and an integral part of the University. This offer was accepted by the Government, and in 1854 Mr. Lyon Playfair, writing as an official of the Board of Trade, proposed to the Town Council and the Senatus a scheme for the creating of a National Museum on the site of the Independent Chapel and the Merchant Maidens' Hospital to the west of the College; this Museum to be one of Natural History and Technology. The Senatus were to make over their Natural History collections, the Professor of Natural History being still Regius Keeper of them, and retaining the use of the specimens for teaching; while a separate Keeper of the Technological side would be appointed. This gave rise to the "Industrial Museum," or, as it is now called, "The Museum of Science and Art," in Edinburgh, the foundation-stone of which was laid by Prince Albert —one of the last public acts of his life—in 1860. But in the meantime a Chair of Technology had been founded in 1855 by the Commission of Queen Victoria to George Wilson.

The Commission stated that it had been thought proper to appoint a Regius Professor of "Technology in the University of Edinburgh," and "that the Director of the Industrial Museum in Scotland should be *ex officio* Professor of Technology therein." This might seem a curious way of putting it, for the Industrial Museum at the date of the Commission had not yet come into existence, and it would therefore appear more appropriate to have said that the

Regius Professor of Technology in the University was to be *ex officio* Director of the Industrial Museum. But the officials of the Home Office knew what they were about in drawing the Commission. They did not wish to give the University a perpetual title to the direction of the Museum. At the outset the scheme agreed upon seemed most favourable, and indeed flattering to the University; the University collections were to be taken over, and maintained at the national expense in a building adjacent to, and considered as an integral part of the University Buildings, and the Museum thus constituted was to be under the management of two University Professors—the Professor of Natural History, and the Professor of Technology, who, in addition to the care of his own department, was to have the general direction of the whole institution. But probably from the first, this arrangement was not intended to be permanent; it was too much opposed to the centralising instincts of the London bureaucracy. Therefore Dr. George Wilson was appointed Regius Professor of Technology "during the Queen's pleasure," and "subject to any regulations in regard to the said Professorship," which might be approved by the Home Secretary, and also to any regulations which might be made "from time to time in respect of the said Industrial Museum." What was intended, or kept in reserve, by these terms, came to light more quickly than the Government officials could have anticipated. For George Wilson was one

> " Within whose delicate being,
> Like light and wind within a summer cloud,
> Genius and death contended."

And within four years after his appointment his brief and brilliant career terminated. On this the Government immediately suppressed the Chair of Technology in the University, and appointed an official of their own choosing to be Director of the Museum. Following up the thoughts which arise on this subject, we may say here that from first to last the University has been to a considerable extent beguiled in the matter of the Museum. In 1852 the University possessed Natural History collections "second only to those of the British Museum," and also a space of ground to the west expressly purchased with the object of securing free light to her buildings from that side. The collections were taken away, and the ground was built over for the Museum, so that the west side of the University quadrangle is rendered nearly useless. She was to administer the new Museum by means of her Professors of Technology and Natural History; but the Professor of Technology was promptly suppressed, and in course of time the official Director of the Museum succeeded in playing the cuckoo to the Professor of Natural History, and in ousting him from his function of Regius Keeper of the Natural History collections. At length it went so far that even the free use of specimens from the Museum for the teaching of the Natural History class was denied. And thus the physical connection of the "Bridge of Sighs" which joins the two buildings of the University and the Museum, now chiefly serves the purpose of being a record of broken pledges.

Assuredly it was not owing to any want of capacity or want of success on the part of the first Professor of Technology that the Chair was abolished, and the University deprived of the Directorship of the Museum. George Wilson had at first very unfavourable circumstances to contend with. The Museum had not yet been built, or even begun, and the specimens intended for it were placed temporarily in the Independent Chapel in what was then Argyle Square and in the Merchant Maidens' Hospital adjoining. But Wilson's zeal in his office of Director knew no bounds, "I am determined," he said, "to let no day pass without doing something for my dear Museum." He begged for it throughout the world, and in four years he added to its collections more than ten thousand objects. In his inaugural address as Professor he told the Students: "With the Industrial Museum, this Chair stands in organic connection. My office, as Professor of Technology, is to be interpreter of the significance of that Museum, and expositor of its value to you, the Students of this University." And he concluded by saying: "Let me commend this new Chair to your good will and kindly aid. With its associated Industrial Museum, it constitutes a great additional centre of Knowledge, from which light will spread over this land and over the world. I can but sow the seed. I have sown it to-day; I am honoured to do thus much; but the prediction, true in reference to all matters, is that 'one soweth and another reapeth.'"

Wilson could not obtain a class-room within the University walls till just before his own death in 1859,[1] and he had to lecture in an inconvenient room outside, but, in spite of all drawbacks, above forty persons attended his first course. His entire syllabus of lectures extended over three years; the first year's course being devoted to Mineral, the second to Vegetable, and the third to Animal Technology. George Wilson defined Technology as "Science in its application to the useful Arts," and on another occasion as " the sum or complement of all the sciences which either are, or may be made applicable to the industrial labours or utilitarian necessities of man." His first course included lectures on Fuel, Building Materials of Mineral origin, Glass and Glass making, Pottery, Metallo-techny, Electro-techny, and Magneto-techny. Under the latter heads were comprised the working of metals, and what was then known of Electrical Engineering.

Such a field demanded an acquaintance with the secrets of all trades, and, in short, an aptitude for universal knowledge, which George Wilson to an extraordinary degree possessed. His mode of exposition was also eminently lucid and attractive, and drew to him an audience, not of candidates for

[1] When the Professor of Music made way for him by moving out into the newly-built Music class-room of which some account is elsewhere given.

degrees, but of persons desiring practical information for the needs of life. In his third session he wrote to a friend : "Students abound this winter, especially juniors. I think myself well off with thirty-five. My class is a very pleasant one. An Indian General, an Artillery Lieutenant who lost a bit of his skull (but certainly none of his brains) at Lucknow, an Engineer Officer, four Indian Surgeons, a Navy Surgeon, a W.S., several young Ministers, and a wind up of Farmers, Tanners, etc." In November 1859, a few weeks before his death, he enrolled a class which had increased to the number of eighty-five.

George Wilson was an exceptional man, and it may be doubted whether a successor to him could have been found possessing all his qualifications. Still the inauguration of a Chair of Technology under him had been a manifest success, and it had been shown that such a Chair contained possibilities of great usefulness. We see now how extremely useful and important would be the existence at the present time of a Chair, part of the province of which would be to expound all the recent developments of Electrical Engineering. All such possibilities, however, were stamped out by the suppression of the Chair of Technology on the death of George Wilson. The Government of that day were no doubt only too eager to transfer the direction of the Museum from the University of Edinburgh to the South Kensington Department of Science and Art. But it must be admitted that the Senatus Academicus, with great short-sightedness, played into their hands. The Professors of Chemistry, Botany, and Natural History, each saw a rival in the Professor of Technology, and they got the Senatus to represent to Government that it would be better, instead of seeking for a new Professor of all the useful Arts, to allow each of the Professors named to lecture separately within the Museum on subjects connected with his own department. The pretext served its purpose, but no substitute was ever really provided for the Chair of Technology.

APPENDIX I. ALEXANDER CUNNINGHAM.

IN the sign-manual of Queen Anne (1707), which created Charles Areskine "Professor of Public Law and the Law of Nature and Nations," it was added that this appointment was to be "without prejudice to Mr. Alexander Cunningham who is already nominated Professor of the Civil Law by Act of Parliament." As above stated, Alexander Cunningham was never a Professor in the College of Edinburgh, though he appears to have been appointed Regent of Humanity in 1769, and of Philosophy in 1689.

He was a man of great ability, and so profound a Latin scholar that he even entered the lists with some success against the great Bentley. He became tutor in the family of the Duke of Queensberry, and, supported by the influence of that family, he petitioned the Scots Parliament in 1698 for an allowance of £200 sterling a year for six years to enable him to carry to completion a work in four volumes folio upon the Civil Law. The two first volumes were to contain the "text of the *Pandects* accurately settled, with notes upon two thousand passages requiring elucidation"; the third volume was to contain the "Reconciliations of Opposite Laws;" and the fourth "a System of the Digests by way of principles and consequences."

Cunningham, with modest assurance, "judged it his duty" to offer this work "to his own country," thereby giving the Parliament to understand that if they declined to encourage him he would go elsewhere. The "Committee for Security of the Kingdom" were desired to report upon the application; which they did by recommending that the "imposition on the tunnage of shipping" should be burdened with £150 sterling, "to be paid to the petitioner as a yearly fee and salary as Professor of the Civil Law in this Kingdom." They also advised that the petitioner should be allowed to go abroad to qualify himself further for carrying on the work. It seems clear that the title of "Professor of Civil Law in Scotland" was invented merely with the object of serving as an item in the Treasury accounts. The "salary" of a National Professor would look less irregular than a yearly grant to an individual to aid him in writing a book. Cunningham was never meant to teach Civil Law, and he never did. By *Stat.* 1698, c. 37, entitled "an Act anent the Tunnage," the impost was burdened *inter alia* with £150 sterling, "as the yearly fee and salary" for five years "granted to Mr. Alexander Cunningham, as Professor of the Civil Law, nominate and designed to that profession." And by *Stat.* 1704, c. 9, this grant was renewed for five years more; in the prelude to this last Act the purpose was specified of "maintaining a Professor of Law at Edinburgh."

It is doubtful, however, whether the allowance from the tonnage dues was ever received by Cunningham, as prior claims upon the dues appear to have exhausted them. Cunningham, enjoying a small patrimonial estate, named Block, in Ayrshire, and also a pension from the Queensberry family, retired to a life of literature at the Hague, where he collected a valuable library. Perhaps on account of not receiving the subsidy which had been voted for his edition of the *Pandects*, he was less persevering than he might otherwise have been with that work, which was never completed. Cunningham went off into fields of lighter literature, and in 1721 brought out his *Animadversiones* on Bentley's *Horace;* also his own edition of Horace; and twenty years later an edition of Virgil. And he won for himself the reputation of being the best chess-player in Europe.

APPENDIX J. GEORGE DRUMMOND.

IT would be difficult to over-estimate what Edinburgh owes to George Drummond. When he began to have influence in the Town Council this city had recently ceased to be the seat of the Scottish Parliament, and therefore was also rapidly ceasing to be a place of residence for the Scottish nobility. It was sinking into the condition of a small superseded capital, or, in fact, of a provincial town, when the genius of Drummond intervened, and by working out a series of great ideas, led the way to the production of the Edinburgh of the present day out of the squalid (though picturesque) " Good Town " of the past.

Drummond's first great service was the development of the Medical School of the University, and connected with this the foundation of the Royal Infirmary, which was opened in 1741. A few years later proposals, signed by him as Lord Provost, were circulated through the country, calling upon all Scotsmen to contribute to the improvement of their metropolis. These proposals included the building of the Royal Exchange, of the City Chambers, of new Courts of Justice, and of better apartments for the Advocates' Library. At the same time a petition to Parliament was proposed for an extension of the royalty of the town both to the north and to the south, with a view to the building of the North and South Bridges, the formation of the New Town of Edinburgh, and the addition of new streets and squares to the south. This was in its entirety a great and bold conception, and George Drummond lived to see considerable instalments of it completed. Since his death the rest has been accomplished quite in accordance with his ideas, but in a manner and to an extent which would surprise him if he could now revisit Edinburgh, for which he did so much. In 1753, as Grand Master of the Freemasons in Scotland, he laid the foundation of the Royal Exchange ; and in 1763, when Lord Provost for the sixth time, he laid the foundation-stone of the North Bridge.

George Drummond was eldest son of John Drummond, " Factor " in Edinburgh, and was born on the 27th June 1687. He does not appear to have graduated at the University, but is said to have been educated " in the schools of Edinburgh," and to have got an early reputation for skill in arithmetic, which led to his being employed when only eighteen years old by the Committee of the Scottish Parliament for settlement of the National accounts, preparatory to the Union with England, to make most of their calculations for them. He did such good service in this capacity that he was selected as accountant to the Excise Office in 1707. In 1717 he was appointed one of the Commissioners of Customs, and also was elected City Treasurer. In 1725-26 (the year of the establishment of the Medical Faculty in the University) he was Lord Provost for the first time.

We pass over George Drummond's services in 1715 and 1745 to the Hanoverian dynasty. It is not necessary here to write his biography. The chief object of this Appendix is to mention a very curious source of information about him which exists in the University Library. This is a portion of the Diary which George Drummond kept with scrupulous care for several years. The earlier portion of the Diary is lost, but we possess two folio volumes of manuscript,[1] written in a beautiful hand: the first volume beginning in the middle of the year 1736 and going to the end of 1737; the second volume beginning with the 1st January and ending with the 25th November 1738. At this last date the Diary abruptly stops, not, however, without furnishing a peculiar but very sufficient reason for its discontinuance.

At the period recorded in the Diary George Drummond had been already twice married: *First*, in 1707, to Mary Campbell of Burnbank, who died in 1718, and by whom he had five children: *Secondly*, in 1721, to Catherine Campbell (daughter of Sir James Campbell of Aberuchil), who died in 1732, and by whom he had nine children. It may be inferred from passages in the Diary that shortly after the death of his second wife, when he was in his forty-fifth year, George Drummond became attached, and, in fact, engaged, to another lady, whose name is not known, but whose initials were R. B. Want of pecuniary resources prevented their union, and their relation to each other assumed the character of a platonic, or rather spiritual, friendship. On the 20th September 1736 he blesses "the Lord for choosing such a partner and in that character giving" him "so valuable a friend

[1] These volumes were picked up somewhere by Principal Lee, and were much prized by him. At the sale of his library they came into the possession of the University.

as R. B." And in 1738 he writes: "The Lord having pointed out R. B. as my partner, and making it utterly unreasonable for us to think of uniting now, might create great uneasiness. But, blessed be God, he has heard prayer and answered it with respect to this; for I see her every day and we converse together in a holy innocence; so it has been for two years past."

The Diary shows George Drummond to have been a man of deep and sincere religious feeling, after the "evangelical" type, and he employs the "evangelical" phraseology in writing. In 1736 he says: "It wants but a few months of thirty-two years since He engaged me in His service;" in other words, Drummond dates his "conversion" from the eighteenth year of his age. We know not when the Diary first commenced, though there is an allusion to an entry made in it in 1734. But it seems not improbable that it took its origin out of George Drummond's relations with "R. B.," and from their agreeing to record and interchange their spiritual experiences. Not only did George Drummond daily register, as one might register a barometer, the rise or fall of his own devotional feelings in family or private worship, but the remarkable thing is that he, the City Treasurer, Commissioner of Customs, Member of the Board of Manufactures, and busy at that time with the promotion of the Infirmary, went through the labour of transcribing " R. B.'s " Diary, and incorporating it into his own. So that about two hundred and fifty large folio pages, in these volumes, are filled with the "confessions" of that lady in the small exquisite handwriting of George Drummond.

There is a slight psychological interest attaching to these records, but it soon vanishes, owing to the great sameness in them. On the whole, one cannot wonder that George Drummond's feelings towards " R. B." should have cooled down to the platonic temperature. She had very delicate health, and the details of her maladies, which she gives, were hardly suitable for the inspection of a lover; she was evidently of a nervous, and, indeed, hysterical, disposition. She believed, and for the matter of that Drummond believed it too, that she had direct personal communication with the Deity. In her Diary she is repeatedly telling how "the Lord has suffered her to lie at his feet wrestling for G. D." And she goes straight to work to ask "the Lord" the most practical questions, such as whether "G. D." shall take tickets in the

Thames Bridge lottery, or whether his salary in the Customs is going to be reduced. She had a great verbal knowledge of the *Authorised Version* of the Bible, and a repertory of texts equal to that shown by John Bunyan in the *Pilgrim's Progress*. When an encouraging text came into her head in answer to one of her inquiries she hysterically took it as the external and direct voice of God speaking to her, or, if she did not really do so, she was a mere vulgar impostor. But the curious thing is that the sagacious George Drummond accepted her ravings as real revelations, and treated her as a spiritual medium between himself and God; so that when some of the promises thus made to him were not realised he half grumbled at the Deity, and only reconciled himself to the dispensation by reflecting that there must be something about it which he did not understand.

Some of " R. B.'s " ecstasies are very nauseous; the following is a sample. "I sought the Lord to Mrs. C., who, J. P. tells me, has taken up a new pet at me, for what I do not know, but she will not come where I am;—and He answered, 'I will speak more fully to you about all her concerns than ever; and I will make her acknowledge that she has wronged you.' Then I said, 'O keep all this for me,' and He answered, 'I will keep it, and I will speak more to you than ever. I will again draw aside the veil and give you a more full discovery of my love than ever you have got. Arise my Love, my fair one, and come away. Thou art all fair, my love, there is no spot in thee.'" But other experiences of hers were not of so encouraging a character. She frequently has entries like the following : " The Enemy so molested me by making noise in the room all night, that I concluded it would be my last; sometimes he tossed the chairs and sometimes pulled the clothes off me. The flood of unbecoming thoughts of God which he darted into my soul, almost distracted me. Both body and soul were on the rack the whole day." This medley of ecstatic and abysmal utterances—from which " G. D." himself is never long left out—George Drummond, honest man, patiently and sympathetically copies out, and indeed calls this work of transcription his "favourite employment." It was all no doubt flattering and soothing to him, and " R. B.," as his *innamorata* and friend, had a great and sincere interest in his affairs, which at that time wore the gloomiest aspect.

In one of the earliest entries, in the midst of his religious chronicling, he says: "I met with several shocking duns in my outward affairs to-day." And at the beginning of 1738 he records: "For almost eighteen years past I have evidently seen the Lord blasting every attempt I made for relief, however much they promised towards it at their setting out. All attempts of that kind since the 1720, have hurt my circumstances instead of bettering them." This evidently refers to unsuccessful speculations, which had brought him into pecuniary embarrassment. As Commissioner of Customs he had received, since 1717, a salary of £1000 a year, which was an extremely handsome income in those days; but towards the close of 1737 he was so much pressed that he writes: "The Lord provided a way for me to-day to pay off my servants and put my sons to their colleges and schools. I bless him for it." Not only was he himself involved, but many of his relatives were in the same condition. The affairs of his father-in-law, Sir James Campbell, form a constant theme in the Diaries both of George Drummond and of "R. B.," and the sale of the estate of Aberuchil is recorded. At least two of his grown-up sons were in pecuniary difficulties, and other near relations were in the same plight. The whole of George Drummond's Diary for 1738 is one continuous wail, interspersed with comforting, but fallacious, promises made by "the Lord" to "R. B."

Matters looked especially bad at the beginning of the year, for in October 1737 the Government had determined to reduce the Commissioners of Customs from seven to five. And George Drummond and Sir James Campbell were the two who lost their appointments. Drummond fancied that this was from a personal enmity entertained towards himself, on account of his religious opinions, by the Earl of Islay. But what was done seems, in reality, to have been an act of kindness to himself. For early in 1738 he was made Commissioner of Excise, and his salary was made payable from the date of his dismissal from the Customs, while those who remained Commissioners of Customs had their salaries cut down from £1000 to £500 a year. The Commissionership of Excise restored to him ample means for supporting his family, but not for clearing him of the difficulties in which he and those belonging to him had become involved. This, however, was effected for him, as the mouse released the lion from his net, by one Mrs. Fenton, the widow of "My old friend, Bailie Fenton;" of whom he writes on the 18th October 1738: "She told me she had been providing a wife for me,—a widow, with an estate large enough to relieve me out of my distresses." This communication threw the simple-hearted George Drummond into great perplexity, for he considered that "the Lord had pointed out another partner" to him; and anyhow he "dared not make one step towards deliverance, either in this way or any other, unless the Lord should open his way."

The next day he loyally communicated to "R. B." what Mrs. Fenton had been saying to him, and "told R. B. all he thought about it." But he does not record what that unfortunate lady had to say on the subject. On the whole, we must conjecture, to her honour, that she sacrificed herself and did not dissuade George Drummond from forming another alliance, else it seems certain that he would have given up the idea. Six days later he writes that he "found the Enemy at work to set this marriage affair before him in an agreeable light." And he only endeavours to dismiss the suggestion by saying: "I know nothing about the woman at all, and how ridiculous would it be for me, in this situation of the thing, to give it a thought." A month afterwards, however, Mrs. Fenton used an argument which was likely to be efficacious with George Drummond, for she declared that in answer to prayer "it was said to her, 'What do you know if this woman's money is not given her to be a blessing to him; and if he is not to be a blessing to her by being the means of her conversion?'" A meeting was now arranged between the parties, and on the 23d November Drummond writes: "I saw the woman at Mrs. Fenton's. There's nothing disagreeable either in her manner or person." Two days afterwards he writes once more of his overwhelming troubles, and adds: "It's mercy that under all this I feel no rancour of mind against the Lord and his way, and though this marriage would probably relieve me out of these distresses, yet, however desirable that would be, upon looking into my heart I find that I dare not make one step in it till I can see the Lord calling me to it." This is the last entry; the Diary now breaks off on the 25th November 1738, and two-thirds of the pages in the huge folio before us remain blank.

George Drummond does not record the process by which he became assured that the "Lord was calling" him to make an advantageous marriage. But we learn from other sources that in January 1739 he married Mrs. Hannah Parson or Livingstone, widow of Major Livingstone. And so, if the year 1738 began for George Drummond with *Hélas! Hélas!* the year 1739 may be said to have begun with *A-ha! A-ha!*[1] It is no wonder if at this point he discontinued the joint-stock diary with "R. B.," and gave up keeping for himself what, after all, was a somewhat morbid record.

By his third marriage Drummond had no children, and Mrs. Livingstone only lived for three years after marrying him. She died in February 1742. Thirteen years later, when he was in his sixty-eighth year, George Drummond took to himself another rich wife; she was the widow of Joseph Green, of the parish of St. Dunstan, Stepney, County Middlesex, who had left her upwards of £20,000. The peculiarity was that she was a Quakeress, and that in the Diary for 1738 Drummond had recorded sentiments about the Quakers which he must have modified before entering into matrimonial alliance with one of them. He had written (and the record explains the origin of his acquaintance with Quaker families): "I dined with Thomas Erskine and three other Quakers from England, at their desire. My sister May lodges in London at one of their houses. I endeavoured to divert it all I could, yet I could not prevent their talking a great deal about their principles, and what they said haunted me when I got from them. I see Satan will suffer mankind to run into any delusion however sublime, provided they don't come to Christ. These people have high pretences to conformity with God and unbounded benevolence to their fellow creatures, which

---

[1] The story is that a lady who had just lost her husband, wrote a long letter, pouring out her grief, to Talleyrand, who sent the brief reply :—
Ma chere Madame,
Hélas! Hélas!
Toujours à vous, Talleyrand.
Not long afterwards the same lady wrote another long letter, announcing that she was going to be married again. To which Talleyrand responded :—
Ma chere Madame,
A-ha! A-ha!
Toujours à vous, Talleyrand.

halts here,—that they don't improve the Lord Jesus for sanctification. They reject the sacraments of Baptism and the Supper, as being but the literal sense of the Scriptures to which they pay but small regard. Their rapturous enthusiasms fill them with spiritual pride and self-conceit. I was unwilling to enter into argument with them, and thought most of the time that I was in their company very ill-spent." When George Drummond came to marrying Mrs. Green he found that he had some scruples on her part, and also some disapprobation on the part of his friends, to overcome. In a letter from him, still extant, to one of his sons-in-law, he says: "She is over her difficulty about the manner of performing the ceremony." "It's to be gone about in the privatest manner and, it may be, is not to be owned for some time either there (*i.e.* in England) or here. Of course I must not recoil from this country; my going won't keep a secret long. My letter for leave of absence must come to the Board (*i.e.* of Excise). I must own I am to go, then; but I tell nobody upon what footing but those I must." All this is very different from the tone of the Diary, and seems to show that during the sixteen years which had elapsed since the days of "R. B." George Drummond had grown more sensible in matters of religion.[1] His fourth wife had no family, and only lived for four years after marrying him. His two last marriages doubtless rendered him very comfortable in his circumstances, and he was enabled to purchase the handsome house which he called Drummond Lodge, and which stood in the centre of what is now Drummond Place.

The fragment which remains of George Drummond's Diary contains very few references to external and contemporary events, and in this respect is disappointing. No allusion is made to the University of Edinburgh. There are some rather interesting entries about the Porteous riot and the action taken thereupon by the Government, but they are not to our present purpose. These are almost the only public matters referred to. The Diary

---

[1] During this time Drummond was greatly under the influence of his son-in-law, Dr. Jardine, Minister of the Tron Church, and Dean of the Thistle, who was regarded as the oracle of the Moderate party. Dr. Somerville (p. 91) quotes the following from some *Contemporary Verses by Lord Dreghorn*:—

"The old Provost, who danced to the whistle
Of that arch-politician, the Dean of the Thistle."

shows Drummond in a depressed and somewhat unnatural frame of mind. But withal it contains indications that, with all the weight of care which he then had at his heart, he was genial and popular, as well as unrelaxing in public business. When he got his appointment as Commissioner of Excise, and first went to the Office, he records: "The undissembled joy I read in the faces of all the folks there, and the Commissioners as much as any, gave me a very sensible pleasure and fixed a contentedness in my mind." There are one or two references to the progress of the Infirmary, of which the following are the most important, though they chiefly show the careful watch which this good man kept over his own motives:—

"22d March 1738.—I have had more work than ever upon my hands this winter and all of it for others. The Royal Infirmary is one of the affairs I have given a great deal of time to. We have got a plan for our house; it's to hold above two hundred patients. I look to the Lord often about it, to make it a blessing to the place and to the nation. The distinguished part I have in it made me afraid that the spring of my action about it might degenerate," etc.

"13th October 1738.—Forwarding the building of the Infirmary is the only amusement I have allowed myself in of a great while, but I have not the same pleasure in it I had, because of late I began to be afraid vanity and not regard to God is become the spring of my activity. At first it was somewhat uphill work, but now it's the favourite undertaking among all ranks of people; and as the fervour of my temper naturally leads me to be very active in every society I am a member of, and as the Lord gives remarkable success to all our applications, I am distinguished and called 'the Father of it, etc.,' with which, alas! I have too much pride and vanity not to be pleased. Yea, I am afraid I am puffed up. Woe's me, I can neither be humble under success, nor bear up under discouragement. O what a poor worthless creature am I! I am sure my eye was single when I set out in this undertaking."

George Drummond's Diary gives us curious information about a particular episode in his life and circumstances, but it does not enable us to know him; the entries in a record of the kind are too one-sided,—it may seem a parodox to say so, but they are too private to be entirely real. The concrete man is something between what a man appears to himself in utter privacy, and what he appears to others in the business of life. Hence, probably, George Drummond was less religious than he thought himself, but more religious than others thought him. On the whole, we get the impression that he was a simple-hearted, somewhat under-educated man, who was for the time greatly under the influence of "R. B.," and was led to sympathise with spiritualistic extravagances, but at the same time always gravitated towards common sense. In his Diary we find no trace of anything mean, and we turn with pleasure from his introverted account of himself to his great public achievements, and to the appearance which he presented to his contemporaries. Dr. Somerville says of him: "The dignity of his person in advanced age, when I knew him, commanded at first sight respect and reverence, insomuch that if a stranger had been introduced to any meeting of the inhabitants of Edinburgh for the consideration of business of the most important nature, his eye would have immediately selected Mr. Drummond as the fittest person to take the lead in council. Every prepossession in his favour was confirmed upon further acquaintance, by the politeness of his manners, and the affability of his conversation."[1]

George Drummond's services to the University have been well summed up by Bower,[2] who says: "That he was the greatest benefactor which the University ever had, will not be called in question by those who are acquainted with his history. From the year 1715 to the time of his death in 1766, nothing was done in the College without his advice or direction. His care of the University not only extended to an accurate investigation how its funds were expended, but he was of much more essential service in procuring men of real talents to be appointed as Professors. In the course of the fifty years during which he managed the city, he may be said to have appointed all the Professors. The following gentlemen were introduced to the University whilst he was Provost, and he served that honourable office six times. In this catalogue the names of the greatest ornaments of the University are included:—

[1] *Life and Times*, p. 45.
[2] *Hist. Un. Ed.*, vol. ii. p. 185.

GEORGE DRUMMOND.
FROM A BUST BY NOLLEKENS.

"Adam Watt, Humanity; Colin M'Laurin, Mathematics; Joseph Gibson, Midwifery; Robert Whytt, Theory and Practice of Medicine; Matthew Stewart, Mathematics; James Robertson, Hebrew; John Goldie, Principal; Robert Hamilton, Divinity; James Balfour, Moral Philosophy, afterwards the Law of Nature and Nations; Robert Dick, Civil Law; William Cullen, Chemistry, and Theory and Practice of Medicine; Thomas Young, Midwifery; Alexander Monro, *secundus ;* Adam Ferguson, Natural and afterwards Moral Philosophy; William Robertson, Principal; Robert Cumming, Church History; Hugh Blair, Rhetoric."

George Drummond died on the 4th December 1766, at Drummond Lodge, and a great procession, including the Principal and Professors of the University, attended him with every mark of respect to his burying-place in the Canongate Churchyard on the 8th of the same month. On that morning Dr. Cullen, in dismissing his class before the conclusion of the hour, apologised to them by saying that he was "called upon by the Principal to attend a Faculty Meeting, the reason of which was that the College were to attend a funeral to-day, to put the highest mark of respect upon the greatest character Edinburgh ever saw. That they were unanimously of opinion too much could not be done by them to show the sense they had of his merit; that Medicine owed more to him than to all the men who ever sat in that Chair; and it was well known he followed them out with every good office in his power in or out of office. Who but himself could erect such an edifice as a Royal Infirmary? What benefit it was to Medicine, besides the relieving the distressed! and therefore he well knew they (*i.e.* the Students) would readily excuse his leaving his Chair in order to join his Brethren, that they in the most public manner might testify to the world what high veneration they had for so noble a character."

In the lobby of the New Royal Infirmary of Edinburgh, whither it has been transferred from the original Infirmary which Drummond built, there is an admirable and characteristic bust of him by Nollekens, with an inscription on the pedestal by Principal Robertson :—

> "George Drummond
> To whom this country is indebted for all the benefit which it
> derives from the Royal Infirmary."

But Scotland owes more to George Drummond than the institution of an Infirmary, and the real monument to him is—modern Edinburgh.

Appendix K. The Natural History Museum of the University of Edinburgh.

The subject of this Appendix is something that was and is not. Its Natural History Museum was once the great glory of the University of Edinburgh, but that has long since been carried off and absorbed into a Governmental institution, which, so far as possible, repudiates all connection with the University. A few brief notes on the history of the Museum once possessed by the University may perhaps here suffice.

The first attempts to get together a collection of Natural History specimens in Edinburgh were made by those two friends to whose zeal and energy we owe (as above related, pp. 217-223) the establishment of the Physic Garden and of the Royal College of Physicians, namely, Dr. Andrew Balfour and Sir Robert Sibbald. Balfour had commenced collecting before Sibbald, and he spent twenty-three years, as Bower says, in amassing natural curiosities from all countries, in the pursuit of which object his wealth and his extensive travels gave him a great advantage. What became of Balfour's collection is not stated, but Sibbald considered the collection which he began making towards the end of the eighteenth century to be a supplement to that of his friend. He proceeded on a less extensive scale than Balfour had done, and aimed especially at collecting indigenous curiosities, such as would throw light on the Natural History of Scotland. In 1697 he presented the specimens which he had got together to the College of Edinburgh, accompanied by a catalogue, which was dedicated to the Town Council, and bore the title of *Auctorium Musæi Balfouriani e Musæo Sibbaldiano*. And this looks as if Balfour's collection had been already given to the College ; only Bower in relating the above-mentioned circumstances (vol. i. pp. 376-78) does not say so.[1] The catalogue contains 216 pages

[1] In 1688, when Morer visited the College of Edinburgh, he was shown such treasures as it then possessed, and he describes them in the following terms : "The staircase before mentioned leads us up to a large room, formerly

in 12mo, and describes the objects in the collection, classified into—I. Minerals; II. The more rare substances taken from plants; III. The more rare productions from the Animal Kingdom; IV. Works of Art, with MSS. and rare books added.

Sibbald's collection having been added to such specimens of Natural History as the College previously possessed, the Town Council a few years later bethought them to provide for the keeping in order of the Museum which had been commenced. As we have seen above (p. 295), they appointed the first Professor of Anatomy in 1705, to "take exact notice and inspection of the rarities of the College," and to give in to the Council "an exact inventory of the same." This interest in the Natural History collections, for want of a Professor of the subject, was not maintained; the objects fell into disorder, deteriorated, or were abstracted. By 1770, when Ramsay was appointed the first Professor of the subject, the Sibbald Museum had disappeared.

When in 1766 Dr. Walker was appointed to be Ramsay's successor, he immediately commenced getting together a new Natural History collection for the use of his class. And in 1783, when the Royal Society of Edinburgh was founded (in the manner which will be related elsewhere), it was laid down by its charter that all the specimens of Natural History belonging to the Society should be placed under the custody of the University. And thus the University got possession of the Huttonian collection of minerals and other valuable collections. On Dr. Walker's death such specimens as he had himself procured for the University were removed by his family as being private property.

The third Professor of Natural History, Jameson, succeeded to the Chair in 1804, and it must be remembered that at that time the University buildings were in a deplorable condition,

their Library, but is now used for a commencement chamber, and is the Common-Hall for all College entertainment and business of moment. Here were several maps, globes, and some books, with a few rarities, as a Palm-leaf two yards and a half long; a Speaking-trumpet made of copper, about three yards in length; a Sea-horse Pissle two yards; an American Shell which the natives make their trumpet; a crooked Horn divers inches long, cut out of a woman's head above the right ear, when she was fifty years old, and lived twelve years after." It may be mentioned that this horn is now in the Anatomical Museum of the University, with a silver plate attached to it, on which the history of the patient is recorded.

parts of the old College having been pulled down, and the new buildings having been arrested for want of funds when only a small instalment of them had been completed. Such curiosities and specimens as the University possessed were still kept in the Upper Hall mentioned by Morer. And here Jameson at once commenced to form, *de novo*, a zoological collection, and for fifty years he continued with the most distinguished success to gather in contributions to it from all parts of the world. This he did by setting his numerous pupils to work for him in whatever country they might be placed. But besides isolated contributions of particular objects, there came in several ready-formed collections for the aggrandisement of the Museum. In addition to the Huttonian collection held for the Royal Society, the University received as a direct gift to itself the zoological collections of Dr. William Thomson, who having got his medical education in Edinburgh, had been made Professor of Anatomy in Oxford, and afterwards retired to reside at Naples, and finally at Palermo.

In 1819 the great Natural History collection of M. Du Frèsne was announced for sale in Paris, and the Senatus having the reversion of General Reid's legacy of £52,000 to look forward to, borrowed the sum of £3000 from some of the Edinburgh Banks [1] on the security of this reversion, and purchased the collection. Next year, in 1820, the "Regius Museum" for the use of the Regius Professor of Natural History, and for the reception of his collections, was completed, occupying the whole of the west side of the University quadrangle, and was most carefully fitted up by Playfair, the architect, under Professor Jameson's instruction. All the splendid zoological display was removed thither, and additions to it continued to flow in. In the same year, 1820, a cordial letter arrived from the Marquis of Hastings, Governor-General of India, forwarding an elephant's skeleton, and promising such duplicates of specimens as there might be in the possession of the Asiatic Society of Calcutta. In 1822 Sir Thomas Brisbane, Governor of New South Wales, sent large contributions of natural objects from that country. Bower, writing in 1830, says of the Museum: "The collection of Birds is very extensive. It is the third in Europe, only being exceeded by those of Paris and Berlin. There are upwards of three thousand

---

[1] These were the Bank of Scotland, the Royal Bank, and Forbes & Co.

different specimens. What greatly enhances the splendour of the sight, is, that every individual throughout the whole Kingdom, which the Museum contains, is in the highest state of preservation, no pains or expense having been spared to accomplish the end in view. The Professor has also studied to introduce scientific arrangement, which renders it more interesting to the philosopher, as well as more agreeable to the mere spectator." Other authorities spoke of the Natural History collection, as a whole, as being in this country "second only to that of the British Museum."

In December 1820 a meeting was held of persons representing the College Buildings Commissioners, the Senatus, and the Town Council, and rules were drawn up for the admission of the public to the Museum now placed in the new buildings. The admission fee was fixed at half-a-crown, in order to provide a fund for keeping up the collections. In 1834 (as we shall see elsewhere) the Town Council reduced the admission fee to one shilling, contrary to the wishes of the Senatus. And in 1839 they proposed to go still further in the direction of popularising the Museum by reducing the price of entry to sixpence. This, however, does not appear to have been carried out.

In 1852, with pardonable want of foresight, the Senatus petitioned Government to take over the Natural History collection of the University, which was overflowing the Museum provided for it, and to convert it into a National collection in a building to be erected to the west of the College, as an addition to and integral part of the University buildings. The Senatus confidingly thought that they could give away their collections and yet still retain them. They even thought that a paternal Government would take the opportunity to build them a Graduation Hall as part of the new building to be erected. How exceedingly deceived they were in their expectations has been to some extent recorded above (p. 357). The whole transaction has turned out in many ways an unfortunate one. If the Science and Art Department of Her Majesty's Government resolved to establish a Museum in Edinburgh—which it was doubtless very proper for them to do—they might have done so without reference to the University. The Treasury now pays above £11,000 a year for the maintenance of their Museum, so that the saving effected by taking over the University's collections was insignificant. On the other hand, the University has undoubtedly lost prestige by the loss of its Museum. All the pledges made by Government at the time of the transfer have been violated. And the very existence of the Government Museum in its actual locality has been a great disadvantage to the University.

APPENDIX L. THE EDINBURGH OBSERVATORY.

STRENUOUS efforts were made by the great Professor M'Laurin to provide an Observatory for the instruction of Students in the University of Edinburgh. In this good purpose he was, doubtless, encouraged by George Drummond, and the matter was progressing favourably when the troubles arising out of the Porteous riot in 1736 put a stop to it. In 1740 Lord Morton, then Lord Clerk Register, handed over to the University £100 towards building an Observatory; other subscriptions came in, and M'Laurin raised some money for the purpose by a course of popular lectures on experimental philosophy. The sum now amounted to £300, and that being considered sufficient, Maclaurin begged of the Town Council "so much of the southern row of the College buildings as would be sufficient," together with certain grants of building materials. This was agreed to, and an Observatory would have arisen under M'Laurin's auspices about the centre of the present University Library had not the Rebellion of 1745 intervened, shortly after which M'Laurin died.

The money which had been collected was placed in the hands of two trustees, "both of whom," says Arnot (writing in 1779), "unfortunately became bankrupt."[1] But a dividend, amounting with interest to about £400, was recovered out of their estates in 1777. At that time a Mr. Short, brother and executor to a London optician, had come to Edinburgh, bringing with him the optical instruments he had inherited, and among them a large reflecting telescope. He wished as a speculation to erect an Observatory in order to receive fees from visitors who might come to indulge their curiosity or to make observations; and he made an application to the Town Council to be allowed to do so. Some of the Professors, especially Alexander Monro *secundus*, endeavoured to utilise this proposal for the benefit of the Uni-

[1] Arnot's *History of Edinburgh*, p. 415. One of the bankrupts was Matthew Stewart, Professor of Mathematics in the University.

versity. And an arrangement was made by which a liferent of half an acre of ground on the Calton Hill was granted to Mr. Short, and the money above mentioned was handed over to him on condition of his building and fitting up an Observatory, which, with all the instruments therein, was to become the absolute property of the Town Council at the death of Short. During his life he was to make what he could out of entrance-fees from the public, but Students of the University were to be admitted on favourable terms.

A design for the Observatory was made by an architect named Craig. The foundation-stone was laid by the Lord Provost, accompanied by the Town Council and Senatus, on the 25th June 1776. But Arnot, a contemporary writer, tells us that "about this time, Mr. Robert Adam" (to whom the city owes so many of its best buildings) "happened to come to Edinburgh. Upon seeing the intended Observatory, founded upon the top of a high and abrupt hill, he conceived the idea of giving the whole the appearance of a fortification. Accordingly the line was chalked out for enclosing the limits of the Observatory with a wall constructed with buttresses and embrasures and having Gothic towers at the angles. The beauty of the design was so much admired that the main object was forgot. The workmen left the Observatory, already half built, and turned themselves to raise the tower on the south-west brow of the hill. This was greatly promoted by Mr. Short, who in the tower saw an excellent accommodation for himself and family. Upon this building was exhausted all the money destined for the Observatory; and besides a considerable arrear was incurred to the tradesmen. To discharge this the Duke of Hamilton, having gained at Leith races, in July 1777, His Majesty's Purse of a hundred guineas, generously bestowed it for that purpose. Still, however, this sum was only applied to discharge arrears already incurred; the building was not advanced an inch." The Town Council, with a supineness very different from the spirit of George Drummond, moved no further in the matter. "And thus," sighs Arnot, "an optical instrument, perhaps the finest in the world, is lost for the want of a proper place to keep it in; and the Observatory stands a half-finished work upon the highest hill in Edinburgh."

This striking instance of mismanagement remained conspicuous to all eyes for more than a quarter of a century, though in the meantime a Professor of Practical Astronomy had been appointed and had no means of teaching his subject. In 1812 a private Society, calling itself the Astronomical Institution of Edinburgh,[1] obtained from the Town Council a grant of the Observatory enclosure on the Calton Hill on condition that the premises should be used solely for the purposes of an Astronomical Observatory; and they commenced building from a design from Playfair, in which it is said that scientific considerations were too much sacrificed to the picturesque. The means of the Society soon ran short, and in 1813 they began applying to the Treasury for assistance, which at last came to them in 1826 in the shape of a grant of £2000 for the completion of the buildings and the purchase of instruments.

The Universities Commission having reported in 1830 on the death of Blair, the first Professor of Practical Astronomy, that his Chair ought not to be filled up till an Observatory could be provided for his successor, the Government negotiated with the Astronomical Institution, who gave "the use of the Observatory created by them and all the instruments therein contained to the Professor of Practical Astronomy." And Henderson being appointed to the Chair in 1834, at once commenced his course of laborious observations. The Astronomical Institution, having ensured that a competent observer would be maintained at the public expense, desired to withdraw from further responsibility as to the building; and in 1847, under sanction of the Treasury, the Commissioners of Woods and Forests accepted a transfer to them of the Observatory and premises on the Calton Hill under three conditions: 1st, that the office of Astronomer-Royal for Scotland should be permanently associated with the Regius Professorship of Practical Astronomy in the University of Edinburgh; 2d, that the Astronomer should be responsible solely to the department of Government by which he should be appointed; 3d, that a Board of Visitors should be constituted for the Observatory similar to those acting at Greenwich or elsewhere, who should annually report and make suggestions to Government.

[1] At that time Playfair, Professor of Natural Philosophy, was President, and Dr. David Brewster Secretary, of the Astronomical Institution.

These arrangements were concluded during the incumbency of the present Professor and Astronomer-Royal, who was appointed in 1846.

We have above related (p. 343) how that gentleman found, or considered, himself unable to perform, the function of delivering lectures in his Professorial capacity; and in his capacity of Astronomer-Royal he constantly represented to Government the inadequacy of his staff, his allowances, his instruments, and his buildings, for prosecuting the important work with which he had been entrusted. In 1876 a small Commission of most able personages (scientifically and otherwise), with Lord Lindsay as Chairman, was appointed by Parliament to inquire into the state of the Observatory. They reported unfavourably upon both building and instruments, and stated their opinion that, in order to obtain complete efficiency, it would be necessary to remove the Observatory altogether, and rebuild it on some other site to the west or south-east of the town. One curious fact was mentioned by them, namely, that the labours of Henderson had been vitiated "by large and at first unaccountable errors which had crept into the results of his observations." It was ultimately ascertained that these were due to the extreme sensitiveness of the Craigleith sandstone composing the piers upon which the transit instrument was mounted. This stone had been chosen by the Astronomical Institution as the very finest and most suitable for their purpose. But the experience of forty years has shown that "in fact the Craigleith sandstone ranks next to cast-iron in the amount of its expansion under heat. The light of a common bull's-eye lamp, thrown upon one of the piers, will cause it to expand to such an extent that the direction of the axis of the telescope is sensibly altered; and a similar phenomenon will be produced, though in a less degree, even by the approach of the human body to the stone. The liability of the piers to tremor was also exhibited to us by Professor Smyth in the process of taking the collimation error by reflection from the mercury trough. And when looking through the telescope at the surface of the mercury, we were able to see the effects of the tapping of the hand, or even of a single finger, on the stone."

APPENDIX M. GENERAL REID.

THE University owes so much to General Reid that it is a pleasing duty to collect any contemporary notices of him, or other particulars, which may still survive. The following fragments of information have been brought to notice by the kindness of Mr. Small, the University Librarian.

We have seen above (p. 350) that General Reid spoke of himself as the last representative of an old Perthshire family. These were the Robertsons of Straloch; and it may seem odd to state that General Reid's father was Alexander Robertson of Straloch. But he and his forefathers for more than three centuries had been styled the "Barons Rua," or "Roy," this designation having arisen from the family having got a royal grant of a barony, and from the first of the line having had red hair. While the head of the family was addressed in all companies as "Baron Rua," his signature was invariably Robertson, until John Robertson—our General—the last of the race, who assumed the nickname, which had grown into a courtesy title, as his surname, and called himself "Reid" (which would be *Anglice* "Red," see above, page 173). This is just what the celebrated Rob Rua Macgregor did, when he signed himself Rob Roy.[1] But the curious thing is that John Robertson called himself Reid during his father's lifetime, when he was not as yet Baron Rua, and was only entitled to the name of Robertson.

He joined the Regiment raised by the Earl of Loudon in 1745, half of which went abroad, and the other half was kept in Scotland as a check upon Prince Charlie's Highlanders. He afterwards joined the 42d Regiment, and served with them in America. He there married Susanna Alexander, whose brother claimed the earldom of Stirling, the title of which was denied to him by the House of Lords owing to his having taken part in the Jacobite rising, but was accorded to him in America.

Major John Reid, as he had now become, acquired—how, is not very clear—an estate in the neighbourhood of New York, which his father, in a letter still extant, describes as "larger than all Perthshire." Bower says that the estate was confiscated, but

[1] These facts are given by Colonel David Stewart, in his *Sketches of the Highlanders*, vol. i. p. 98.

it seems more probable that he was allowed to sell it, for his father speaks of him as having this estate, but no ready money; whereas at his death, in 1807, he left £52,000 invested in consols.

Reid's daughter, who in 1775 was described by her grandfather as "a handsome girl, going fourteen years," married her cousin, Dr. Stark Robertson. General Reid's Highland pride made him look down on the medical profession; he was extremely averse to the marriage, and used to speak of his son-in-law as a "vile apothecary." It was this feeling, combined with the circumstance that Mrs. Stark Robertson never had any children, which procured the Reid bequest for the University.

There appears to have been a good deal of poetry and music among both the soldiers and the officers of the 42d Regiment. Reid himself was a most accomplished flute-player, and also a composer, and the men "were much attached to him for his poetry, his music, and his bravery as a soldier."[1] At his Birthday Concert, every year now on the 13th February, the orchestra perform a pastoral movement of his, a minuet, and the martial song called "The Garb of Old Gaul." Stewart, in his *Sketches of the Highlanders*, states that the words of this song were originally composed in Gaelic, and afterwards translated into English. But it seems more probable that the reverse of this process took place. The first two lines of the song are fine:—

"In the garb of old Gaul, with the fire of old Rome,
From the heath-covered mountains of Scotia we come."

But the inspiration of the poet failed him there; and the rest of the words are justly characterised by Graham in his *Songs of Scotland* (vol. iii. p. 113) as "very trashy." The author of the song as we have it in English was Lieut.-General Sir Henry Erskine of Alva, Bart., who brought it out in a volume called *The Lark* in 1765. Shortly after this time the "Black Watch" returned to Scotland, and Colonel Reid, as he then was, set the song to music. Certainly one of the men in the Regiment wrote Gaelic words for it, but it seems more probable that he should have made a Gaelic version of the English song which his Colonel had set to music, than that Sir Henry Erskine, whom we do not know to have been a Gaelic scholar, should have

[1] Stewart's *Sketches of the Highlanders*, vol. i. p. 360.

translated the Gaelic words into English. However, Stewart quotes the testimony of an officer in the Black Watch, that though he could not "recollect the name of the man who composed the 'Garb of old Gaul,'" he "thought his manner of singing the Gaelic words of it preferable to the English."

Of Colonel Reid, as a flute-player, we have an enthusiastic contemporary description preserved in a letter of Mrs. Cockburn, the authoress of "The Flowers of the Forest."[1] Writing to some lady friend, she says: " Of all the sounds I ever heard—and my soul has soared to heaven before now—of all the sounds I ever heard, Colonel Reid's flute—well, it is amazing the powers of it; it thrills to your very heart. He plays in any taste you please, and composes what he plays. You know my taste is the *penseroso*, and so it is his. He played me five acts of a tragedy that went to my heart, and I spoke in to myself all the words of it. I would not let him speak the epilogue. You must hear him, Sylph. Oh, how I regretted your absence to-night! But here is a letter that will bring harmony enough to you. My niece Clark was so good as entertain me with Colonel Reid to-night. He is a gentle, melancholy, tall, well-bred, lean man; and for his flute, it speaks all languages; but these sounds that come from the heart to the heart! I never could have conceived it. It had a dying fall, I was afraid I could not bear it, when I heard it perfectly. I can think of nothing but that flute,—so good night, good Sylph."

From the Matriculation Album of the University we find that "John Reid" attended the Logic Class of Professor Stevenson in the Session 1743-44. What other classes he attended is not on record.

[1] Given in Miss Tytler's *Songstresses of Scotland*, vol. i. p. 130.

END OF VOL. I.

www.ingramcontent.com/pod-product-compliance
Lightning Source LLC
Chambersburg PA
CBHW030559300426
44111CB00009B/1039